Chef Sameer Gupta
Pratibha Jain

Relishing Rajasthan

Time-honoured vegetarian recipes
from a chef's home kitchen

Published by Westland Books, a division of Nasadiya Technologies Private Limited, in 2026

No. 269/2B, First Floor, 'Irai Arul', Vimalraj Street, Nethaji Nagar, Alapakkam Main Road, Maduravoyal, Chennai 600095

Westland and the Westland logo are the trademarks of Nasadiya Technologies Private Limited, or its affiliates.

Chef Sameer Gupta and Pratibha Jain assert the moral right to be identified as the authors of this work.

The views and opinions expressed in this work are the authors' own and the facts are as reported by them, and the publisher is in no way liable for the same.

ISBN: 9789371977906

10 9 8 7 6 5 4 3 2 1

Typeset by Jojy Philip

Printed at Thomson Press (India) Ltd

Relishing Rajasthan is not just a cookbook—it's an odyssey through time, taste and tradition. Chef Sameer Gupta doesn't merely share recipes; he resurrects memories, people and places that have flavoured his fifty years in Rajasthan. You can almost hear the hiss of ghee hitting a hot kadhai as the Jodhpuri Mirchi Vada turns golden, smell the saffron rising from a simmering pot of Maanglik Laapsi, and see a grandmother's hands shaping Bajre ki Roti beneath the desert sun. Each page feels sun-kissed by the dunes, fragrant with memory, alive with stories from kitchens where generosity was a way of life. This is food as philosophy, cooking as culture and hospitality as heritage. Pratibha Jain's lyrical touch elevates the chef's recollections into literature, and every dish becomes an act of devotion. Together, they remind us that recipes are not instructions but inheritances. This book belongs on every table that still believes food can heal, unite and inspire wonder.

Suvir Saran
Chef, Author and Columnist

I have long admired Pratibha's cookbooks, which have received the prestigious Gourmand awards. The recipes in *Relishing Rajasthan* are very well written and clear enough even for a novice cook. Chef Sameer offers useful tips and anecdotes alongside the recipes, addressing every doubt a reader might have. I wish this book all the very best.

Chandra Padmanabhan
Bestselling cookbook author

For any newcomer fascinated by Rajasthani cuisine, *Relishing Rajasthan* is a dream—rich with intricate details, precise measurements and helpful nuances, such as placing a heavy tawa underneath to achieve the ideal texture. The illustrations are excellent. I especially appreciate that the dishes are shown just as we make them at home, not 'dressed up' merely for visual appeal. Pratibha and Sameer, you have truly risen to great heights in the making of this book—congratulations!

Chithra Viswanathan aka Chitvish
Cookbook author and social blogger

I am genuinely excited about Chef Sameer Gupta's cookbook, *Relishing Rajasthan*, beautifully documented in collaboration with Pratibha Jain. A living legend, he has created a unique brand that brings traditional Rajasthani dishes to life through thoughtful, contemporary pairings while preserving the centuries-old heritage of rich, sumptuous vegetarian delicacies.

Kamlesh Mehta
Chairman, Forsythe Multimedia Group, LLC
The South Asian Times, New York

In celebration of taste and togetherness …

To Late Shri Subodh Raisurana, an ardent food connoisseur and a truly remarkable human being.

And Smt. Neeta Raisuarana, for her deep love of words, food and the desert state. We deeply cherish her for the flavours she preserves, the memories she evokes and the legacy she continues to inspire.

Relishing Rajasthan is not just a cookbook—it's an odyssey through time, taste and tradition. Chef Sameer Gupta doesn't merely share recipes; he resurrects memories, people and places that have flavoured his fifty years in Rajasthan. You can almost hear the hiss of ghee hitting a hot kadhai as the Jodhpuri Mirchi Vada turns golden, smell the saffron rising from a simmering pot of Maanglik Laapsi, and see a grandmother's hands shaping Bajre ki Roti beneath the desert sun. Each page feels sun-kissed by the dunes, fragrant with memory, alive with stories from kitchens where generosity was a way of life. This is food as philosophy, cooking as culture and hospitality as heritage. Pratibha Jain's lyrical touch elevates the chef's recollections into literature, and every dish becomes an act of devotion. Together, they remind us that recipes are not instructions but inheritances. This book belongs on every table that still believes food can heal, unite and inspire wonder.

Suvir Saran
Chef, Author and Columnist

I have long admired Pratibha's cookbooks, which have received the prestigious Gourmand awards. The recipes in *Relishing Rajasthan* are very well written and clear enough even for a novice cook. Chef Sameer offers useful tips and anecdotes alongside the recipes, addressing every doubt a reader might have. I wish this book all the very best.

Chandra Padmanabhan
Bestselling cookbook author

For any newcomer fascinated by Rajasthani cuisine, *Relishing Rajasthan* is a dream—rich with intricate details, precise measurements and helpful nuances, such as placing a heavy tawa underneath to achieve the ideal texture. The illustrations are excellent. I especially appreciate that the dishes are shown just as we make them at home, not 'dressed up' merely for visual appeal. Pratibha and Sameer, you have truly risen to great heights in the making of this book—congratulations!

Chithra Viswanathan aka Chitvish
Cookbook author and social blogger

I am genuinely excited about Chef Sameer Gupta's cookbook, *Relishing Rajasthan*, beautifully documented in collaboration with Pratibha Jain. A living legend, he has created a unique brand that brings traditional Rajasthani dishes to life through thoughtful, contemporary pairings while preserving the centuries-old heritage of rich, sumptuous vegetarian delicacies.

Kamlesh Mehta
Chairman, Forsythe Multimedia Group, LLC
The South Asian Times, New York

In celebration of taste and togetherness...

To Late Shri Subodh Raisurana, an ardent food connoisseur and a truly remarkable human being.

And Smt. Neeta Raisuarana, for her deep love of words, food and the desert state. We deeply cherish her for the flavours she preserves, the memories she evokes and the legacy she continues to inspire.

What Led to This Book

Chef Sameer Gupta

The process of shaping this book has been touched with the same magic as the process of raising a child. As a parent, I have poured my life, my experiences and my learnings into my children. I have also experienced many challenges and struggles, and grown tremendously as a result of them. I have had the opportunity to do it all over again with this book. Each page, each recipe, has been a process of giving and learning. A process of balancing spontaneous and delightful flow with focus and dedication. A process of being kind to mistakes while gaining confidence. A process of sharing my knowledge and experience in a way that is useful and enlivening to someone else.

Many moons ago, in 2010, I met Pratibha-ji for the first time in the city of Bangkok. I was a chef at an Indian wedding, and she was a dynamic lady with a smiling face and serene gaze. I met her several times over three days and found she was true to her name, Pratibha, which means 'talent' in Hindi. I was delighted to know that she was a writer, with equal command of Hindi and English. Her recipe book *Cooking at Home with Pedatha*, co-authored with Jigyasa Giri won the award for Best Vegetarian Cookbook in the World 2006.

Each page, each recipe, has been a process of giving and learning. A process of balancing spontaneous and delightful flow with focus and dedication.

This was the moment when the faint tune of wanting to write a book that I had started humming as a child emerged as a full-throated song in my mind. As a child, I would string together unpenned words in my head and think that someday I too would write a book like one of my favourite authors. Bankimchandra, Vimalmitra, Acharya Chatursen, Rahul Sankrityanan, Gaura Pant Shivani, Amrita Pritam, Mahadevi Varma, Mahasweta Devi and other famous writers of that time kindled my love for the written word.

In the magical world of writing, where there is no difference between a king and a beggar, where an old man becomes a child and a child becomes an adult, where sometimes one can spread wings on the blue expanse of the open sky while at other times swim in the bottomless waters of the ocean like a golden fish, where fairy tales look like the real world while at other times truth seems to fall flat on its face, and where even the most suppressed frustrations find wings of hope, you find all those things that are beyond your imagination.

If writing a book seemed like a childhood fantasy, writing a cookbook was not even in my wildest imagination. Meeting Pratibha-ji allowed me to nurture the writer in me who had got lost in the daily routine of life and where the chef in me had emerged over the years. In her presence, I also began to enjoy a new-found confidence in my writing skills. This compilation of recipes is an outcome of that interaction.

While today's children don't even ask for a newspaper from the neighbours, we had an endless list of requests that were simply and generously fulfilled.

While the writer in me was born during my childhood, so was the chef in me. Growing up, families in a locality lived like a large community. If ever food was not cooked at home or took too long to prepare, none of us children ever hesitated to ask for some pulses and vegetables from Ma Saheb next door, or Bhabhisa, Badki Jiji or Chutki Bai. While today's children don't even ask for a newspaper from the neighbours, we had an endless list of requests that were simply and generously fulfilled. This kindled my love to share food joyfully with others.

I was also blessed to easily learn many skills from families living around me that otherwise require tireless effort. Some families made papad, badi and pickles at home to earn some extra income. Playfully helping them in their work, I learnt these skills without any conscious effort. And when my palms would slightly swell and redden due to rolling the papads, I would try to hide them, which only exposed them further. My sister Rajrani's affectionate anger would then pour over me, and I would make a promise never to repeat the action, only to break it the very next day. I guess it was not surprising that I naturally ventured into the field of cooking when I grew up.

I don't know if it was the blessings of my ancestors, the guidance of my teachers or divine grace that led my first workplace to be a five-star hotel. I started as a bill clerk, and over the decades, I watched the ups and downs of the hotel industry while I climbed my way to becoming a chef. The wise say that one must let go of painful memories and remember only the good tidings. Like scribbled letters on a slate, I want to erase the memories of my struggle in those years, yet retain the ones where I evolved and established myself in the culinary arts. At the risk of sounding arrogant, I want to share that my talent for cooking and learning new things always received praise, which in turn inspired me to learn a lot more.

I feel it my soulful duty to mention all the hotels and restaurants, cities and countries, and all those people who have been a part of my journey.

This includes Gangali Bai, who I am sure has forgotten her real name, Ganga, from whom I learnt the ordinarily extraordinary moong dal, which is my signature dal today.

Then there is Rosa, an eighty-year-old Italian resident, who came to Rimini (a small town in Italy) to meet me after travelling for three hours to teach me her recipe of Macarronese de ungia—a hand-rolled and hand-shaped pasta with beautiful dots— and learn how to make grape chutney. She also carried with her memories of her childhood stay in India, and even today, I giggle when I remember how I helped her wear a sari. It was a clear in the case of the blind leading the blind!

Also, Firaki Kaka of Nawalgarh Jhunjhunu, from whom I learnt to prepare a chutney with raw garlic and kachri (a berry), and Kisni Kaki whose Aalan ki Sabzi and Bajre ki Roti, and many other dishes, were proof of her divine bond with God.

I remember Dr Bansal of New York, because of whom I could present my cooking along with Mrs Madhur Jaffrey at the James Beard Foundation. She made it possible for me to cook a majestic dinner in the President's Circle of the Asia Society of America, and it was Dr Bansal who referred me to many famous people who form very special memories for me: Pepsi's Indra Nooyi; filmmaker Meera Nair; singers Rajan and Sajan Mishra; celebrity chef the late Floyd Cardoz; Indian Ambassador Nirupama Rao; Michelin Star chef Suvir Saran; Western Union CEO Hikmet Ersek; Harvard Business School Dean Nitin Nohria and many more names whose long list is fresh in my mind.

I am also indebted to Roopa Bari, the home manager of Dr Bansal, who prepared the vegetable of gourd peels; Ghasi Maharaj who was the most famous chef for Jaipur weddings from whom I learnt Chakki ki Sabzi; Suryakanta Mamisa, Kanchan Mamisa, Golu Mama, Mrs Rashmi Chatur, Sena Bhabhi-ji Bothra, Mrs Madhu Birani, and Manju Bhabhi-ji for their various homemade delicacies such as Fogla ka Dhokla, Khelre ki Sabzi, Jaipuri Kadhi, Ambariya, Kakdi Angoor ki Sabzi and many varieties of pickles.

Meera Bhabhi and the late Nirmal-ji Lodha Saheb are not only connoisseurs of gemstones but also had such a fine sense of taste that they could tell by the smell whether a dish was over or under-salted, and whether a dish was cooked in ghee or oil. I have rarely met anyone with such discerning taste. I will always remember Asha-ji Daga who opened up her home in California to me and taught me the unforgettable Mandiya dish. I feel blessed that I carry an iota of their aesthetic in my palms.

There is a saying that marriages are made in heaven. Surely that must be true for other relationships as well. God has blessed me with a strong relationship with the Raisurana family. They are not my biological family, but Raisurana-ji, Neeta-ji, Rachna and Siddharth were like a father, mother, sister and brother to me. They always treated me like their own. My deepest gratitude is to Neeta-ji Raisurana, whom I call Mummy-ji. Both of us often talk about the food of Rajasthan. Her father, Shri Shubhakaran-ji Bothra, was a great man with extensive knowledge and mastery of many languages. Her maternal grandmother, Laadbai, was a lady of immense poise from whose kitchen one could never return hungry. During mealtimes, while she paid full attention to everyone seated at the chowki, she also managed to quickly organise some hot dal and rotis for the domestic help who may have just walked in. Not just humans, but other creatures were also her focus of attention. This included feeding grains to the pigeons, flour to the ants, fresh halwa made with oil and jaggery for the street dog that had just birthed her puppies, the first roti for the cow and the last one for the dog! Despite limited means, how she managed all this is indeed baffling.

Not just humans, but other creatures were also her focus of attention ... the first roti for the cow and the last one for the dog!

Neeta-ji never fell short of sharing many insightful incidents from the past. There were countless stories in her box of memories, but the most important thing for me was that in her presence, I got a front-seat view of traditional cooking methods. Raisurana-ji was the creator of the delicacy Katbel Pachak ki Chutney, while it was from Neeta-ji that I learnt Nana Saheb's favourite Papad Goli, which I served at a party at Shri Lakshmi Mittal's London house and won many accolades.

Their daughter Rachna, who has now settled in the United States, would experiment with new recipes on her birthday, and in the evening when her friends came over, talk about that food and exchange recipes amidst loud chatter and noisy fun. These were my early days when the art of cooking was slowly gaining my attention. In my later years when I visited the US every year, with the help of Rachna and her husband Deepak, I learnt a lot about international cooking.

Rachna's brother, Siddharth, who has inherited the love for good food from his father, also actively participates in our dining table conversations, which always centre around food. As a blessed coincidence, Siddharth's lovely wife Pooja is also deeply interested in cooking and hospitality. This is another shining example of my belief that relationships are indeed a divine conspiracy. If this was not true, then why would I have met so many kindred souls? This is not just a coincidence, it is life's biggest blessing.

… relationships are indeed a divine conspiracy. If this was not true, then why would I have met so many kindred souls?

In this infinite journey of learning, I have travelled within the country and to distant countries many times like a nomad. But it remains to me a mystery why since childhood, no other place has influenced me as much as the land of Rajasthan! Perhaps there is a link to some previous birth or an unfulfilled thirst which pulls me to this land again and again. This pink city of Jaipur, the lake city Udaipur, the blue aura of Jodhpur, the reticular mansions of Jaisalmer, the golden dunes of the desert, the temples of Nathdwara and Ekling ji, the bravery of Padmavati, the devotion of Meera, the struggle of Maharana Pratap, the mysterious stories of forts and palaces! For me, there is a sense of completeness at every turn, even in the sparse and minimal.

There is so much more I wish to share about the people of Rajasthan, the rich tapestry of its cuisine and the countless memories that fill my heart. Nostalgia overtakes me. Jaipur, where I live—or perhaps our entire country—is alive with conversation. Silence feels unfamiliar; words flow as effortlessly as the air we breathe. Maybe that is why our prayers are not whispered but spoken with devotion, as if filling the space around us with faith and belonging.

For me, the journey of this book would feel incomplete without sharing the story of its creation, though I confess that narrating it stirs emotions I can hardly contain. My only defence is that this book is a dream realised, and I cannot help but be carried away speaking about it.

Finally, I must acknowledge my wife, Sudha—without whose unwavering dedication, there would be no Chef Sameer. And to our children, Vipul and Natasha, who always believed in my ability to bring this book to life, I am deeply grateful.

– **Sameer**

CONTENTS

A NOTE FOR VEGANS

The world of plant-based alternatives has expanded beautifully, offering rich and flavourful options for those who follow a vegan lifestyle or prefer dairy-free choices. Today, vegan ghee, made from coconut and plant-based fats, brings the same rich aroma and depth as traditional ghee. Dairy-free butters, crafted from nuts and seeds, offer a smooth and creamy texture. Plant-based milks—whether almond, oat, soy or coconut—blend seamlessly into recipes, while vegan buttermilk, easily made by curdling plant-based milk with lemon juice or vinegar, provides the same tangy touch essential for many dishes.

While our recipes often call for ghee, butter, milk or buttermilk, we encourage you to explore these wonderful alternatives and find what works best for your preferences. Cooking is about creativity and adaptation, and with the variety of vegan options available today, you can enjoy traditional flavours while staying true to your dietary choices. Whether you choose dairy or plant-based ingredients, we hope these recipes bring you joy, nourishment and a sense of connection to timeless culinary traditions.

A Rajasthani Couplet

कोस-कोस पर पानी बदले
चार कोस पर वाणी
छट कोसया खाणो जुदी
अठ कोसया पर धाणी

Walk one kosa and the water tastes different;
another four kosa to hear a different language;
six for a change in cuisine;
and eight will bring you to another hamlet.

A leaf of mint.
A touch of love.
That's all it takes to make a meal sing.

MY FIFTY YEARS IN RAJASTHAN

Food is a precious storehouse of memories, history and love. My family is from Uttar Pradesh, but I was born and raised in Jaipur, where my fondest memories revolve around Rajasthani cuisine. Entering my kitchen takes me back to childhood: the fragrance of sautéed onions, stacked earthen pots of dried mangoes and lemons, and my grandmother's sari fluttering over ker and kumatiya drying under the sun. These echoes, combined with the generosity of people I've met and my love for exploring, inspired this book.

I met Pratibha-ji over a decade ago at a wedding I catered in Bangkok. An award-winning cookbook author and sparkling conversationalist, we became well-acquainted over those three days—it was destiny, I believe. As we got talking, I shared with her my keen interest in learning forgotten recipes from elders, and she remarked, 'Start documenting, Sameer-ji. You have a book, more than one, inside you.' I have always been an avid reader, and I also enjoy penning my thoughts. However, I never considered writing a book, let alone a cookbook. The writer within me, if there was one, was long lost in the everyday race of life. But her words instilled within me the aspiration and self-confidence to pursue writing. This compilation of recipes is an outcome of that long and joyous journey.

I've long felt the need for a well-researched book capturing authentic Rajasthani food. Beyond Dal Baati Churma and Ker Sangri, the desert's cuisine reflects ingenuity: the Bheel community's Paaniya made from tree leaves, the cooling spicy chutneys of the Banjaras and the one-pot meals of the Gadiya Luhars. I have met urban families who continue to preserve seasonal vegetables, and who eat wild shrubs and berries as part of a standard meal. I have met Rajasthanis living overseas who have carefully passed spice boxes and kansa utensils down generations. I am fortunate to have inherited some from my grandmother's collection. All of these remind me time and time again of how rich and precious my heritage is.

Many recipes here are generations old, while others are my creations or tweaks for modern tastes. I have suggested variations to suit individual tastes and explained the reasons behind specific steps, staying true to the essence of each dish. I chose traditional names to honour the diversity of recipes born from shared ingredients and wove in details about Rajasthani kitchen utensils, unfamiliar ingredients and cherished food stories.

Through it all, I've stayed true to the flavours of the desert I love, my dreams forever filled with its beautiful sand dunes.

Chef Sameer Gupta
December 2025

CHEF AND KITCHEN, HOMEMAKER AND LAND

If I had another title for this book, it would be *Serendipity*. As a Rajasthani born in Chennai where I have also lived most of my life, my Tamilian heart reaches for Rasam and Thayir Saadam when in need of comfort. Growing up, annual visits to my nanihaal in Jodhpur created powerful memories but were not enough to secure my identity as a Rajasthani. When I met Chef Sameer Gupta, a Baniya from Uttar Pradesh, who was born and brought up in Jaipur and whose natural affinity is towards everything Rajasthani, the decision to write this cookbook together was fuelled by my inner child wanting to return home.

This story is not uncommon in India, a land of myriad flavours allowing every soul many homes.

When we first started on this journey together, our roles seemed predestined. Sameer-ji, as an established chef, would furnish the recipes, while I, as an author, would weave them into a book. However, very quickly, his poetic essence started to flow through. As I listened to stories of his childhood and descriptions of dishes and experiences, I asked him to pen down his thoughts. He began sharing his notes, sometimes in English, often in Hindi—lyrical, evocative paragraphs that were a pleasure to read.

Simultaneously, as I tried out the recipes at home, the depth of Rajasthani flavours and breadth of the land's cuisine established themselves deep in my bones. My family welcomed the forgotten but familiar tastes, and as my confidence grew, I found myself totally involved in the recipes, suggesting modifications to proportions and sound alternatives to ingredients.

And so this book is a true collaboration, between a chef who writes and an author who cooks. Heartfelt, grounded, serendipitous.

Pratibha Jain
December 2025

MITHAI

Sweets—Everyday and Festive

Chef Sameer Gupta attributes the wide variety and complexities of Rajasthani sweets to the legacy of Maharaja Sawai Jai Singh, the revolutionary Rajasthani leader. He ruled over Amber when he was just eleven years old and later, also founded one of India's first planned cities, Jaipur. A great administrator with a keen interest in architecture and astronomy, Maharaja Jai Singh was also a food lover. Under his patronage, sweet makers from all across Rajasthan thronged to Jaipur in hopes of winning favour with him. Even today, we find sweet shops on almost every street in Jaipur, each selling its signature mithai.

Many delicious sweets were also created at home at the time. Home cooks were experts at creating delicacies such as Laapsi with broken wheat, Kankri Mirch with edible gum and Bajri ki Tikdi with millet flour. These, along with quick and easy crowd-pleasers such as Meethi Poodi, Mishri Mawa and Matar ka Halwa form the first section of this book.

It is said that the desert we see in Rajasthan today was once a vast seashore, and that early wells dug in the region bore saline water. This led to the tradition of welcoming guests with water sweetened with sugar candy, and serving sweets as the first course in a meal. Try the sweets in this collection and you may want to follow suit.

However, before the recipes, we begin with an ode to the golden saffron, which infuses its warm colour and aroma into many preparations, especially Rajasthani sweets. It is rich and subtle, incomparable to anything else. If asked to describe one ingredient that represents Rajasthan, it would be saffron.

An Ode to Saffron

The golden hues of the desert land, the blood of its brave warriors
The yellow-stained turbans, the flowing orange skirts
The deep muddy clay, the henna-stained palms
Sunsets over the forts and grand houses
All caressed by the hand of my saffron sweetheart

The startling coloured centres of the white parijat flowers
The turmeric blessings cleansing the to-be newlyweds
The river parting the centre of a hopeful bride's hair
The sacrifice of every mother, the courage of every child
All glowing under the gaze of my saffron sweetheart

The delicately infused almonds, the deeply smudged lips of royalty
The golden festival feasts, the tinted tea of a beloved visitor
The ornate, rich, sweet offerings to a benevolent God
The simple renunciation of the sadhu
All equally at home in the embrace of my saffron sweetheart

सुनहरी केसर

ये राजस्थान की धरती का कमाल है या यहाँ के रण बाँकुरों का, पीली पाग का जादू है या केसरिया ओढ़नी का, हल्दी घाटी की पीताभ मिट्टी का या हाथों में रची मेहंदी का, जैसलमेर के क़िलों, हवेलियों और रेत के टीलों में पसरी सुनहरी दमक का या एक मनुहार भरे आमंत्रण का - केसरिया बालम आओ नी पधारो महारे देस का, मैं नहीं जानता।

पर यह ज़रूर जानता हूँ कि राजस्थान में केसर ख़ूब खायी और खिलायी जाती है। केसर गुलाबी बैंगनी फूलों का पराग है जिसका केसरिया रंग वैराग्य का प्रतीक भी है, बलिदान और वीरता का भी, ज़रा बासंती राग का भी। यह मसाला भी है और औषधि भी।

कुसुम्भी शेफालिका (पारिजात पुष्प) नाल के से रंग वाला यह रंग संभवतः सबसे महँगा रंग है। आमेर के किले की केसर क्यारी उसी की स्मृति है जहाँ उसे उगाने का कभी असफल प्रयास किया गया था। मेरी इन तमाम रेसिपीज़ के अलावा व मिठाइयों के बाद, कई ख़ास व्यंजनों में, भगवान के प्रसाद से लेकर माथे पे सजने वाले तिलक में, दूल्हा या दुल्हन की शगुन की हल्दी में, बींद या बींदणी के पहले कँवर कलेवे या बहू भात में, जवाई या समधी के आने पर, ख़ास मेहमान की चाय में और शादी व अन्य उत्सवों में सुबह के नाश्ते में परोसे जाने वाले भीगे बादाम एवं मिश्री के साथ भी केसर डाली जाती है। और तो और, राजसी केसर की दारू में भी इसका उपयोग होता है। क्या केसर के इतने विभिन्न रूप अन्यत्र कहीं देखने को मिलते हैं!

— समीर

 MAANGLIK LAAPSI *Auspicious Sweet with Broken Wheat* (*pic on p. 19*)

Festivals and celebrations call for dishes that are 'maanglik', meaning auspicious. Whether it is a bride setting foot for the first time into her new home, the birth of a baby, the start of the harvest season or days reserved for worshipping different forms of a Goddess, each observation is incomplete without the offering of auspicious dishes, such as Laapsi. In this recipe, grains are roasted on low heat while the aroma of pure ghee and cooked jaggery pervades the house. Garnished with golden saffron and slivered nuts, this wholesome dish is a comforting, spiritual delight.

Serves 4 to 6

1 cup daliya (broken wheat),
   see Step 1
¾ to 1 cup crushed jaggery
4 tbsp ghee
½ tsp cardamom powder
1 tbsp khopra (dry coconut),
   thinly sliced
½ tsp saffron strands
1 tbsp almond slivers
1 tbsp pistachio slivers

Cooking tip: You can prepare this dish in a rice cooker or pressure cook it for 4 whistles. Take care not to overcook it. When cooked, the grains may look sticky, but as soon as you gently turn them with a fork, they separate.

1. Clean and sift the daliya to eliminate any fine powder (this can be reserved for other recipes). Measure out 1 cup of the sifted daliya.

2. Mix jaggery with 1 cup boiling water and stir until the jaggery dissolves. Strain in a fine sieve to remove any grit.

3. In a heavy-bottomed pan, heat 2 tbsp ghee. Add daliya and roast for 5–7 minutes on medium heat, or until the grains turn golden brown.

4. Alongside, boil 2½ cups water in a pan. Add to the roasted daliya, stir continuously and bring to a boil. Reduce to low heat, cover and cook for 7–8 minutes, stirring occasionally to prevent the daliya from sticking to the bottom. Check the daliya to see if it is soft and cooked. If not, add more boiling water to the daliya and continue cooking until all the water has been absorbed.

5. Once the daliya is cooked, pour the jaggery liquid into the mixture and gently mix it in. Cover the pot and continue cooking for an additional 8–10 minutes, or until the liquid has dried up.

6. Place this pan of laapsi on an iron skillet (tawa) and drizzle the remaining 2 tbsp ghee on top. Add cardamom powder and mix gently. Cover the laapsi and simmer for about 15 minutes on low heat. Stir a few times to ensure that it is not sticking to the bottom. Turn off the heat.

7. Set aside for about 20 minutes, then gently toss it with a fork to fluff it up. Garnish with khopra, saffron strands, and almond and pistachio slivers.

Serve at room temperature or just warm without reheating, ideally at the start of a meal on festive days, or as a filling breakfast dish.

Ask Chef Sameer
Pratibha: In Step 6, why do you place the pan on a tawa?
Sameer: It helps prevent the grains from sticking to the bottom and dries the moisture completely.

MEETHA KHEECH   *Milky Porridge with Hulled Wheat*

Also known as Doodhiya Kheech, meaning a milky porridge, this healthy, rejuvenating dish is prepared with hulled wheat. Traditionally, Rajasthan was a region where wheat and millets, not rice, grew in abundance. Accordingly, locals made kheer and porridge with wheat, unlike many other regions where rice was the grain of choice.

Serves 4 as one-meal dish, or 6 as sweet dish in a meal

1 cup hulled wheat*
6 cups milk
6 tbsp sweet condensed milk (or ¾ cup jaggery or palm sugar)
½ tsp cardamom powder
½ tsp (15–20) saffron strands
1 tbsp almond slivers
1 tbsp pistachio slivers

* Hulled wheat: Also known as gehun ka kheech, this is readily available both as whole wheat and pounded wheat. Some families prefer pounded wheat but we recommend whole wheat which lends this dish a deliciously chewy texture.

1. Wash the hulled wheat a couple of times and soak in water for 5–6 hours. Put it in a strainer.

2. In a heavy-bottomed pan, bring 2 cups water to a boil. Add the hulled wheat to the boiling water. Boil for 10 minutes on high heat.

3. Add 6 cups of milk and bring to a boil. Turn the heat to low and cook for around 1 hour, without covering. Stir now and then as the milk reduces to a thick consistency.

4. Add condensed milk, mix and cook for another 5 minutes. Turn off the heat.

5. Add cardamom powder. Mix in half the saffron strands, almond and pistachio slivers and use the remaining as garnish.

Serve warm or chilled as a sweet dish in a meal, or as a filling breakfast dish.

Chef Sameer says

To reduce cooking time, in Step 3, you can cook the hulled wheat in 4 cups water in a pressure cooker for up to 3 whistles. Then add 4 cups milk and cook until fully absorbed. Continue with the rest of the recipe.

✿ DESI SATTU   *Nourishing Sweet with Roasted Gram*

A must-have during the lunar month of Shravan, Sattu is a delightful treat—easy to make and even more fun to decorate. Children especially love topping it with colourful sweets, even Cadbury Gems! The third day after Rakshabandhan is fondly known as Sattu-waali Teej, a celebration that highlights this beloved seasonal dish. Sameer enjoys adding a crunchy twist with gond (edible gum) for that extra punch.

Makes 12–15 sattu

1 cup bhuna chana (roasted Bengal gram)
2 tbsp gond (edible gum) crystals
¾ cup powdered sugar
½ cup ghee
1 tbsp almond slivers
1 tbsp pistachio slivers
½ tsp cardamom powder
¼ tsp saffron strands, rubbed to a fine powder

1. Heat 2 tsp ghee in a thick-bottomed pan over medium heat. Add the chana and roast for 2–3 minutes. Cool slightly and grind into a fine powder. Set aside.

2. In the same pan, heat the remaining ghee. Fry the gond crystals, a few at a time. As they puff up, remove them with a slotted spoon and transfer to a bowl. Fry all the gond in this manner. Once cooled, crush them into a coarse powder.

3. Mix the powdered gram and sugar and pass it through a fine sieve. Return it to the pan along with the ghee used for frying. Do not turn on the flame—no further cooking is required.

4. Add the crushed gond, slivered nuts, cardamom and saffron (reserving a few strands for garnishing) and mix well. Shape the mixture into 12–15 lemon-sized balls using your palms. If needed, add a little more ghee to help bind the mixture. Lightly flatten each sattu and taper the edges. Decorate with the remaining saffron strands.

Serve any time of the day.

Shelf life: Store in an airtight container in a dry place for up to a month.

JHAJHARIYA   *Sweet Dish with Tender Corn*

Also known as Dudhia Makki ki Mithai, Jhajhariya is a favoured dessert of the Chhitod-Merta-Udaipur belt. The natural sweetness of milk and tender corn combine well with spices like cardamom and saffron. Buy a batch of tender corn when in season, remove the kernels with a sharp knife or grate to separate from the cob. Use straight away or freeze to make delicacies with tender corn round the year. Veena-ji Gelda, an Oswal Jain from the Udaipur region and a close family friend, specialises in churning out many delicacies with corn, among which this sweet preparation is Sameer's favourite.

Serves 4 to 6

3 cups tender corn kernels
2 tbsp ghee
3 cups milk
½ cup condensed milk
   or sugar
¼ tsp cardamom powder

For garnish
8–10 saffron strands
½ tbsp almond slivers
½ tbsp pistachio slivers

1. Grind corn kernels into a fine pulp, without adding any water. Strain this pulp through a medium-holed strainer to get a smooth paste. Discard the husk that stays on top of the strainer.

2. In a pan, heat ghee and add the corn pulp. Cook for 10–12 minutes on medium heat while the pulp thickens, turns golden brown and almost turns dry.

3. Add milk and bring to a boil. Reduce to low heat and simmer for 15 minutes while stirring occasionally.

4. Add sugar (or condensed milk) and cardamom powder, and cook for another 10 minutes. Make sure you stir frequently to prevent it from sticking to the bottom. The consistency of this dish is like thick kheer.

5. Garnish with saffron strands and almond and pistachio slivers.

Serve warm or chilled as a sweet dish any time of the day. It's an ideal addition to your party menu.

# INSTANT MISHRI MAWA   *Crunchy Milky Sweet*

One would think that a traditional sweet believed to be the favourite of royalty would need hours of slaving to produce. Enjoy this demystified, instant version of the famous milk fudge much loved by Raja Mansingh, the erstwhile ruler of Jaipur. The secret to this deceptively simple recipe lies in the paneer (cottage cheese). Use fresh, soft, good quality paneer and press it between a kitchen towel to remove any excess water for best results.

All dishes need a balance of flavour as well as texture. For instance, adding a crunch to soft dishes like halwa or fudge. Usually, this is achieved by adding nuts, but as the traditional Mishri Mawa recipe does not include any, sweet makers of yore creatively used coarse rock sugar instead. The perfect Mishri Mawa is an interesting combination of textures: juicy, granular and crunchy.

Serves 4 to 6

2 cups fresh, soft paneer, grated
1 cup milk powder
¾ cup condensed milk
1 tsp lemon juice
1 tsp mishri (rock sugar), coarsely
   crushed

1. Mix paneer, milk powder and condensed milk in a non-stick or heavy-bottomed pan. Cook on medium-high heat for 2 minutes, stirring continuously. (It may take longer if the paneer has excess water content.)

2. As it begins to thicken, add lemon juice. Cook for 1–2 minutes. As soon as it turns granular, transfer to a serving bowl.

3. Sprinkle crushed mishri on top just before serving to enjoy its crunch.

Serve warm during winter and chilled during summer.

 Variations

Rose Mishri Mawa
Add crushed ice to a small earthen bowl, and top it with 2 tbsp Mishri Mawa. Drizzle some rose syrup on top, garnish with rose petals and serve at once.

Mango Mishri Mawa
Add ¾ cup chopped ripe mango and ¼ cup thick mango pulp to the prepared Mishri Mawa for another summery twist.

 INSTANT CHURMA *Roasted Flour with Khoya and Nuts* (*pic on p. 98*)

Due to its strengthening and energising properties, this dish earned its fame as the food of warriors, who would store it for weeks in leaf bowls, dipping in for a quick pick-me-up when their energy levels flagged. The original churma recipe is a time-consuming process. After many experiments, Sameer developed this easy recipe, which is equally flavourful and aromatic.

Serves 4 to 6

6 tbsp melted ghee
2 cups coarse wheat flour*
½ cup crumbled khoya (reduced milk)
½ cup sugar (preferably boora sugar; add more, as you prefer)
½ tsp cardamom powder
½ tsp (15–20) saffron strands
2 tbsp almond slivers
2 tbsp pistachio slivers

* The wheat flour in this recipe is as coarse as sooji (semolina). It is readily available as mota aata or baati ka aata. Alternatively, whole wheat kernels can be ground in a mill.

1. Reserve 2 tbsp ghee and heat the rest in a pan. Add the coarse wheat flour and roast on medium heat for 6–8 minutes, or until the flour turns golden brown and aromatic. Set aside to cool.

2. In a heavy-bottomed pan, roast khoya on medium heat for about 5 minutes, or until it becomes thick and dry. Turn off the heat. Wait until it cools down, then add the roasted flour and mix well with your fingers.

3. Add sugar, cardamom, saffron, and almond and pistachio slivers. Add the remaining 2 tbsp of melted ghee and mix well by rubbing gently with your palms.

Serve at room temperature as a sweet dish, any time of the day. Dal Baati Churma is the most beloved Rajasthani feast.

Shelf life: Traditionally stored in leaf bowls known as donna, you can store churma for several days in a clean, dry container.

> **Variations**
>
> **Rose-flavoured Churma**
> After Step 3, add 2 tbsp dried and crushed rose petals, 2 tbsp gulkand (a relish made with rose petals; available in stores) and 1 tbsp rose water. Mix well with your fingers.
>
> **Besan Churma**
> Substitute coarse wheat flour with coarse besan (gram flour) and follow the recipe.

EASY BADAM KATLI   *The Classic Almond Diamonds*

In this sweet delight, nostalgia blooms, evoking memories of a close-knit community where all the food was homemade. During weddings and celebrations, men from the neighbourhood would gather to peel heaps of soaked almonds, engaging in jovial conversations as they uncovered the lustrous kernels. The kernels were then ground into a paste and cooked in sugar syrup to form a dough. After kneading and rolling the dough into circles, a touch of opulence—silver or gold leaf known as varak—adorned the katli before it was cut into flawless diamond shapes.

The inspiration for this simplified recipe came from Sameer's Iranian friend Dilshad, who compared katli to a Persian delicacy. Delighted by their no-cook method, Sameer ingeniously developed this quick Badam Katli recipe.

Makes 12 Badam katlis

2 cups almond flour*
½ cup powdered sugar
¼ tsp cardamom powder (optional)
2–3 tbsp chilled rose water
8–10 saffron strands

* Almond flour is readily available at gourmet stores. To make at home, blanch 2 cups almonds in boiling water for 2 minutes. While still hot, quickly remove the skin. Place the almonds on a kitchen towel, cover with a muslin cloth and leave them overnight to dry completely. Grind into a fine flour the next morning.

1. Sieve the almond flour, powdered sugar and cardamom powder together. Add rose water spoon by spoon to make a soft, pliable dough. Set aside for 5 minutes. (Place it in the refrigerator if the weather is hot).

2. Alongside, soak saffron in 1 tsp warm water for a few minutes and crush to make liquid saffron.

3. Place the almond dough between two plastic sheets and roll it out to a ½-inch thickness. Trim the sides to make a neat rectangle. Cut into diamond-shaped katlis. Dot the centre of each katli with liquid saffron.

Serve as a sweet delicacy any time of the day. It's an ideal addition to a festive or party menu.

Shelf life: Store in an airtight container. It stays fresh for up to 2 days at room temperature. It can be refrigerated for up to a week. (You don't need to warm it up before serving.)

Variations

Almond Pistachio Rolls
Instead of rolling the almond dough into a circle, divide it into 10–12 portions and roll each into a ball. Flatten each of the balls and place 1 tsp pistachio dough in the centre. You can make pistachio dough with ¼ cup pistachio flour just like almond dough. Shape each of the balls gently into a log of 1 cm thickness. Roll them in the pistachio flour. Trim the ends to make neat and even rolls.

Almond Gulkand Rolls
Tweak the above recipe by using 1 tsp chilled gulkand for the filling instead of pistachio. Then, roll the log in crushed dried rose petals to add a pinkish-red colour.

MEETHE GULGULE *Wheat Flour and Jaggery Fritters*

Also known as Meethe Vade or Meethe Pue, these golden fried dumplings are prepared from a simple batter of wheat flour and jaggery. They are prepared as an offering on Basoda, and also on Makar Sankranti, which celebrates the spirit of universal coexistence. On this special day, youngsters, guided by their elders, perform a ritual of feeding the first batch of Meethe Gulgule to crows and other birds. The belief behind this act is that these birds always call out to the rest of their tribe when they find food. This symbolic gesture of sharing food represents the harmonious relationship between humans and nature. These sweet fritters are often served alongside spicy Dal ki Pakodi (see p. 26), making it a perfect sweet–spice combination.

Makes 24 gulgule

1 cup crushed jaggery
1 cup wheat flour
1 tbsp curd, beaten
1 tsp saunf (fennel) seeds, coarsely
  crushed
1 pinch soda bicarbonate
Ghee or oil for deep-frying

To prepare the batter

1. Heat ¾ cup water. Just before it begins to boil, add jaggery and turn off the heat. Dissolve jaggery and strain the liquid using a fine sieve.

2. While still warm, add the wheat flour, curd and saunf. Beat well with a hand whisk or spoon for about 2 minutes. Add soda bicarbonate and mix well. The consistency should be like cake batter, ideal for making pakodas. Set aside for at least 10 minutes.

Frying the gulgule

3. Add ghee or oil in a pan for frying and turn up the heat to medium. Drop spoonsful of the batter into the pan, leaving space in between each dollop. You can also use your fingers for this—just remember to wet them or the spoon with water to help the batter slide off easily.

4. Fry the gulgule in batches of 7–8. Ideally, they should float to the surface as soon as they hit the hot oil. Fry them on medium heat, flipping occasionally. Once they turn golden brown, transfer them to a plate lined with kitchen paper to drain. Repeat this process for all the gulgule.

Serve the gulgule hot or at room temperature. You can serve them plain or jazz them up with a sprinkle of powdered sugar or cinnamon powder. You could also do a drizzle of condensed milk. Enjoy as a sweet snack any time of the day.

 AAM KA KALAKAND *Milk Fudge with Mango*

A luscious twist on the classic milk fudge, this summer delight is infused with the golden richness of ripe mangoes and melts in the mouth with every bite. Use Alphonso or Pairi mangoes, as their smooth fibreless pulp needs no straining. Choose mangoes with a sweet-sour flavour—the slight tartness helps curdle the milk naturally and adds a delicious depth to the final taste.

Serves 4 to 6

1 litre full-fat milk (4 cups)
2 cups mango pulp, smooth and
    fibreless
2–4 tbsp curd
1 cup sugar
8–10 strands saffron
¼ tsp cardamom powder
1 tbsp pistachio slivers

1. In a heavy-bottomed pan, bring the milk to a boil. Once it rises, stir in the mango pulp and curd. Continue to cook over medium heat, stirring gently. The milk will begin to curdle. If the mangoes are not sour enough, add more curd to aid curdling.

2. Allow this mixture to simmer while stirring occasionally to prevent it from sticking to the bottom of the pan. Let it cook until the liquid evaporates completely—this may take about 30 minutes. Once the mixture is dry, add the sugar and cook further. Avoid adding the sugar too early, as it may cause the mixture to splatter before it thickens.

3. When the sugar has dissolved and the mixture turns granular, turn off the heat. Stir in the saffron strands and cardamom powder. Cover the pan and allow the aromas to infuse for about 5 minutes.

4. Garnish with pistachio slivers. Allow it to cool completely before serving.

Serve chilled in small dessert bowls or set in a tray and cut into soft pieces.

Shelf life: Stays well for 3–4 days when refrigerated.

 DILJANI *Orange Pudding with Boondi* *(pic on p. 19)*

Diljani means sweetheart, and the name truly reflects how loved this pudding-like mithai is. Chef Sameer discovered Diljani in the royal kitchens of Udaipur where it was prepared with marble-sized gulab jamun and orange-flavoured boondi. Also known as Nukti, boondi refers to tiny fried pearls of besan. Sameer created a simpler version of this dish by replacing the gulab jamun with orange segments.

Use only seasonal, sweet oranges for this delicacy. Otherwise, the orange syrup will lack the desired flavour and sweetness.

Serves 4 to 6

For syrup
1 cup fresh orange juice
3 tbsp sugar (or more, if oranges are not very sweet)
1 tsp orange zest
A few drops of orange food colour

For boondi layer
1 cup plain, unsalted boondi
2 cups orange segments, chilled
3 tbsp condensed milk

For topping
Few drops orange blossom water or 1 tsp rose water
2 tbsp pistachio slivers

1. Place the boondi in a sieve and shake off any spice powder or salt. Rinse with water and set aside.

2. In a pan, boil orange juice with sugar on high heat until the sugar melts, then simmer on medium heat for about 8 minutes.

3. Cool this syrup to room temperature and mix in the orange zest and food colour.

4. In a serving dish, mix boondi, orange segments and condensed milk.

5. Over this layer, pour the orange syrup and mix well.

6. Sprinkle the orange blossom water (or rose water) and garnish with pistachio slivers.

Serve chilled. To serve it warm, bake the boondi layer of Step 4 in a preheated oven at 180°C for 5 minutes and top it with the orange syrup.

Tip: You can add a dash of lemon to the orange syrup for a hint of tangy punch.

KANKRI MIRCH   *Peppery Health Crunch with Edible Gum and Nuts*

This mixture creates a truly satisfying sweet dish with a hint of pepper, perfect for the winter months. It is popularly referred to as Falodi, originating from the word 'foolya', which means puffed up, in connection to the puffed edible gum used in the recipe. The combination of edible gum, rock sugar and pepper lends the dish a grainy texture, hence earning its name 'kankri', which translates to tiny pebbles. In the vibrant land of Rajasthan, locals often kickstart their cold mornings with a few handfuls of this delicious treat. Not only does it warm and energise the body but it also curbs sweet cravings, making it a perfect start to the day.

Makes about 3 cups

½ cup ghee
½ cup gond (edible gum) crystals
½ cup almonds, roughly crushed
   (with mortar and pestle)
1 cup wheat flour
1 tsp peppercorns, coarsely crushed
1 tsp dried ginger powder
¾ cup sugar (preferably boora
   sugar; add more, as you prefer)
1 tbsp mishri (rock sugar), coarsely
   crushed

1. Heat ghee in a thick-bottomed pan on medium heat. Fry the gond crystals, a few at a time. As they puff up, remove them with a slotted spoon and transfer to a bowl. Fry all the gond in this manner. Crush them roughly.

2. In the same ghee, add crushed almonds. Lightly fry for a minute, remove from the pan and set aside.

3. In the same ghee, add wheat flour and roast for 2–3 minutes, stirring continuously. Add the fried gond back to the pan. Add crushed pepper and continue to roast for another 2–3 minutes, or until the flour turns golden brown.

4. Add ginger powder, turn off the heat and set aside.

5. Once it cools down completely, add the fried almonds, sugar and mishri. Mix well.

Serve in tiny bowls any time of the day, ideally mornings.

Shelf life: Prepare this mixture in larger quantities and store it in an airtight container in a dry place for up to a month.

Chef Sameer says
You can roll this mixture into small lemon-sized balls. For this, add a few tablespoons of warm melted ghee to bind it into shape.

INSTANT DAL KA HALWA   *Easy Recipe for Traditional Lentil Fudge*

A heart-warming comfort dish enjoyed in frosty Rajasthani winters, this is a much-awaited delicacy at weddings and festivities. The traditional process of soaking and grinding moong dal into a coarse paste and then cooking it to a rich golden colour can be tedious, so Sameer came up with a simpler recipe without compromising on colour, texture, flavour or taste. By substituting dal with its flour, and liberally using ghee, fragrant cardamom and aromatic strands of saffron, he ensured this novel version retains its authenticity.

Serves 4 to 6

½ cup ghee
½ cup flour of yellow moong dal*
¼ cup khoya (reduced milk) or
    malai (milk cream)
1¼ cups warm milk
½ cup sugar (or less, as you prefer)
½ tsp cardamom powder
½ tsp (15–20) saffron strands
1 tbsp almond slivers
1 tbsp pistachio slivers

---

* In Rajasthan, flour of moong dal is readily available. If you want to make it from scratch, rub a cup of yellow moong dal with a damp cloth to clean it, and then air-dry until it is completely moisture-free. Grind the dried dal at home or in a mill ensuring the powder remains slightly coarse, like sooji.

1. Reserve ¼ cup ghee and heat the rest in a heavy-bottomed pan. Add moong flour and roast on medium heat for 4–5 minutes, stirring continuously or until it turns aromatic and golden brown.

2. Crumble the khoya and add to the pan. Add milk and cook for about 3 minutes, stirring continuously. Turn the heat to medium-high. Add sugar and continue to cook for 2–3 minutes or until it thickens like a fudge.

3. Add the remaining ghee and continue to stir and cook for about 4 minutes. As the ghee starts leaving the sides of the pan, turn off the heat.

4. Mix in cardamom powder and saffron strands, and half of the almond and pistachio slivers. Garnish with the remaining slivers.

Serve hot as a sweet dish in a festive or elaborate menu. Else, enjoy it as a filling breakfast dish in winters.

> ## Variation
>
> **Dal Badam ka Halwa**
> For a rich, nutty flavour, you can roast ¼ cup chopped almonds along with the moong flour.

BESAN MALAI KA HALWA   *Fudge with Gram Flour and Milk Cream*

Neeta-ji Raisurana, who is like a mother to Sameer, created this unique recipe by mixing besan with homemade malai and cooking it in ghee. As the malai mixes with the besan, the texture transforms, becoming almost grainy when roasted. Sameer has also substituted malai with fresh cream, and says that both work equally well. The texture mimics that of traditional Dal ka Halwa and elevates the taste of the dish. You have to make it to believe it.

Serves 4 to 6

½ cup besan (gram flour)
½ cup malai (milk cream)
¼ tsp cardamom powder
12–15 saffron strands
½ cup ghee
½ cup sugar
½ tbsp almond slivers
½ tbsp pistachio slivers

1. Mix besan and malai into a smooth mix and set aside for 15 minutes.
2. Boil 1½ cups water. Add cardamom powder and saffron strands and set aside.
3. Reserve 1 tbsp ghee and heat the rest in a heavy-bottomed pan. Add the besan-malai mix to the pan and roast on medium heat for 5–6 minutes, or until it turns deep golden.
4. Add the cardamom and saffron-flavoured water and cook, stirring continuously, until it starts bubbling and becomes soft like a fudge, and ghee starts leaving the sides of the pan.
5. Add sugar and cook for 4–5 minutes, or until it thickens again. Add the reserved ghee and cook for 2 more minutes. Turn off the heat.
6. Garnish with almond and pistachio slivers.

Serve hot as a filling breakfast dish or as a sweet dish as part of a special meal.

MATAR KA HALWA   *Sweet Fudge with Green Peas*   *(pic on p. 17)*

Jaipurites are very possessive of their winter peas, and why not! The peas are more tender and sweeter than one can possibly imagine. In the winter months, the market is filled with these green pearls. Home cooks make hundreds of varieties of main and side dishes, snacks and even sweets out of them. As long as peas are in season, there will be at least one dish a day that highlights this delicate vegetable. Here is an ode to the beautiful winter peas: Matar ka Halwa.

Serves 4 to 6

2 cups fresh green peas
1 cup milk
½ cup ghee
½ cup khoya (reduced milk),
    crumbled
½ cup sugar
½ tsp cardamom powder
2 tbsp pistachio slivers

1. Blanch the green peas in hot water for 3 minutes and then rinse in chilled water to preserve the fresh green colour. Cook the peas in milk for 3 minutes. Strain the cooked peas and grind into a coarse paste. (Use the strained milk to knead the dough for roti or some other preparation.)

2. Reserve ¼ cup ghee and heat the remaining in a pan. Add the peas paste and cook on medium heat for 7–8 minutes. Stir continuously to prevent it from sticking to the bottom.

3. Add khoya and cook for 3–4 minutes, then add sugar and cook for 1–2 minutes. At this stage, the halwa might become slightly runny as the sugar dissolves. Continue to cook until it reaches a fudge-like consistency.

4. Add the reserved ghee gradually, 1 tbsp at a time and cook for about 5 minutes, until the halwa begins to leave the sides of the pan. Turn off the heat.

5. Sprinkle cardamom powder and mix well. Remove any excess ghee floating on top of the dish with a spoon (and use it in any other preparation). Garnish the halwa with pistachio slivers.

Serve hot as a sweet dish any time of the day. It's an ideal addition to a festive or party menu.

Ask Chef Sameer

Pratibha: Why do you boil the peas in milk and then discard the liquid?

Sameer: Peas have a strong, overpowering, protein-rich taste, and milk helps mellow and balance this flavour, which can otherwise alter the taste of the sweet dish. This is why the milk is discarded. But it can be used in other preparations.

Matar ka Halwa p.16

Diljani p.12

18

Matar ka Halwa p.16

Diljani p.12

Maanglik Laapsi p.3

19

Paneer Roll p.29

20

NAMKEEN

Savoury Snacks and Street-style Bites

Whenever I recall my childhood holidays spent with my cousins in Jodhpur, the memories of steaming koftas and kachoris from the nearby snack shop appear front and centre. I have never been much of a sweet lover, so the golden jalebi or Mawa ki Kachori, which the rest of my family devoured, didn't interest me. It was the varieties of namkeen, or savoury snacks, that had my mouth watering. These were not just eaten at tea-time but were often served as appetisers with the main meal. I owe the cultivation of spice in my palate to the tongue-tingling savoury snacks of those holidays.

Although these snacks were always at hand, I rarely saw them made at home. They were so easily available at affordable prices that it allowed my aunt, who was the primary cook, to focus on churning out simple, comforting dishes for a small army at every meal.

With these tasty additions coming from the local snack shop, I grew up with a mix of home and shop food. This changed after meeting Sameer. A chef by profession and also the primary cook at home, he is equally skilled at simple comforting dishes as well as complex culinary treats. This section features savoury snacks of both kind. We hope you enjoy them.

An Ode to Childhood Flavours

As the suspended metal rectangle
Was struck and struck again
We'd run gleefully out of the school gates
Ready to bargain

Sweet and sour berries
And fruit and vegetable chaat
Pomegranate-flavoured golis
Hot chai to warm our heart

Spiced icy popsicles
Licked from the elbow up
Raw mango with chilli powder
From an overflowing cup

The hundred-wrinkled grandfather
The lady with a toothless smile
The rickety wooden cycle carts
Lined up longer than a mile

Not one fancy burger
Or pizza in our sight
Mirchi vada and kofta
Remind me of the delight

खट्टी मीठी

मुझे अपने स्कूल के दिन याद आते हैं जहाँ ना आज की तरह फ़ैन्सी केंटीन होते थे, ना ही होते थे पिज़्ज़ा और बर्गर। इंटरवेल में स्कूल के बाहर होते थे कोफ्ते और कचौरी के ठेले वाले, चेहरे पर हज़ार झुर्रियों व पोपले मुँह वाली बूढ़ी माई के लाल-लाल बेर और हरे डांसरे, सर्दियों में गाजर मूली और अमरूद की मसाले वाली चाट तो गर्मियों में ठंडक देते थे, बर्फ़ की चुस्की वाले गोले, जिसका आधा रस चूस कर थोड़ा और रस लेने का बालसुलभ लोभ, चूरण और गोली वाला जिसके पास होते थे अनारदाना, कोकम, अमचूर व कटबेल पाचक यानि काठौडी।

मैं तो इन सबको भूल सा गया था, पर राय सुराना पापा के यहाँ ये विस्मृत स्वाद जैसे पुनः जीवित हो गया। पापा जब रसोई में जाकर कटबेल का पाचक बनाते और शौक़ से हमें चखाते तो उनके चेहरे की चमक देखने लायक़ होती थी।

समीर

JODHPURI MIRCHI VADA   *Fried Chillies with Potato Filling*   *(pic on p. 38)*

An all-time favourite snack to satisfy your craving for spicy, rich and robust flavours, this Jodhpur speciality is available at every street corner of the city. Large, succulent chillies are filled with a potato filling, dipped in golden besan batter and then fried to perfection. If you want a fiery start to your day, follow the local tradition and eat it for breakfast!

Makes 6 mirchi vadas

6 large green chillies (long, thick variety, which is not very spicy)

For tadka
1 tbsp oil
1 pinch hing (asafoetida powder)
½ tsp cumin seeds
1 tsp saunf (fennel) seeds, coarsely crushed
1 tsp coriander seeds, coarsely crushed

For potato mix
1½ cups boiled, mashed potatoes
1 tsp fresh ginger, finely chopped
½ tsp salt
½ tsp black salt
½ tsp red chilli powder
1 tsp chaat masala or amchur (dried mango) powder
½ tsp Marwadi garam masala (p. 193)
2 tbsp coriander leaves, chopped

For batter
1½ cups besan (gram flour) (and more for dusting)
1 pinch soda bicarbonate
½ tsp salt
½ tsp turmeric powder
¼ tsp ajwain (carom) seeds, hand-crushed

For deep-frying
Oil

1. To make the filling, heat 1 tbsp oil in a pan and add the ingredients for tadka. As the seeds crackle, add the potato mix and cook for 2–3 minutes on medium-high heat, mixing it well. Set it aside to cool down.

2. Wash and pat dry the chillies, keeping the stalks. Slit lengthwise to remove the seeds. Divide the filling into 6 portions, stuff the chillies and dust with dry besan.

3. Whisk together the ingredients for the batter in a bowl with about 1 cup water, taking care to make it lump-free like cake batter.

4. Heat oil for frying in a pan. Dip the stuffed chillies in the batter and fry them, two at a time, on medium heat for 2–3 minutes, or until the batter sets well on the chillies.

5. Once all the chillies are fried, dip them again in the batter and refry them on medium-high heat for 3–4 minutes, flipping occasionally so they turn golden brown all over.

Serve hot with Green Chutney (p. 162) and any Tamarind Chutney (p. 163).

Ask Chef Sameer

Pratibha: Can the second frying be done after a few hours?
Sameer: No, the second frying must be done while the Mirchi Vada is still warm from the first round of frying. If you allow a longer gap, it will absorb too much oil when you refry.
Pratibha: How can this Mirchi Vada be made Jain-friendly?
Sameer: In many such delicacies, Jain families use raw plantains instead of potatoes—it retains the texture and flavour well.

❧ TANATAN KOFTA *Instant Savoury Balls with Bhujia Sev*

Aloo bhujia, also known as Tanatan bhujia, isn't just a delightful savoury snack, but an ingredient with versatile uses. Chef Sameer's favourite, he uses this bhujia in many dishes, including this recipe to craft koftas, which are incredibly easy to make and tasty too.

Makes 8 koftas

For kofta

1 cup aloo bhujia (about 100 gm)
2 tbsp onions, finely chopped
2 tbsp tomatoes, finely chopped
1 tsp green chillies, finely chopped
1 tsp fresh ginger, finely chopped
2 tbsp coriander leaves, chopped
1 tsp coriander seeds, coarsely
  crushed
1 tsp saunf seeds, coarsely crushed
½ tsp chaat masala
½ tsp red chilli powder
¼ tsp black salt

For batter

3 tbsp maida (all-purpose flour)
1 tbsp sooji (semolina)
½ tsp black cumin seeds or ajwain
  (carom) seeds

For deep- frying

Oil

1. Mix the ingredients for kofta in a bowl. Mash the mixture gently to bind it together. If the mixture seems too dry, sprinkle up to 1 tbsp water. Divide the mixture into 8 equal portions and shape each one into a tight ball.

2. To make the batter, mix maida, sooji and black cumin in ½ cup water. The batter should be just thick enough to coat the back of a spoon.

3. Heat oil for frying in a pan. Dip 3–4 balls in the batter carefully and drop them in the hot oil. Fry on medium-high heat for about a minute until light golden. Transfer to a dish lined with kitchen paper to absorb any excess oil. Fry the remaining kofta balls.

Serve hot with Green Chutney (p. 162) as a tea-time snack or party starter.

> 🌿 **Variations**
>
> ❀ **Tanatan Poodi**
>   Use the kofta mixture instead of the popular urad dal filling to make Bedwi Poodi.
>
> ❀ **Tanatan Kachori**
>   Fill kachoris with the kofta mixture instead of the traditional dal filling.
>
> ❀ **Tanatan Kofta Curry**
>   For a rich sabzi, you can serve these koftas in any gravy of your choice.

PREM PRAKASH SAMOSA   *A Cult Classic from Cinema's Golden Days*

On one of my trips to Jaipur, my brother-in-law Gautam Seth—who shares a truly special food bond with me—introduced me to these samosas with the words, 'You've never tasted samosas like these.' Naturally, I had to ask Chef Sameer—since he knows just about every Rajasthani recipe there is.

This is a tribute to the iconic Prem Prakash Talkies (now Golecha Cinema) of Jaipur, where this samosa was once sold. Its flavour is unlike the typical spicy samosa—no red chilli, no chaat masala—just an honest, deeply satisfying taste. Even today, street vendors and local shops across Jaipur continue to sell it by its original name—Prem Prakash Samosa, or simply PP Samosa. Unpretentious yet flavourful, it carries the memories of old cinema halls, rustling wrappers and shared bites under flickering interval light.

Makes 12 mini samosas

For filling
2 tbsp oil
1 tbsp ginger, finely chopped
2 tbsp green chillies, finely chopped
2 tbsp coriander leaves, finely chopped
2 cups boiled potatoes, roughly mashed
1 tsp salt
1 tsp white or black pepper powder
a pinch citric acid (or 1 tsp amchur powder)

For dough
1¼ cups maida (all-purpose flour)
2 tbsp melted ghee
½ tsp salt

For sealing and deep-frying
1 tbsp maida
Oil

1. To make the filling, heat oil in a pan over medium flame. Add the chopped ginger, green chillies and coriander leaves. Stir for about 30 seconds. Add the mashed potatoes and cook for 5–7 minutes, stirring and roasting. If any of the mixture sticks to the bottom and forms a crust, don't discard—scrape it off and mix it back in. It adds a delicious crusty flavour. Add salt, pepper and citric acid, and mix well. Turn off the heat and set the filling aside to cool.

2. To prepare the dough, mix maida with ghee and salt in a paraat (wide-rim plate). Add cold water in small amounts, kneading into a semi-tight dough. Cover with a damp cloth and set aside for 15–20 minutes.

3. In a bowl, mix 1 tbsp maida with ¼ cup of water to make a thin batter.

4. Knead the dough once more for 10 seconds, divide it into 6 portions and roll into balls. Roll each portion into an oval and cut it in half. Form a cone with one half, fill with some of the cooled potato mixture and seal the edge with the maida batter. (If shaping the samosas feels tricky, you can also make potli-style samosas by gathering the edges like a small pouch and sealing them at the top.)

5. Refrigerate the samosas for 30 minutes in the summer, or air-dry them in the winter for a crispy crust.

6. Heat oil in a pan for frying. Add 2–3 samosas and fry on low heat initially. Gradually raise the heat to medium-high until golden and crisp. Remove to a plate and fry the remaining samosas in batches.

Enjoy this samosa with a cup of chai for the perfect tea-time bite—no chutneys needed, so you can savour its distinct flavour.

DAL KI PAKODI *Lentil Fritters*

Dal ki Pakodi is a year-round favourite, but it gains special significance in the month of Paush as per the Vikram Samvat Calendar. This pakodi is prepared in most Rajasthani homes during the kite festival of Makar Sankranti. In temples, it is offered as prasad in the form of slightly larger-sized vadas, known as Paush Vada.

Makes 18 to 20 small pakodis

For grinding
½ cup chawli dal (split cow peas)
½ cup yellow moong dal
1 tsp coriander seeds
1 tsp saunf (fennel) seeds
4 cloves
4 peppercorns

Other ingredients
1 tbsp fresh ginger, finely chopped
1 tbsp green chillies, finely chopped
1 tbsp coriander leaves, finely chopped
1 tsp red chilli powder
1 tsp kuti mirch (coarse chilli powder)
¼ tsp hing (asafoetida powder)
1 tsp salt

For deep-frying
Oil

Tip: You can add 2–3 tbsp of seasonal greens such as fresh dill, mustard or garlic greens to the batter.

1. Wash together the ingredients for grinding and soak in water for 4–5 hours. Drain and grind into a coarse mixture with as little water as required (up to 2 tbsp water).

2. Add all the items listed under other ingredients to the batter, and mix well.

3. In a pan, heat oil for frying until it turns hot, but not smoky. Reduce the heat. Using your hands or a spoon, drop 5–6 dollops of the batter, about 1 tbsp each, into the oil, one by one. Fry for 3–4 minutes on medium heat, and then for 1–2 more minutes on high heat, or until they turn golden brown.

4. Transfer these pakodis to a plate lined with kitchen paper. Make more pakodis using the remaining batter.

Serve hot with Green Chutney (p. 162) as an anytime snack. A favourite during winters.

> **Variation**
>
> **Jhol ki Pakodi**
> A village favourite from Rajasthan, this quick treat features pakodis soaked in 'pitkaali ka jhol'—a tangy-spicy water. Mix ½ tsp hing, 1 tsp chilli powder, 2 tsp salt, and juice of 1 lemon in 1 litre water. Soak pakodis in this spicy water, known as jhol, for at least 2 hours. Serve 1–2 pakodis in a cup of the jhol. You might just find everyone asking for more of this spicy water!

PYAAZ KI KACHORI   *Fried Pies with Spicy Onion Filling*   *(pic on p. 38)*

This beloved dish has gained popularity beyond its Jodhpur origin. For instance, Maya Chaat shop in the Sowcarpet area of Chennai has recreated this kachori perfectly, and Rajasthanis from across the city testify to its authentic taste. Most people prefer to buy this snack from their favourite chaat shop rather than making it at home. But it is time to change that. Follow this recipe precisely, and you will be patting yourself on the back while serving the perfect kachori! Nothing compares with a freshly fried kachori; yet, it is possible to make these ahead of time and crisp them up in the oven just before serving.

Makes 8 kachoris

For dough
1½ cups maida (all-purpose flour)
3 tbsp oil
½ tsp salt

For tadka
2 tbsp oil
1 pinch hing (asafoetida powder)
½ tsp cumin seeds
½ tsp saunf (fennel) seeds, crushed
½ tsp coriander seeds, crushed
½ tsp kuti mirch (coarse chilli powder)

For filling
1 cup onions, finely chopped
1 tbsp green chillies, finely chopped
1 tsp garlic, finely chopped
1½ tbsp besan (gram flour)
½ cup boiled, mashed potatoes
¾ tsp salt
1 tsp red chilli powder
1 tsp amchur (dried mango) powder
½ tsp Marwadi garam masala (p. 193)
5 to 6 fresh mint leaves, chopped
2 tbsp coriander leaves, chopped

For deep-frying
Oil

1. Mix maida, salt and 3 tbsp oil in a paraat (wide-rim plate). Knead into a semi-soft dough using about ½ cup warm water. Cover with a damp cloth, set aside for 15 minutes.

2. Heat 2 tbsp oil in a pan and add the ingredients for tadka. As the seeds crackle, add onions, green chillies and garlic, and fry for 2–3 minutes on medium-high heat.

3. Add besan and cook for 30 seconds. Add the mashed potatoes and remaining ingredients for the filling. Cook for 1–2 minutes, mixing it well. Set it aside to cool down.

4. Knead the dough again for a minute, divide into 8 equal portions and shape into balls. Divide the filling into 8 portions.

5. To make a kachori, pat one ball of dough into a circle of 3-inch diameter. Place one portion of filling in the centre. Bring together the edges of the circle on top, seal tightly and pinch off any excess dough from the top. Now shape it into a circle of 2.5-inch diameter, ensuring the filling does not spill out. You can use some dry flour to pat it into shape. Repeat with the remaining balls and filling to make all the kachoris.

6. Heat oil for frying in a pan. Add 2–3 kachoris at a time and fry on high heat for about a minute, or until tiny bubbles appear on them. Remove them to a plate.

7. Once all the kachoris are fried, refry them immediately on medium heat for 5–7 minutes, flipping occasionally so they turn golden brown all over. Transfer to a serving plate lined with kitchen paper.

Serve hot with Green Chutney (p. 162) and any Tamarind Chutney (p. 163) as an anytime snack.

Ask Chef Sameer

Pratibha: Why do you fry these kachoris twice?

Sameer: As explained in the recipe, you should remove the kachori from oil as soon as tiny bubbles appear on their surface. This halts the cooking process that takes place during frying. When you refry the kachori, it develops that crispy and flaky, yet soft crust, a texture expert chefs achieve through this secret two-step process.

KAPURA PITOD   *Fresh Pasta Snack with Besan*   *(pic on p. 39)*

With besan at home, the Rajasthani housewife has no dearth of dishes to serve the sudden guest. Kofta, pakodi, cheela—all of them use besan as the base. Kapura Pitod ranks supreme amongst dishes cooked with besan. Resembling golden pasta sheets garnished with tadka, you cannot resist picking up a couple of pieces on the go.

Note: For this dish, keep in mind that you have to prepare the pitod beforehand.

Serves 4

2 cups pitod (recipe on p. 201)

For tadka
2 tsp oil
¼ tsp hing (asafoetida powder)
½ tsp mustard seeds
1 tsp white sesame seeds (optional)

Final ingredients
1 tsp jeeravan masala (p. 195) or
   chaat masala
1 sprig of coriander leaves,
   chopped
1 lemon, cut into wedges

1.   Arrange the pitod pieces on a serving platter.

2.   In a small pan, heat oil on medium heat, and add hing and mustard. As mustard crackles, add sesame and immediately drizzle this tadka over the pitod.

3.   Sprinkle jeeravan masala, garnish with coriander leaves and serve with lemon wedges.

Serve at room temperature with Green Chutney (p. 162). This is an ideal party snack or as a dry side dish in a meal.

PANEER ROLL *Pan-fried Cottage Cheese Roll* *(pic on p. 20)*

A delectable and nutritious snack made with paneer (cottage cheese), featuring a one-of-a-kind filling of bhujia, chutney and nuts. Unleash your culinary creativity with this filling, perfect for stuffed paratha, stuffed tinda and even the traditional luchi. Luchi is a Bengali-style fried poodi typically made without any filling, but Sameer surprised his guests by adding a delicious filling to it and turning it into a delightful treat! Ensure the paneer is firm, yet soft and pliable so it rolls easily without breaking.

Serves 4

200 gm (about 2×4 inch) block of paneer
1 tsp oil, for brushing the pan

For filling
2 tbsp green chutney (p. 162)
25 raisins (preferably lemon-soaked, p. 209)
12–15 cashew nuts, broken into bits
4 tbsp bhujia (preferably aloo bhujia)
½ tsp salt
1 tsp red chilli powder
1 tsp amchur (dried mango) powder
1 tsp cumin seeds, roasted and crushed

1. Cut the block of paneer into 6 to 8 thin, even slices.
2. Grind the ingredients for filling into a thick and coarse paste, without adding any water.
3. Heat a non-stick pan and brush with oil. Cook each slice of paneer, one by one, on medium-high heat for a few seconds (without flipping). Take care that it remains soft and does not get roasted or turn crisp. Transfer to a plate.
4. Spoon some filling onto one end of the paneer slice and roll it gently like a carpet. Do this with all the paneer slices and arrange the rolls on a plate, seam side down.

Serve warm or chilled as a tea-time snack. A much-loved dish for your party menu.

BADI KI TIKKI *Cutlets with Lentil Nuggets*

Badi, also known as mangodi, are sun-dried nuggets of soaked and ground lentils mixed with spices. Although many families make them at home, these are readily available and are used in sabzi and pulav. This innovative recipe converts the humble badi into exotic kabab. Use good quality badi to get the perfect texture and crispness.

Makes 12 tikkis

For batter

2 cups badi (lentil nuggets)*
1 tsp salt
1 tsp red chilli powder
½ tsp Marwadi garam masala (p. 193)
1 tsp chaat masala or amchur (dried mango) powder
½ tsp cumin seeds, roasted and crushed
1 tsp coriander seeds, coarsely crushed
1 tsp saunf (fennel) seeds, coarsely crushed
1 tbsp kasuri methi (dried fenugreek leaves)
1 tbsp green chillies, finely chopped
1 tbsp fresh ginger, finely chopped
1 tbsp coriander leaves, finely chopped

For roasting

2–3 tbsp oil

*Available in online stores as Marwadi badi or mangodi.

1. Crush badi and soak in just enough hot water for 10–15 minutes. It will absorb most of the water; in case of any excess, drain it out. Grind the soaked badi into a coarse paste.

2. Add remaining ingredients of the batter to the badi paste and mix well.

3. Heat a tawa, preferably non-stick, and brush with oil. Drop 4–6 spoonsful of the batter, leaving space in between. Use the back of the ladle to spread them into 2-inch round tikkis and drizzle oil around them. Cover the pan with a lid and roast the tikkis on medium-high heat, around 2 minutes on each side.

4. Transfer these tikkis to a plate and make the remaining tikkis.

Serve hot with Green Chutney (p. 162) or any Garlic Chutney (p. 165) as a party snack.

PANEER PAPAD KURKURE   *Cottage Cheese Fingers in a Crunchy Crust*

Seeing Sameer dip and roll the paneer fingers into the batter and crushed papads is quite a pleasing sight—it looks effortless, but it takes a bit of practice and is well worth the effort. This delightful snack works any time of the day—at breakfast, with evening tea or as a party starter when guests drop in. The fun (and a little challenge) lies in getting the coating just right—evenly and quickly.

Serves 4

200 gm (about 2×4 inch) block of
    paneer
1 tbsp pickle masala (p. 194)
1 tbsp ginger paste
1 tbsp green chilli paste
½ tsp salt
2 tsp oil
¼ cup maida (all-purpose flour)
3 unroasted Bikaneri papads
Oil for deep-frying

1. Cut the paneer into half and then cut into 16 fingers.

2. On a plate, mix the pickle masala, ginger paste, green chilli paste, salt and oil. Coat the paneer fingers with this mixture. Set aside.

3. Crush the papads by hand into a coarse mixture. If needed, air-dry them for about an hour to make crushing easier. You may also use a mixer, but take care not to grind them into a powder.

4. In a bowl, mix maida with 1/3 cup water to make a smooth batter (also known as a slurry).

5. At a time, dip 5–6 marinated paneer fingers into the maida batter, then roll them in the crushed papads to coat them well. Repeat with the rest. Freeze for 10–15 minutes to set the coating.

6. Heat oil in a pan over medium-high heat for deep-frying. Fry the coated paneer fingers in batches until golden and crispy. Transfer to a dish lined with kitchen paper.

Serve hot with Green Chutney (p. 162). A crunchy, spicy bite perfect for tea-time!

 CHAWLI KA BHAPIYA *Steamed Dumplings with Cow Peas* *(pic on p. 39)*

Bhapiya is a term that evolved from bhaap, meaning steam. A close cousin of the Gujarati dhokla and Maharashtrian pandoli, many variations of bhapiya are made by soaking and grinding certain lentils and grains, and steaming the batter to make savoury cakes. Whole or split chawli (cow peas or black-eyed beans) forms the base of this healthy, tasty, low-calorie bhapiya. Ideal as a breakfast snack with spicy green chutney, it also does well as a starter for any party. It can be prepared in advance and served at room temperature.

Serves 4 to 6

2 cups white chawli (cow peas)
1 cup curd
1 tsp cumin seeds
1 tsp salt
2 tsp sugar
2 tsp ginger paste
2 tsp green chilli paste
2 tbsp oil
2 tsp Eno fruit salt
2 tbsp coriander leaves, chopped

Tip: Add ginger and green chilli paste to the batter for a warming flavour. You can also add a fistful of greens such as fresh dill, spinach or fenugreek.

1. Wash chawli and soak in water for about 6 hours. Strain and set aside the water. Grind the chawli into a fine paste with curd, cumin seeds and as little of the strained water as required. The consistency should be like cake batter.

2. Transfer the batter to a deep bowl and mix in salt, sugar, ginger paste, green chilli paste and oil. Mix well, preferably with a hand whisk.

3. To steam the batter, fill a pan (about 8x10-inch in size) with 2 cups water and bring to a boil. Place a ring or stand in the pan tall enough to surface above the water. Keep ready a steel plate, large enough to be placed over the ring, and grease it lightly with oil. You can also make the bhapiya in a steamer or idli maker.

4. Alongside, add Eno fruit salt into the batter and mix well, allowing it to rise evenly. With a spoon, quickly drop rounds of 1 tbsp batter on the greased plate, keeping enough space between the rounds to allow them to spread while steaming. (Drop the batter without spreading it with the spoon, it will spread on its own.)

5. Place the plate on the ring, in the pan. Cover the pan with a lid and steam the rounds for 8–10 minutes on medium heat. Remove the plate from the pan and set aside for 1–2 minutes, then remove the steamed bhapiyas with a wet spatula or flat spoon. Garnish with coriander leaves.

Serve hot with Green Chutney (p. 162) or plain curd or spiced curd. You can sprinkle a tsp of jeeravan masala (p. 195) for some spice. Some families add a tadka of mustard and sesame seeds just before serving.

 Variation

> **Moong Dal Bhapiya**
> Substitute chawli with yellow or green moong dal and follow the recipe.

 MEWA CHAAT   *Dry Fruit Munch*

As lovers of rich food, it's no surprise that this robust, tangy, crunchy chaat made with the finest nuts is one of the most anticipated starters at Rajasthani weddings. Known for their craze for dry fruit and nuts, people of Rajasthan fuss over procuring the best quality and serve them to guests with pride. Many dishes, especially those served at special occasions, include almonds and pistachios. In this protein-rich chaat, the nuts are roasted to perfection in salt, mixed with spices and enriched with the smoky flavour of caramelised sugar.

Serves 4 to 6

For nut mix
½ cup kala chana (brown chickpeas)
1 cup salt (to roast nuts)
¼ cup almonds
¼ cup cashew nuts
¼ cup walnuts
¼ cup raisins
¼ cup dates, cut into tiny bits

For caramelising
1 tbsp ghee or oil
1 tbsp honey (or agave syrup or maple syrup)
1 tbsp sugar

For seasoning
½ tsp salt
½ tsp black salt
½ tsp red chilli powder
½ tsp pepper powder
½ tsp yellow chilli powder (optional, but adds a punch)
1 tsp chaat masala
1 tsp cumin seeds, roasted and crushed
1 tbsp lemon juice

1. Wash chana and soak overnight. Pressure cook chana with ½ tsp salt and a pinch of turmeric for 3–4 whistles. It should be well cooked, but not become mushy. Drain and set aside to cool.

2. Heat a cup of salt in a wide pan for about 5 minutes on high heat. Reduce to low heat and roast the nuts in this salt, one by one: almonds for 3 minutes, cashews for 2 minutes and walnuts for 1 minute, or until they turn golden brown. Stir continuously so they are evenly roasted. Remove each of the nuts with a slotted spoon before adding the next one. Sieve them through a metal strainer to remove the salt.

3. Transfer the nuts to a plate, cool and break them into small pieces (almost the size of chickpeas). Add raisins and chopped dates. Mix in the cooked chana. Set this nut mix aside.

4. For caramelising, melt ghee in a wide iron pan or skillet on medium heat. Add 1 tbsp water along with honey and sugar. Cook for about 2 minutes, stirring continuously, as the liquid starts bubbling and turns frothy. Add the nut mix and continue roasting for a few minutes, stirring gently. When the nut mix turns a little smoky, turn off the heat.

5. Sprinkle the ingredients for seasoning, except the lemon juice, over the nut mix. Mix well, then add lemon juice.

Serve in mini leaf bowls, shot glasses or in a paper cone as an anytime munch.

Chef Sameer says
You can cook the chana and roast the nuts in advance. Do the steps for caramelising and seasoning just before serving.

SHEKHAWATI KAANJI VADA   *Lentil Dumplings in Fermented Mustard Water*
(pic on p. 99)

The Shekhawati region is renowned for its recipes, offering a journey back to the roots. Among these gems, Shekhawati Vadas stand out, often overshadowed by the popularity of urad vadas, but definitely worth trying. A combination of lentils gives these vadas a distinctive texture and an irresistible taste. An ideal addition to an elaborate menu, these vadas can be enjoyed in multiple ways, as you'll discover in this recipe.

Note: Plan this dish two days in advance as the kaanji fermentation takes 24–36 hours.

Makes about 25 vadas

For kaanji
1 litre water
2 tbsp kaanji masala (p. 195)

For vada
½ cup yellow moong dal
½ cup white chawli dal (split cow peas)
½ cup whole moth (dew beans)
2 tsp coriander seeds
2 tsp saunf (fennel) seeds
1 black cardamom
4 cloves
6 peppercorns
2 dried, long red chillies

To soften vada
1 litre water
¼ tsp hing (asafoetida powder)
1 tsp salt

For deep-frying
Oil

1. To make kaanji, boil 1 litre of water and let it cool to room temperature. Add kaanji masala, stir well with a wooden spoon and transfer to a glass or ceramic jar. Cover with a cloth and set aside for 24 hours, stirring occasionally. It should develop a sharp, sour taste with the mustard now floating on top. In winter, allow an extra 12 hours for fermentation. The kaanji is now ready.

2. Alongside, wash the three dals and soak them in water for 4–5 hours with the remaining ingredients for vada. Drain and grind the soaked dals and spices into a slightly coarse paste with very little water. Transfer to a bowl and beat well. If the batter is too thick, add 1 tbsp water and beat again.

3. Heat oil in a pan to fry the vadas. When the oil is just medium hot, wet your palm and shape 2 tbsp of the batter into a 2-inch disk, and slide it into the oil. Repeat to add more vadas to the oil. You can fry 5–6 vadas at a time. Fry for 4–5 minutes on medium heat, and then for 2 minutes on high heat. Transfer to a plate and fry the next lot of vadas. Cool them down to room temperature.

4. Heat 1 litre water with ¼ tsp hing and 1 tsp salt. As the water begins to boil, turn off the heat. Drop in the vadas and leave them for 4–5 hours. Then, squeeze out water from the vadas by pressing each one between your palms.

5. Soak the vadas in the fermented kaanji for 3–4 hours. You can also infuse a smoky flavour to this dish using the dhungaar method (p. 202).

Serve 2–3 vadas per person, along with the kaanji, in shallow bowls, at room temperature or chilled.

Shelf life: You can refrigerate the fermented kaanji for up to a week. If you add vadas to the kaanji, refrigerate and consume within 2 days.

> ## 🌿 Variations
>
> 🌸 **Shekhawati Vada**
> To enjoy the fried vadas as a snack, follow only Steps 2 and 3, but remember to add salt and hing to the batter.
>
> 🌸 **Shekhawati Dahi Vada**
> Follow the recipe from Step 1 to 4. Dip the vadas in beaten curd, drizzle with Tamarind Chutney (p. 163) and Green Chutney (p. 162). Sprinkle some spices on top.

Ask Chef Sameer

Pratibha: Why do you add salt and hing to the water instead of the batter?

Sameer: Frying mellows the aroma of hing. Therefore, add salt and hing to the water and soak the vadas in this flavoured water. This simple tip will enhance the flavour of the vadas in this water-based dish.

Pratibha: When you grind the mixture coarsely, what happens to the cardamom and cloves? Is it all right if they are not ground fine?

Sameer: When whole spices are soaked, they go soft and become pasty on grinding.

PAPAD POTATO ROLL   *Indian Spring Roll with Papad*   *(pic on p. 37)*

In this innovative recipe, the versatile papad takes centre stage, being transformed into a lip-smacking snack, drawing inspiration from the Chinese spring roll. Sameer's experiments led to this culinary composition, where he ingeniously uses papad as a spring roll sheet and fills it with a spicy potato mixture. (To know more about papad, read p. 212.) Be warned, handling papad is an art. Try it a few times to gain expertise before you add it to your party menu.

Makes 12 to 16 potato rolls

For tadka

1 tbsp oil
1 pinch hing (asafoetida powder)
½ tsp cumin seeds
½ tsp saunf (fennel) seeds, coarsely crushed
½ tsp coriander seeds, coarsely crushed
6 cashew nuts (or peanuts), broken into bits

For potato mix

2 cups boiled, mashed potatoes
½ tsp salt
½ tsp black salt
½ tsp red chilli powder
1 tbsp green chillies, finely chopped
1 tbsp fresh ginger, finely chopped
10 raisins (preferably lemon-soaked, p. 209)
½ tsp Marwadi garam masala (p. 193)
½ tsp chaat masala
2 tbsp coriander leaves, chopped

For frying

1 tbsp maida (all-purpose flour)
4 unroasted Bikaneri papad
Oil for deep-frying

1. For the tadka (the Indian cooking technique of tempering, also known as baghaar), heat 1 tbsp oil in a pan on medium-high heat. Add all the ingredients for tadka and stir for 10 seconds.

2. Add all the ingredients for potato mix, stir and cook for 2–3 minutes. Set aside this filling to cool down.

3. In a bowl, mix maida in ¼ cup water to make a thin batter.

4. Keep ready a board and a bowl of warm water. Dip a papad for just 10 seconds, then lay it flat on the board. Place one-quarter of the filling near the bottom of the papad, leaving space at the edges. Fold in the two sides over the filling, roll up gently into a 4-inch log and seal with the maida batter.

5. Alongside, heat oil for frying in a pan. Add the papad roll and fry on medium-high heat for a minute until crispy. Transfer to a dish lined with kitchen paper. Make the remaining rolls in the same manner. Fry each roll one at a time to avoid breaking the papad.

6. Cut each roll into 3–4 pieces before serving

Serve hot with Green Chutney (p. 162) as a tea-time snack, or a party starter.

 Variation

🧠 **Papad and Raw Plantain Roll**
For a Jain alternative to potatoes, substitute them with raw plantain.

Papad Potato Roll p.36

Pyaaz ki Kachori p.27

Papad Potato Roll p.36

Paneer Roll p.29

Mirchi Vada p.23

38

Chawli ka Bhapiya p.32

Kapura Pitod p.28

Makki ka Dhokla p.44

DHOKLA AND DHOKLI

Savoury Doughnuts and Dumplings

When I sent this manuscript to my friend Annapurna, she exclaimed, 'A section on dhokla? I thought dhokla is the name of one particular dish!' For most people, the word 'dhokla' conjures the image of a soft, spongy, savoury cake. That is the Gujarati dhokla. The Rajasthani dhokla, in contrast, is dense and more wholesome.

In this section, you will find many varieties of dhokla made with flour such as wheat, maize and jowar. The common ingredient in any dhokla is 'papad khaar', an alkaline salt used in making papad of all kinds. Some of my friends and family have substituted it with soda bicarbonate, but not Chef Sameer. He states that the papad khaar lends a distinct flavour and texture to dhokla, which really makes it worth procuring.

In winters, Rajasthanis frequently make Khaar ka Dhokla and Makki ka Dhokla, while summers call for Khichiya ka Dhokla and Fogla ka Dhokla. This section also features dhokli, which is teasingly called 'dhokle ki bahan', meaning dhokla's sister, in Rajasthan, and 'dal ki dulhan', meaning dal's bride, in Uttar Pradesh. Unlike the doughnut-shaped dhokla, the dhokli is formed into small nuggets or pasta-like pieces that float in a lentil or vegetable broth.

Serving Tips
How to make the most of a dhokla

Serve any of these dhoklas, including Khaariya, in the following manner:

- With warm ghee or oil for a simple, comforting meal.
- With ghee and sugar (preferably boora sugar) for a sweet taste.
- With Jeeravan Masala (p. 195), or a dash of Chilli Ghee (p. 196), or any Garlic Chutney (p. 165) for a spicy flavour.
- With Panchmel Dal (p. 103) or Moong Chana Dal (p. 105) for a sumptuous lunch.

Serve with ghee in the summers and sesame oil in winters.

❧ KHAAR KA DHOKLA   *Savoury Steamed Cake*

This steamed, savoury cake made with flour and lentils is an impressive dish to serve even on days you do not want to cook a lavish meal. It is easy to make and has a delicious nutty texture due to the addition of soaked lentils. You can experiment with other flours in this recipe depending on seasonal availability.

Makes 8 dhoklas

For dough*

1 tbsp chana dal

1 tbsp yellow moong dal

2 cups bajri (pearl millet) or wheat flour

1½ tsp papad khaar (an alkaline salt)

2 tbsp oil

1 tsp cumin seeds

1½ tsp salt

2 tsp red chilli powder

1 tbsp coriander seeds, coarsely crushed

1 tbsp fresh ginger, finely chopped

1 tbsp green chillies, finely chopped

2 tbsp onions (preferably onion greens), finely chopped

2 tbsp coriander leaves, chopped

For serving

1 tbsp ghee or sesame oil, per dhokla

1. Wash and soak chana dal and moong dal for at least 2 hours. Strain the water and set aside.

2. Sieve the flour of bajri or wheat and transfer to a large bowl for mixing.

3. Mix papad khaar and oil in a small bowl with ¼ cup water.

4. Add the remaining ingredients of dough to the flour bowl. Add the soaked dals. Add papad khaar and oil (along with the water) and knead into a semi-soft dough using up to 1 cup lukewarm water.

5. Divide the dough into 8 equal portions. Roll and flatten them in your palms to make 2.5-inch rounds (like small cakes), known as dhokla. Make a deep dent in the centre of each dhokla so that it will cook evenly.

6. Cook the dhokla in a lightly greased steamer plate or idli steamer for 15–20 minutes on medium-high heat.

Serve each dhokla slightly crumbled, drizzled with 1–3 tsp of warm ghee or sesame oil. For other serving ideas, see tips on p. 42.

* You can add ½ cup chopped greens such as fresh fenugreek, garlic, mustard or onion greens while kneading the dough.

MAKKI KA DHOKLA   *Spicy Maize Flour Cake*   *(pic on p. 40)*

Maize is a healthy, gluten-free alternative that is extremely satiating. This savoury doughnut with maize flour is a favourite among Rajasthanis during winters. Add any seasonal greens to bring a freshness to the dish every time you serve it.

Makes 8 dhoklas

For dough

2 cups makki (maize) flour

1 to 1½ tsp papad khaar (an alkaline salt)

2 tbsp oil

1 tsp cumin seeds

1½ tsp salt

2 tsp red chilli powder

1 tbsp coriander seeds, coarsely crushed

1 tbsp ginger, finely chopped

1 tbsp green chillies, finely chopped

2 tbsp coriander leaves, chopped

2 tbsp onions, finely chopped

½ cup chopped greens (optional)*

½ cup coarsely crushed peas or corn kernels (optional)

For serving

1 tbsp ghee or sesame oil, per dhokla

1. Sieve the flour of makki and transfer to a large bowl for mixing.

2. Mix papad khaar and oil in a small bowl with ¼ cup water.

3. Add the remaining ingredients of dough to the bowl of flour. Add papad khaar and oil (along with the water) and knead into a semi-soft dough using up to 1 cup lukewarm water.

4. Divide the dough into 8 equal portions. Pat each portion into 2.5-inch rounds (like small cakes), known as dhokla. Make a deep dent in the centre of each dhokla so that it will cook evenly.

5. Cook the dhoklas, in one or two batches, in a lightly greased steamer plate or idli steamer for 15–20 minutes on medium-high heat. You can also steam the dhoklas in a pan by placing them in a colander over a stand.

Serve each dhokla slightly crumbled, drizzled with warm ghee or sesame oil. For other serving ideas, see tips on p. 42.

* You can add ½ cup chopped greens such as fresh fenugreek, garlic, mustard or onion greens while kneading the dough. You can even make this recipe without any greens.

KHICHIYA KA DHOKLA   *Simple Rustic Wheat Cake*

This recipe is actually the starting point for making a type of papad, known as 'khichiya' in Rajasthan. Once the dough is prepared, it is rolled into circles and sun-dried until entirely moisture-free. These crispy round khichiya are stored for months and can be roasted or fried when required.

Perhaps the dhokla as a snack was an accidental invention! At some point in the khichiya-making process, someone possibly tasted the cooked dough and realised how delicious it was! Eventually, a creative cook may have served it with an assortment of accompaniments. Now and then, the humble dough is savoured as a light meal on its own.

Makes 8 dhoklas

For dough

1½ tsp papad khaar (an alkaline salt)

1½ tsp salt

1 tsp cumin seeds

2 cups wheat flour

2 tbsp ghee preferably, or oil

1 tsp ajwain (carom) seeds, optional

2 tbsp coriander leaves, chopped

For serving

1 tbsp ghee or sesame oil, per dhokla

1. Heat papad khaar, salt and cumin in 2 cups water and bring to a boil.

2. In a large bowl, mix the wheat flour with the ghee, ajwain and coriander leaves. Use a sturdy whisk (the round handle of a wooden whisk works very well) to mix in the boiling papad khaar water. Whisk vigorously for just a minute to make a lump-free mixture which is like a semi-thick dough. Cover and leave aside for 10 minutes.

3. Knead the dough again for 30 seconds and divide into 8 equal portions. Wet your hand with water to pat each portion into 2.5-inch rounds (like small cakes), known as dhokla. Make a deep dent in the centre of each dhokla so that it will cook evenly.

4. Cook the dhoklas, in one or two batches, in a lightly greased steamer plate or idli steamer for 15–20 minutes on medium-high heat. You can also steam the dhoklas in a pan by placing them in a colander over a stand.

Serve each dhokla slightly crumbled, drizzled with 1–3 tsp warm ghee or sesame oil. For other serving ideas, see tips on p. 42.

# FOGLA KA DHOKLA *Steamed Cake with Wild Desert Flower* *(pic on p. 58)*

In a world where cultures are becoming increasingly interconnected, it is a rarity to come across ingredients that are truly unique and deeply rooted in specific regions. One of these can be found in the lands surrounding Bikaner Churu and Bidasar in Rajasthan; it is a shrub known as fogla. This small- to medium-sized woody plant, with multiple stems and flowers containing tiny grains and a husk, is highly valued for its ability to cool the body. The fogla crop is typically harvested in March, shortly after the festival of Holi. Available year-round in its dried form, it is commonly used in preparing dishes like dhokla and raita (p. 153), and even a roti. This Fogla ka Dhokla stands as a tribute to the forgotten recipes of the desert state.

Makes 8 dhoklas

For dough

1 cup fogla (desert shrub)
1 cup wheat flour
¼ cup moth (dew beans) flour
¼ cup bajri (pearl millet) flour
1½ tsp papad khaar (an alkaline
  salt)
1 tsp salt
2 tsp kuti mirch (coarse chilli
  powder)
2 tbsp oil
¼ cup chopped dill greens
  (optional)
¼ cup chopped garlic greens
  (optional)

For serving

1 tbsp ghee or sesame oil, per
  dhokla

1. Wash the fogla as explained in the tip below. Strain and set aside.

2. Add the remaining ingredients of dough and mix well. Knead into a soft dough with water.

3. Divide the dough into 8 portions. Shape and flatten them with your palms to make 2.5-inch rounds, known as dhokla. Make a deep dent in the centre of each dhokla so that it will cook evenly.

4. Cook all the dhoklas in a steamer for 15–20 minutes. You can use a lightly greased steamer plate or an idli steamer for this. Since these dhoklas tend to dry up fast, it is best to serve them directly from the steamer so that they remain moist.

Serve each dhokla slightly crumbled, drizzled with 1–3 tsp warm ghee or sesame oil. For other serving ideas, see tips on p. 42.

How to clean the fogla

Transfer to a wide plate to check and remove any hard straws or stones. Sieve the fogla so that most of the grit is removed. Soak the fogla in water for 5 minutes, then gently rub it with your fingers to loosen any straw pieces, which will sink to the bottom. Let it sit for 5 more minutes while the grit settles at the bottom. Without disturbing the water, remove the fogla from the top. Repeat this 3–4 times so the fogla is completely grit-free.

KHAARIYA   *Savoury Fudge*

We call this dish 'choti bhookh ka khana', meaning something light to eat. It is known as Saajiya in some regions of Rajasthan, and Khichu in the neighbouring state of Gujarat. Unlike a dhokla dough, which can be shaped into doughnuts, the Khaariya batter is slightly runny, resulting in a different texture. A complete and satisfying meal by itself in all seasons, prepare this with seasonal flour and greens.

Serves 4, as a light meal

1 cup flour*
1 heaped tsp papad khaar (an
    alkaline salt)
½ tsp red chilli powder or chopped
    green chillies
1 tsp cumin seeds, coarsely crushed
1 tsp salt
½ cup chopped greens**

For serving
1 tbsp ghee or sesame oil, per
    serving

---

* For the flour, you can choose among rice, bajri (pearl millet), jowar (sorghum), makki (maize) or wheat flour.

** For greens, choose from fenugreek, garlic, mustard or onion greens.

1. Pour 4 cups water in a deep, heavy-bottomed pan. If you like the dish to be softer, you can add an additional cup of water.

2. Add the flour and whisk it (preferably with a hand blender or balloon whisk) well to make a lump-free batter.

3. Add papad khaar, chilli powder, cumin, salt and greens to the batter.

4. Place the pan on the stove and turn on the heat to high. Stir the batter continuously for about 5 minutes until it thickens.

5. Cover and cook on low heat for another 8 minutes. (If using a pressure cooker, do not add the whistle.) Turn off the heat.

Open the lid, mix gently and serve hot with ghee or oil. For other serving ideas, see tips on p. 42.

☘ DAL DHOKLI *Wheat Pasta in Lentil Broth*

This dish is crafted by rolling out a wheat-based dough and cutting it into diamond shapes. These are then immersed into a delicious dal with aromatic spices. As the dough absorbs the dal, it transforms into a sumptuous and satisfying one-pot wonder. Dal Dhokli is not merely a culinary creation; it embodies the art of transforming the ordinary into the extraordinary.

Serves 4, as a one-pot meal

For dal*
¼ cup chana dal
¼ cup green moong dal
¼ cup white urad dal
¼ cup tuvar dal
¼ cup chawli dal (split cow peas)
1½ tsp salt
1 tsp turmeric powder

For dhokli
1¼ cups wheat flour
¼ cup besan (gram flour)
2 tbsp ghee preferably, or oil
½ tsp ajwain (carom) seeds, crushed
½ tsp salt

For tadka
3-4 tbsp ghee preferably, or oil
¼ tsp hing (asafoetida powder)
2 bay leaves
¼ tsp cumin seeds
¼ tsp mustard seeds
1 tbsp red chilli powder

Other ingredients
1 tbsp fresh ginger, chopped
1 tbsp green chillies, chopped
½ cup tomatoes, chopped
1 tsp amchur (dried mango) powder
1 tsp dal masala (p. 194) or any
  garam masala
2 tbsp coriander leaves, chopped
1 lemon, cut into wedges

For serving
1 tbsp ghee or oil, per serving

1. Wash and soak the five dals for 30 minutes. Drain and pressure cook with salt, turmeric, and 6 cups water for 3 whistles. Set aside.

2. In a bowl, mix the ingredients for the dhoklis. Knead into a semi-tight dough using water. Cover with a damp cloth and rest for 10 minutes.

3. Knead the dough again for a minute, divide into 5 equal parts and shape into balls. Roll each into an 8-inch roti, dusting with wheat flour. Cut into 1-inch strips, then cut on an angle to make diamond-shaped dhoklis. Transfer to a plate.

4. Alongside, boil 1 litre water in a deep pan. Add the dhoklis gently, one by one, and cook on medium heat for 10–12 minutes. The dhoklis will start floating to the top when cooked. Carefully transfer the dhoklis to a colander. Retain the strained liquid.

5. Open the cooker and churn the dal to a creamy consistency. Simmer on medium heat without the lid. If the dal is too thick, add the reserved liquid. Add the cooked dhoklis and simmer for 3 minutes.

6. For the tadka, heat ghee in a pan on medium heat. Add hing, bay leaves and cumin. After a few seconds, add mustard. As the seeds crackle, add chilli powder.

7. Immediately, add ginger, green chillies and tomatoes. Cook for a minute and pour into the Dal Dhokli.

8. Stir in amchur powder, dal masala and 2–3 tbsp ghee. Turn off the heat and garnish with coriander leaves.

Serve hot, drizzling some melted ghee and lemon juice on top.

---

* You can make this dish with just tuvar dal; or with green moong dal and half its quantity of chana dal. Tweak the choice of lentils to suit your preference.

❀ SABZI DHOKLI *Homely Pasta in Vegetable Broth*

This comforting one-pot meal comes to life every time it rains—especially when prepared by my co-sister, Sadhana Chordia, a passionate home cook with a flair for traditional flavours. With hand-cut wheat dhoklis simmered in a broth of spinach and ever-changing vegetables—sometimes potatoes, sometimes string beans and seasonal favourites—it's a bowlful of warmth and home.

Serves 4, as a one-pot meal

For dhokli
1½ cups wheat flour
½ tsp ajwain (carom) seeds, crushed
½ tsp salt

For vegetables
½ cup bottle gourd, peeled and
   cubed
½ cup carrots, peeled and cubed
¼ cup shelled peas
¼ cup beans, cut into ½-inch pieces
½ cup cucumber, peeled and cubed
2 cups spinach, finely chopped

For tadka
2–3 tbsp oil
¼ tsp hing (asafoetida powder)
¼ tsp cumin seeds
¼ tsp saunf (fennel) seeds
¼ tsp mustard seeds

Basic spices
1½ tsp salt (adjust to taste)
1 tbsp red chilli powder
½ tsp turmeric powder

For serving
1 tbsp ghee or oil, per serving
1 lemon, cut into wedges

1. In a bowl, mix the ingredients for the dhoklis. Add enough water to knead into a semi-tight dough. Cover with a damp cloth and rest for 10 minutes.

2. Knead the dough again for a minute and divide into 5 equal parts and shape into balls. Roll each ball into an 8-inch roti, dusting with wheat flour as needed. Cut into 1-inch strips. Then cut on an angle to make diamond-shaped dhoklis. Transfer to a plate.

3. For the tadka, heat oil in a deep, thick-bottomed pan on medium heat. Add hing, cumin and saunf. After a few seconds, add mustard. As the seeds crackle, add chilli powder.

4. Immediately, add 1 litre water to the pan. As it comes to a boil, add the dhokli pieces one by one and cook on medium heat for 5–7 minutes.

5. Now add the chopped vegetables (except cucumber and spinach) to the pan. Stir gently. Add salt, turmeric and coriander powder. Cover and cook for 10–12 minutes on medium heat until the vegetables are cooked. Add the chopped cucumber and spinach, cook for a minute and turn off the heat. Allow to sit for about half an hour.

Serve hot, with a spoon of melted ghee and a wedge of lemon on each portion.

 PHALI DHOKLI *Multigrain Dumplings in Cluster Bean Curry*   (pic on p. 59)

This healthy and easy dish is made with round dumplings prepared from a combination of flours, mixed into a gravy of cluster beans. As the gravy thickens, it transforms into a flavourful one-dish meal.

Note: As this rustic dish was adapted by urban families, the dhoklis became smaller and thinner. Many families make up to 100 dhoklis from this same quantity of dough. These will take lesser time to cook, so adjust the cooking time accordingly.

Serves 4, as a one-pot meal

2 cups cluster beans, see Step 1
1 cup buttermilk

For dhokli
¾ cup wheat flour
¾ cup mixed flour*
1 tsp salt
½ tsp turmeric powder
½ tsp red chilli powder
½ tsp cumin seeds, coarsely crushed
½ tsp saunf (fennel) seeds, coarsely crushed
½ tsp ajwain (carom) seeds, hand crushed
2 tbsp ghee preferably, or oil
1 pinch soda bicarbonate

For tadka
2 tbsp oil
¼ tsp hing (asafoetida powder)
½ tsp cumin seeds

Spices
1 tsp salt
1 tsp turmeric powder
2 tsp red chilli powder
3 tsp coriander powder
1 tsp amchur (dried mango) powder or kachri (wild berry) powder
½ tsp Marwadi garam masala (p. 193)
2 tsp rai-saunf masala (p. 192)

For serving
1 tbsp ghee or oil, per serving

1. Wash and chop cluster beans into 1 cm pieces (about 2 cups).

2. In a bowl, mix the ingredients for dhoklis. Knead into a semi-tight dough using water. Cover with a damp cloth and rest for 10 minutes.

3. Knead the dough again for a minute, divide into 20 equal portions and shape into balls. Flatten into 2-inch rounds and set aside.

4. Alongside, boil 1 litre water in a deep pan. Add the dhoklis gently, one by one, and cook on medium heat for 8–10 minutes. The dhoklis will start floating to the top when cooked. Remove from the stove and set aside.

5. For the tadka, heat 2 tbsp of oil in a pan. Add hing and cumin seeds. When the seeds crackle, add cluster beans, salt and turmeric. Stir on high heat for a minute, then cover and cook on medium heat for 5 minutes. Sprinkle water if needed. Add chilli and coriander powders with 1–2 tbsp water. Cook for a minute.

6. Add the buttermilk and cook for 2 minutes. Add the cooked dhoklis with ¾ of the liquid (or all, for more soupy). Bring to a boil.

7. Stir in amchur, garam masala, and rai-saunf masala. Simmer for 3 minutes.

Serve hot, adding melted ghee on top.

---

* Take ¼ cup each of any three flours: Choose from besan (gram flour), jau (barley), makki (maize), bajri (pearl millet) and jowar (sorghum). Some families make these dhoklis with just wheat flour. Tweak the flour options to suit your preference.

RANDHEEN

One-pot Meals and Porridges

Slow cooking food at low temperatures is not a new phenomenon in the culinary world. This technique enhances flavours and makes food easy to digest. There are many words for slow cooking across regions, such as stewing, simmering and braising. In Rajasthan, we use the word 'randhana' for slow cooking, and dishes with grains and lentils cooked in such a way are called 'randheen', roughly translated as porridge.

There are innumerable porridge varieties in Rajasthan, most of which are simple, healthy and easy to make. Each one, called by its special name, has a unique texture and comes with special tips, variations and cooking instructions.

While we were growing up, a common question every morning was 'What is today's randheen?' Even today, some variety of porridge is a daily feature in many Rajasthani families. One trick to perfecting the taste of a randheen is the addition of warm ghee just before serving. It is generally the elders in the family who mix the ghee into the steaming hot porridge, with their fingers in a quick whisking motion. It is a knack for sure, known as 'faintna' in Hindi, meaning whisking. If you cannot handle the heat with your fingers, use a spoon. When mixed, the ghee lends its flavour and enhances the taste of the dish.

We promise that once you try these recipes, you'll be convinced that the humble porridge can be so much more.

GEHUN KA KHEECH   *Porridge with Hulled Wheat*

Hulled wheat cooked in buttermilk transforms into a lip-smacking porridge in this recipe. The addition of flour lends a smooth silky consistency. As with any minimalistic dish, source the best quality of ingredients you can, and maintain an unhurried pace while cooking.

Serves 4 as a one-meal dish, or 8 as part of a meal

1½ cups hulled wheat*
¾ cup green or yellow moong dal
1 tbsp wheat flour
1 tsp salt
1 tsp cumin seeds, coarsely crushed
1 tbsp ghee
1 cup buttermilk or milk

For serving
1–2 tbsp warm, melted ghee, per serving

---

* Hulled wheat is available in Indian grocery stores as gehun ka kheech. Some families insist on whole wheat while others prefer it pounded into smaller bits. To prepare the grain at home, wash wheat and soak in water for 4–5 hours. Drain and towel dry. Lightly crush the wheat and use a sieve to separate and remove the husk.

1. Wash the dal and soak with the hulled wheat in water for 10 minutes. Strain and discard the water.

2. Boil 7 cups water in a pressure cooker. Add salt, cumin seeds and 1 tbsp ghee. Add hulled wheat and dal, and wheat flour to the boiling water. Stir well and pressure-cook for up to 4 whistles.

3. Turn off the heat and allow the pressure to settle down. Open the cooker and mix in buttermilk. Cook for 10 more minutes on low heat without placing the lid. Preferably, you can place an iron skillet over low heat and place the cooker on it. This will allow the kheech to cook slowly without overheating.

Serve hot with warm, melted ghee for a simple, comfort meal. You can also sprinkle boora sugar (or jaggery) for a sweet taste; or enjoy it with sips of Aamalvaniya (p. 184) or Kairi Panaa (p. 186) for a tangy taste.

 Variation

 Jau ka Kheech
Substitute hulled wheat with hulled barley, and wheat flour with barley flour. Follow the remaining recipe.

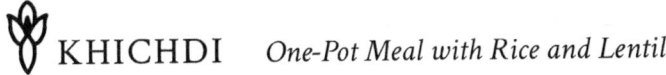

KHICHDI   *One-Pot Meal with Rice and Lentil*

Here is a simple, comforting dish from Rajasthan. The combination and quantity of grains and lentils differ from region to region, and family to family. Some like both to be in equal measure, some prefer more rice, and others more lentil. The perfection of a khichdi lies in its texture: fully cooked yet not mashed like baby food.

Serves 4

¾ cup rice
¾ cup green or yellow moong dal
1 tsp salt
½ tsp turmeric powder
6 cups water

For tadka

1 tbsp ghee
1 bay leaf
¼ tsp hing (asafoetida powder)
½ tsp cumin seeds
2 cloves

1. Wash the rice and dal together and soak in water for about 30 minutes. Wash again and strain.

2. In a pressure cooker (or thick-bottomed pan), heat 1 tbsp ghee with bay leaf and hing. As the ghee warms up, add cumin and cloves.

3. As the cumin splutters, add 6 cups water. Add salt and turmeric and bring to a boil.

4. Add the soaked rice and dal and cook for up to 4 whistles. Turn off the heat. Once the steam settles down, open the lid and mix well.

Always serve khichdi piping hot, topped with a generous helping of melted ghee.

Chef Sameer says

There is a popular saying about khichdi: खिचड़ी के हैं चार यार: दही, पापड़, घी, अचार, meaning khichdi has four buddies: curd, papad, ghee and pickle. It can also be eaten with any of these four depending on whether you like it bland or spicy.

MAKKI KI GHAAT *Porridge with Broken Maize*

A warm, comforting porridge made with broken maize, gently cooked to a soft, hearty consistency—simple, wholesome and especially nourishing in the winter season.

Serves 4

2 cups makki ka daliya (broken maize)
1 tsp salt
1 tsp cumin seeds
7 cups water

1. In a pressure cooker, add 7 cups water and salt and bring to a boil.
2. Add the daliya and cumin seeds and stir gently for a few minutes. Place the lid and cook for up to 1 whistle on high heat and 3 whistles on medium heat.

Serve hot with warm, melted ghee. Serve with boora sugar for a sweet flavour, or with green chutney, raita or kadhi to make a complete meal. You can also serve it with Jaipuri Kadhi (p. 109) and plain chawli (cow peas, cooked with just salt and turmeric).

BAJRI KI GHAAT *Porridge with Pearl Millet*

A rustic pearl-millet porridge simmered in sour buttermilk, offering a tangy, nourishing bowl—perfect as a light and warming winter meal.

Serves 4

2 cups hulled bajri (pearl millet, broken as fine as semolina)
1 tsp salt
7 cups sour buttermilk

1. In a pressure cooker, add all the ingredients and stir gently for a few minutes. Bring to a boil. Place the lid and cook for up to 1 whistle on high heat and 4 whistles on medium heat.

Serve hot with warm, melted ghee. You can also enjoy it with curd, papad or pickle, or with all three, as you like.

Chef Sameer says
The texture of a perfect ghaat should be like a risotto, not too thick but not pourable either. Always check the consistency before serving. If it has turned thick, add 1 cup hot water and cook for a few more minutes.

GEHUN KI THULI   *Porridge with Broken Wheat*

A fragrant, roasted broken-wheat porridge enriched with moong dal, slow-cooked to an earthy softness and enjoyed all year round.

Serves 4

2 cups broken wheat
1 tbsp green moong dal (optional)
1 tsp salt
7 cups water

1. Roast the broken wheat in 1 tbsp ghee on medium heat for 2–3 mins.

2. Alongside, add 7 cups water in a pressure cooker and bring to a boil. Add in the ingredients and stir gently for a few minutes. Place the lid and cook for up to 1 whistle on high heat and 3 whistles on medium heat.

Serve hot with warm, melted ghee. You can also enjoy it with any Garlic Chutney (p. 165) for a spicy treat, or with plain badi ki sabzi to revive a traditional combination.

 CHAWAL KI GHAAT   *Easy Porridge with Cooked Rice*

Light on the stomach, this dish is ideal when vegetables are scarce or even when you want to use up leftover rice.

Serves 4

2–3 tbsp ghee
2 bay leaves
¼ cup jau (barley) or wheat flour
4 cups buttermilk
1 tsp cumin seeds
1 heaped tsp salt
2 cups cooked rice
1–2 tbsp warm, melted ghee, per serving

1. Heat ghee in a thick-bottomed pan over low heat. Add the bay leaves and flour and roast for 1–2 minutes, stirring briskly until aromatic.

2. Gradually add 3 cups of buttermilk and cumin seeds, stirring continuously to avoid lumps.

3. Increase the heat slightly. Add salt and cooked rice, mixing well. Stir and cook for 8–10 minutes until the mixture thickens to a porridge-like consistency.

4. Turn off the heat, cover and let it rest for 10 minutes.

Serve hot with a drizzle of warm ghee and a sprinkle of roasted cumin powder. For a sweet touch, add boora sugar or jaggery. Sameer pairs it with kachumbar—a salad of finely chopped cucumber, onions, green chillies, ginger and coriander, seasoned with salt and roasted cumin. A refreshing contrast that balances the meal perfectly.

BAJRI KA KHICHDA *Porridge with Pearl Millet* *(pic on p. 57)*

In this recipe, pearl millet combines with lentils to make a randheen, which is a comforting, nourishing treat. Cooking randheen in milk or buttermilk lends it a creamy softness. The recipe is simple and straightforward, so follow it unhurriedly for best results.

Serves 4 as a one-meal dish, or 8 as part of a meal

1 cup hulled bajri (pearl millet)*
½ cup chawli dal (split cow peas)
½ cup yellow moong dal
1 tsp salt
2 cups milk (or buttermilk)

For serving
1 to 2 tbsp warm, melted ghee, per serving

* Hulled bajri is readily available as broken bajra or bajre ka daliya, also known as kuti hui bajri. To make this at home, clean the bajri, moisten it by sprinkling water and set aside for 1 hour. Crush it lightly, preferably using a mortar and pestle, or else, roughly crush in a mixer-grinder. Tap and shake firmly to remove the husk.

1. Wash the chawli and moong dal and soak in water for 10 minutes in a bowl.

2. Boil 6 cups water in a pressure cooker. Add bajri, chawli, moong dal and salt to the boiling water. Stir well for a few minutes and pressure-cook for up to 3 whistles.

3. Turn off the heat and allow the pressure to settle down. Open the pressure cooker and add in the milk (or buttermilk).

4. Cook again for 10 more minutes on low heat, without the vent weight (whistle). Preferably, you can place an iron skillet over low heat and place the cooker on it. This will allow the grains to cook perfectly.

Serve hot with warm, melted ghee for a simple, comfort meal.

Chef Sameer says
For a sweet twist, serve this dish with white butter and jaggery—or boora sugar. In winter, it pairs beautifully with Jaipuri Kadhi (p. 109) and a seasonal sabzi such as Dhungaari Mogri (p. 66) or Taazi Matar ki Sabzi (p. 65). A traditional way to enjoy it is in stages: start with a few bites drizzled with warm ghee, move on to kadhi and sabzi, and end with a touch of jaggery.

Bajri ka Khichda p.56

Dhungaari Mogri p.66

57

Fogla ka Dhokla p.46

Phali Dhokli p.50

Aloo Pyaaz Jaipuri p.63

GARDEN FRESH SABZI

With Fresh and Seasonal Produce

Before the advent of refrigerated transportation, access to fresh fruit and vegetables was rare in Rajasthan. During specific seasons, only a limited number of vegetables grew in the unfertile desert soil, so these were treated like precious jewels. Once harvested, each part of the plant was put to good use. This task fell to the ingenuity of the women of the household.

Sameer says that while the bulk of the vegetable was turned into sabzi, its peel, stalk, and seed were also used to make delicacies. For instance, the peels of mango, bottle gourd, ridge gourd, watermelon and the tender pods of fresh green peas were used in chutneys and curries. Melon and tamarind seeds were cleverly converted into mouth fresheners!

Even today, when almost everything is available round the year in Rajasthan, many families continue to honour the gifts of nature, eating seasonally and maximising the utility of every part of a fruit or vegetable.

❦ MALAI PYAAZ *All-Time Favourite Onion Curry*

In Rajasthani homes, this curry with baby onions is the go-to-sabzi when short of fresh vegetables. It is especially handy during the hot months when green vegetables are in shortage due to the summer heat. Quick and easy to make, you cannot go wrong with this recipe. Instead of baby onions, you can use either the white bulbs of onion greens or shallots (known as sambar onion in south India).

Serves 4 to 6

For onions
15–20 baby onions, about 1 inch
    in diameter
½ tsp salt
5 tbsp ghee

For tadka
½ tsp cumin seeds
½ tsp saunf (fennel) seeds
½ tsp kalonji (nigella) seeds
2 dry red chillies, broken

For gravy
½ cup freshly made tomato puree
1 tbsp ginger paste
1 tbsp green chilli paste
1 tsp salt
½ tsp turmeric powder
2 tsp red chilli powder
2 tsp coriander powder

Other ingredients
1 cup malai (milk cream), beaten
2 green chillies, cut into 1-inch
    pieces diagonally
1–2 tsp kasuri methi (dried
    fenugreek leaves), lightly roasted
½ tsp Marwadi garam masala (p. 193)
2 sprigs of coriander leaves,
    chopped

1. Peel the baby onions, keeping the root intact, so that the layers do not fall apart while cooking. Wash and boil them in water with ½ tsp salt for about 5 minutes. Drain and set aside.

2. When cooled, sauté the onions in 1 tbsp ghee for 1–2 minutes. This will lend a nice sheen and smoky flavour to the onions.

3. For the tadka, heat 3 tbsp ghee in a pan on medium heat. Add the ingredients for tadka and sauté for about 10 seconds.

4. As the seeds crackle, add the ingredients for gravy. Cook for 3–4 minutes on medium heat, or until the ghee separates.

5. Add malai and cook for 2 minutes, mixing it well. Add the sautéed onions and cook for a minute.

6. Add green chillies and kasuri methi, and cook for 3–4 minutes. Add a few tablespoons of boiling water if the gravy is too thick.

7. Add garam masala, half of the chopped coriander leaves and remaining ghee. Mix and turn off the heat. Garnish with the remaining coriander.

Serve hot with any roti of your choice, especially Bejhad Roti (p. 126).

❧ Variations

❧ **Malai Tinde | Malai Corn**
Substitute baby onions with tender tinde (apple gourd), baby corn or fresh corn kernels. Follow the rest of the recipe.

ALOO PYAAZ JAIPURI   *Demystified Baby Potato and Onion Curry*   *(pic on p. 60)*

Undoubtedly, this sabzi with baby potatoes and baby onions is one of the most cherished dishes of Jaipur. The original recipe demands infinite patience. For decades, food lovers and chefs have fried the potatoes and onions in ghee and then spent another hour frying the gravy to perfection. What compelled Sameer to demystify this dish was the demand of young women who attended his cooking workshops, many of whom were newly married and wanted to learn traditional favourites. He stumbled upon the idea of frying the onions to golden brown before grinding them, which reduced the overall cooking time from 1 hour to just 15 minutes without any compromise in taste. Try it and enjoy the compliments you receive from your guests.

Serves 4

10 baby potatoes, about 1 inch in
  diameter
10 baby onions, about 1 inch in
  diameter
½ cup ghee preferably, or oil
½ cup curd, beaten

For onion paste

1½ cup onions, thinly sliced
½ tsp cumin seeds
¼ tsp black cumin seeds
2 bay leaves
1-inch cinnamon stick
3 cloves
3 green cardamoms
½ inch piece of mace, crushed

For tomato gravy

2 tbsp garlic paste
1 cup freshly made tomato puree
1 tsp salt
1 tsp turmeric powder
2 tsp red chilli powder
1 tsp Kashmiri chilli powder
2 tsp coriander powder
2 tbsp ginger paste
2 tbsp green chilli paste

Other ingredients

2 tsp kachri (wild berry) powder
1 tsp Marwadi garam masala (p. 193)
3 green chillies, cut into 1-inch pieces
1 tsp kasuri methi (dried fenugreek
  leaves), lightly roasted
2 sprigs of coriander leaves, chopped

1. Wash and peel the baby potatoes. Peel the baby onions and chop away the tops, but keep the root intact so that the onions remain whole and do not fall apart in layers.

2. Boil the potatoes and onions separately in salted water, until they are fork-tender. Drain the water and set aside. In a pan, sauté them separately in 1 tbsp ghee each, for about 3 minutes. Transfer to a bowl.

3. In the same pan, heat 2 tbsp ghee and add the ingredients for the onion paste. Cook on medium-high heat for about 5–6 minutes, or until onions turn golden brown. Transfer to a bowl, sprinkle 1 tbsp water, and leave to cool down. Discard the bay leaf and grind the mixture into a fine paste with 2–3 tbsp water. The caramelised onion paste is ready.

4. In a large pan, heat 4 tbsp ghee on medium-high heat to make the gravy. Add garlic paste and cook for 15 seconds. Add the remaining ingredients of the tomato gravy along with ¼ cup water. Cook for 5 minutes, or until the oil separates.

5. Add the onion paste along with curd and continue cooking for 5 minutes. Add sautéed onions and potatoes and cook for 3 minutes. If the gravy is too thick, add some hot water.

6. Finally, add kachri powder, garam masala, green chillies and kasuri methi. Mix well for a minute and turn off the heat. Garnish with coriander leaves.

Serve with any roti of your choice; chef's suggestion is Bejhad Roti (p. 126).

DAHI KI BHINDI *Fried Lady's Fingers in Curd Gravy*

Available round the year, lady's finger, also known as okra, is a much-loved vegetable for people of all ages. In this recipe, bhindi is coated with flour and fried before adding to a home-style curd gravy. A sure success for any occasion, prepare this sabzi when the bhindi is fresh and tender.

Serves 4

For frying
400 gm tender lady's fingers
2 tbsp besan (gram flour)
2 tbsp rice flour
10–15 fresh mint leaves
Oil for deep-frying

For curd mix
1 cup thick curd
1 tsp salt
½ tsp black salt
2 tsp red chilli powder
3 tsp coriander powder

For tadka
4 tbsp oil
¼ tsp hing (asafoetida powder)
1 tsp cumin seeds
1 tsp mustard seeds
1 tsp turmeric powder
1 tbsp ginger paste
1 tbsp green chilli paste

For topping
1 tsp jeeravan masala (p. 195) or
    amchur (dried mango) powder
    or chaat masala

1. Wash the lady's fingers and gently pat dry. Cut and discard the head and tail ends. Cut each lady's finger lengthwise into 4 thin strips.

2. Mix besan and rice flour in a plate. Coat the lady's fingers with this flour mix. Usually, lady's fingers are moist enough to hold on to the coating. In case they are too dry, you can sprinkle 1 tsp water on the lady's fingers and then coat them with the flour mix.

3. Heat oil for frying in a pan. Fry the lady's fingers and fry them in 3–4 batches on medium-high heat until crispy. Transfer to a dish lined with kitchen paper.

4. In the same oil, fry mint leaves carefully. You can place them in a metal sieve which can be dipped in the hot oil for a few seconds until crisp.

5. Add all the ingredients of the curd mix to any leftover flour, that was used to coat the lady's fingers.

6. For the tadka, add oil and hing in a pan over medium-high heat. As the oil warms, add cumin, and after a few seconds, add mustard. As the seeds crackle, add turmeric powder, ginger paste and green chilli paste. Stir for about 10–15 seconds.

7. Add the curd mix and cook on high heat for 3 minutes, stirring continuously. Turn off the heat.

8. While serving, arrange the fried lady's fingers in a shallow serving dish. Top it with the cooked gravy. Sprinkle jeeravan masala and fried mint leaves.

Serve hot with any roti of your choice.

> 🌱 **Variation**
>
> **Kurkuri Bhindi**
> Serve the fried lady's fingers without the gravy. After frying, sprinkle some jeeravan masala or chaat masala, a generous pinch of black salt and a dash of lemon juice. Serve immediately.

TAAZI MATAR KI SABZI *Freshly Tempered Winter Peas*

Also known as Suswa Matar, this sabzi with fresh green peas is a true delicacy. The term 'suswa' refers to an instant sabzi with seasonal vegetables. Tender, pearl-sized green peas that barely require a minute to cook are the stars of the dish. Some vendors in Jaipur even separate the peas using a particular kind of strainer through which only the perfect pearl-sized peas pass, making them three times more expensive. Such attention to detail defines the Jain Oswal and Baniya communities, and the royal kitchens of Jaipur. This dish is usually prepared just as everyone sits down to begin their meal. It arrives piping hot at the table, aromatic and bursting with flavour, just as hot rotis are served.

Serves 4

2 cups fresh green peas (choose only tender peas)

Basic spices
¾ tsp salt
¾ tsp turmeric powder
2 tsp red chilli powder
3 tsp coriander powder

For tadka
2 to 4 tbsp ghee preferably, or oil
¼ tsp hing (asafoetida powder)
½ tsp cumin seeds

Final ingredients
½ tsp amchur (dried mango) powder or 1 tbsp lemon juice
½ tsp Marwadi garam masala (p.193)

1. Mix the basic spices in ¼ cup water and set aside for 5 minutes. This is known as kaccha masala (p. 208).

2. For the tadka, add ghee and hing in a pan on medium heat. As the ghee warms up, add cumin.

3. As the cumin crackles, add the spices mixed in water. Cook for 2–3 minutes, or until the ghee separates.

4. Now add green peas along with amchur and garam masala and give a quick stir. Turn off the heat.

Serve immediately with steamed rice or Phulka (p. 122).

 Variations

 Instant Mogri | Instant Mint | Instant Onion Greens
This suswa-style recipe is also popular with mogri (radish pods), mint leaves or onion greens. Substitute peas with any of these and follow the recipe.

Tip: For a special touch, add 1 tbsp beaten malai (milk cream) while adding green peas.

# DHUNGAARI MOGRI   *Radish Pods Infused with Charcoal Flavour*   *(pic on p. 57)*

Here is a winter favourite—a must in every home and at every winter gathering. This dish celebrates one of Rajasthan's most loved seasonal ingredients: mogri, or radish pods. Fresh, aromatic and full of character, the pods are delicately tempered, spiced just right and finished with a touch of charcoal smoke.

Serves 4

2 cups fresh mogri (radish pods)

For tadka
3 tbsp oil
¼ tsp hing
1 tsp cumin seeds
½ tsp mustard seeds

Spices
¾ tsp salt
½ tsp turmeric powder
1 tsp red chilli powder
3 tsp coriander powder
1 tsp amchur powder
1 tsp rai-saunf masala (p. 192)

For dhungaar
1 small piece of charcoal (about
    1×1 inch)
½ tsp melted ghee
1 pinch hing (asafoetida powder)

1. Break off the ends of the mogri and finely chop them.

2. For the tadka, heat oil in a pan. Add hing, cumin and mustard, and sauté for 10 seconds.

3. Add the chopped mogri and sauté for 1 minute. Add salt, turmeric, red chilli powder, coriander powder and amchur powder.

4. Mix well and cook for about 3 minutes, until the mogri is slightly tender yet still crisp.

5. Mix in the rai-saunf masala and turn off the flame.

6. For the dhungaar, place a small earthen or metal bowl at the centre of the prepared mogri. Heat the charcoal on the stove until red hot. Using tongs, place the charcoal in the bowl. Pour the ghee and a pinch of hing over it. Immediately cover the dish with a large plate to trap the smoke. Let it sit for 1–2 minutes to absorb the flavour. Uncover and allow the smoke to settle before serving.

Serve immediately. Best enjoyed with Khichda, Sogra or any Randheen.

---

* For more on the distinctive smoky 'Dhungaar' effect and some easy recipes, turn to p. 202.

AALAN KI SABZI   *Curry with Seasonal Greens*

Also known as Aalaniya, this dish refers to a curry where the gravy is thickened with flour. It can be prepared with a wide range of greens and flours. Sameer's first choice is to combine onion greens with jowar flour in this recipe. Experiment with different combinations to discover your own seasonal preferences.

Serves 4

5 cups chopped greens*

For gravy

4 tbsp flour**
2 tbsp curd
1 tbsp fresh ginger, finely chopped
1 tbsp green chillies, finely chopped
2 tsp red chilli powder
1 tsp turmeric powder
1 tsp salt

For tadka

4 tbsp oil
½ tsp hing (asafoetida powder)
½ tsp cumin seeds
½ tsp coriander seeds, coarsely
  crushed
5 dried, long red chillies, broken

Other ingredients

½ tsp Marwadi garam masala (p. 193)
1 tsp lemon juice
4 tbsp ghee

1. Rinse the greens several times until the water is clear. Squeeze out most of the water and chop the greens. This should amount to about 5 cups.

2. Mix together the ingredients for the gravy with 4 cups water and set aside.

3. For the tadka, add oil and hing in a pan on medium-high heat. As the oil begins to warm up, add cumin seeds, crushed coriander seeds and red chillies.

4. As the seeds crackle, add the chopped greens and cook them for 5–6 minutes, or until wilted.

5. Add the gravy mix, reduce the heat to medium, and cook for 8–10 minutes, stirring continuously. If you find the gravy too thick, add a little hot water.

6. Add garam masala, lemon juice and ghee. Mix well and turn off the heat.

Serve hot with any roti of your choice, ideally with Sogra (p. 128).

* Options for greens: Choose from radish greens, onion greens, mustard greens or amaranth greens. For mustard greens or amaranth greens, add another 2–3 minutes of cooking time.

** Options for flour: Choose from flour of bajri (pearl millet), jowar (sorghum) or makki (maize).

🌸 AAM KI SABZI   *Ripe Mango in Spicy Gravy*

While catering a wedding in New York, Sameer was requested to set up an entire counter dedicated to mango, the king of fruits. His team put together a range of dishes celebrating mangoes—drinks, starters, pulav, desserts and the showstopper: a sweet mango curry in spicy gravy. It is one of his most popular dishes and always in demand, so it gives us great pleasure to share it with you. The secret lies in using firm, sweet mangoes of fine quality. This much-loved curry makes a complete meal with roti or steamed rice. You can give all other accompaniments the day off!

Serves 4

3 cups ripe mangoes, see Step 1

For gravy
2 onions
8–10 garlic cloves
1 inch piece of fresh ginger
4 medium-sized tomatoes

For tadka
4–6 tbsp ghee preferably, or oil
¼ tsp hing (asafoetida powder)
1 tsp cumin seeds
½ tsp kalonji (nigella) seeds
½ tsp fenugreek seeds

Basic spices
¾ tsp salt
½ tsp black salt
2 tsp red chilli powder
1 tsp turmeric powder

Other ingredients
4 green chillies, slit
½ tsp Marwadi garam masala (p. 193)
15 fresh mint leaves (or ½ tsp dried
    mint powder)

1. Wash, peel and chop the mangoes into 1-inch chunks. You will need 3 cups of mango chunks.

2. For the gravy, make a fine paste of onion, garlic and ginger with 1–2 tbsp water and set aside.

3. Grind the tomatoes into a smooth puree and set aside.

4. For the tadka, add ghee and hing in a pan on medium-high heat. As the oil warms up, add cumin, kalonji and fenugreek seeds.

5. As the seeds crackle, add the onion-garlic-ginger paste. Cook for 2–3 minutes, or until the raw smell disappears.

6. Reduce the heat to medium, add all the basic spices and cook for another 2 minutes.

7. Add tomato puree and cook for 2–3 minutes, or until the oil separates. Add 1–2 tbsp water if the gravy is too thick. Add the final ingredients and cook for a minute.

8. Alongside, arrange the mango chunks in a serving bowl. Pour the gravy evenly over the mangoes. Let it sit for about 5 minutes, allowing the flavours to meld and infuse.

Serve hot with steamed rice or any roti of your choice, ideally with Bejhad Roti (p. 126).

🌿 **Variation**

🍉 **Tarbooz ki Sabzi**
This is another fruit-based curry. Try swapping the mango with 3 cups ripe watermelon cubes (remove seeds as much as possible). You can also use watermelon juice instead of water in this recipe.

CHANAKYA SPECIAL *Delicate Medley of Fox Nut and Fruit* (pic on p. 79)

Sameer created this curry in the early 1990s for Chanakya, a famous vegetarian restaurant in Jaipur. Received with much love by the guests, it became one of the best-liked dishes on the menu. A rich dish flavoured with saffron, cardamom and beautified with silver leaf; it was a key item when the restaurant served up meals to celebrities. Try a real shahi curry from a city of royalty and richness.

Serves 4

For makhana-fruit mix
¾ cup makhana (fox nuts)
½ cup tender green peas
½ cup mixed fruit (from canned fruit cocktail)
¾ cup paneer (cottage cheese) cubes
2 tsp green chillies, finely chopped

For tadka
4 tbsp ghee
¼ tsp cumin seeds
¼ tsp black cumin seeds
2 green cardamoms, lightly crushed

For gravy
½ cup milk
¾ cup crumbled khoya (reduced milk)
½ tsp salt
¼ tsp turmeric powder
½ tsp red chilli powder
2 tbsp fresh cream
8-10 saffron strands (soak in 1 tsp warm water)

Other ingredients
½ tsp Marwadi garam masala (p. 193)
¼ tsp cardamom powder
1 vark (silver leaf)
1 tbsp rangat (glaze) (p. 196)
1 sprig of coriander leaves, chopped

1. Soak the makhana in water for 30 minutes. Squeeze out the water.

2. Blanch the peas for 3–4 minutes in boiling water.

3. Collect the fox nuts, peas, mixed fruit, paneer cubes and green chillies in a bowl.

4. For the tadka, heat ghee in a pan on medium-high heat. Add cumin, black cumin and cardamom.

5. As the seeds crackle, add milk and bring to a boil. Add khoya, mix well and cook for about a minute. Add salt, turmeric and chilli powder and cook for a minute.

6. Add the ingredients of makhana-fruit mix. Cook for 2–3 minutes until it thickens. Add cream and saffron strands and cook for 2 more minutes.

7. Add garam masala and cardamom powder. If the gravy is thick, add 2 tbsp warm water or milk.

8. Transfer to a serving dish. Top with silver leaf, drizzle some rangat and garnish with coriander leaves.

Serve at once to relish the flavours to their best. A delicious standalone dish, you can also serve this with any of the Basic Rajasthani Rotis (p. 122).

DAHI WALI TURAI   Ridge Gourd in Home-style Curd Gravy

In Rajasthani homes, many different methods have been adopted to enhance the taste of each seasonal vegetable and avoid monotony. Vegetables that children commonly dislike, such as ridge gourd, bitter gourd, pumpkin and bottle gourd, were considered a treat in Sameer's home. He says, 'Growing up, my favourite was the humble yet delightful Dahi Wali Turai. This cherished recipe, inspired by Pratibha-ji Maini—a close family friend whose culinary wisdom has always enriched me—continues to hold a special place in my heart.'

Serves 4

½ kg ridge gourd

For tadka
4 tbsp ghee
2 bay leaves
¼ tsp hing (asafoetida powder)
½ tsp cumin seeds
1 tbsp green chillies, chopped

Basic spices
¾ tsp salt
½ tsp turmeric powder
1½ tsp red chilli powder
2 tsp coriander powder

Other ingredients
½ cup curd
1 tsp besan (gram flour)
2 tsp rai-saunf masala (p. 192)
   (optional)
1 sprig of coriander leaves,
   chopped

1. Peel and cut the ridge gourd into round or half-moon slices.

2. For the tadka, add ghee, bay leaves and hing in a pan on medium-high heat. As the oil warms up, add cumin seeds. As the seeds crackle, add green chillies and sauté for a few seconds.

3. Add the chopped ridge gourd and cook for a minute. Add salt and turmeric powder, reduce the heat to medium-low, place a lid over the pan and continue to cook for 5–7 minutes. Remove the lid. Add chilli powder and coriander powder, and cook for a minute.

4. Whisk the curd with besan and add to the pan, stirring continuously to prevent curdling. Cook for about 3 minutes on high heat, or until the ghee separates.

5. Finally, add rai-saunf masala and cook for a minute. Turn off the heat and keep covered for 5–7 minutes. Garnish with coriander leaves.

Serve with any of the Basic Rajasthani Rotis (p. 122). This is traditionally enjoyed with roti and dal, all mixed and crushed gently with the fingers and eaten together.

Variations

Dahi Wale Aloo
Substitute ridge gourd with boiled potato cubes in this recipe.

Dahi Wale Kele
Substitute ridge gourd with boiled cubes of raw plantains in this recipe.

Dahi Wali Lauki
Substitute ridge gourd with boiled cubes of bottle gourd in this recipe.

❧ GWARPATHA KI SABZI *Aloe Vera Curry*

Here is a traditional sabzi with aloe vera, a succulent cactus in the desert state of Rajasthan. This simple, healthy sabzi with the perfect blend of spices represents the wisdom of elders in using local produce. Choose a fleshy, firm leaf with a healthy green colour, whether buying from a store or harvesting from your garden.

Serves 4 to 6

For aloe vera
2 cups aloe vera cubes, see Step 1

Basic spices
1 tsp salt (and ½ tsp for boiling aloe vera)
1 tsp turmeric powder (and ½ tsp for boiling aloe vera)
2 tsp red chilli powder
3 tsp coriander powder

For tadka
4 tbsp oil
¼ tsp hing (asafoetida powder)
2 bay leaves
½ tsp cumin seeds
½ tsp mustard seeds
½ tsp fenugreek seeds
½ tsp saunf (fennel) seeds

Other ingredients
2 tbsp (or more) crushed jaggery or sugar
2 tsp amchur (dried mango) powder

1. Rinse the aloe vera leaves a couple of times. Cut about an inch of the leaves from the tail end and place them straight up in a tumbler or narrow container for a couple of hours. The yellow sap-like liquid from the aloe vera will collect at the bottom of the container. Discard the liquid and wash the aloe vera leaves 2–3 times. Cut away the sharp spikes. Now, slice the leaf into long strips and then into 1-inch cubes.

2. Boil the aloe vera cubes with ½ tsp salt and ½ tsp turmeric for 5–8 minutes, or until the outer skin turns fork-tender and darker. Drain and rinse the aloe vera well.

3. Mix the basic spices in ½ cup water and set aside for 5–10 minutes.

4. For the tadka, add oil, hing and bay leaves in a pan on medium-high heat. As the oil warms up, add cumin, and after a few seconds, add mustard, fenugreek and saunf seeds.

5. As the seeds crackle, add the spices mixed in water. Cook for 2–3 minutes, or until the oil starts floating on top. Add the cooked aloe vera, mix and cook for 2 minutes.

6. Add jaggery and amchur powder, mix and cook for a minute. Turn off the heat and set aside for about 10 minutes so the flavours are well infused.

Serve at room temperature with any roti of your choice.

MOOLI KI SABZI *Curry with Tender Radish and Radish Greens*

According to Ayurveda, radish is believed to possess various medicinal properties. It is considered effective in regulating blood pressure, treating urinary disorders and improving immunity. This makes Mooli ki Sabzi a sought-after option during the winter season. However, one challenge with radish is that it is not easily digestible. As the folk proverb goes, radish digests everything, but to digest radish, consume it with jaggery. Hence, Sameer has added a dash of jaggery to this sabzi for a perfect balance.

Serves 4

2 cups tender radish, see Step 1
2 cups radish greens, see Step 1

For tadka
4 tbsp oil (preferably mustard oil)
¼ tsp hing (asafoetida powder)
½ tsp ajwain (carom) seeds
½ tsp mustard seeds

Other ingredients
1 tsp salt
1 tsp turmeric powder
2 tsp red chilli powder
3 tsp coriander powder
1 tsp amchur (dried mango) powder
1 tbsp crushed jaggery

1. Thoroughly wash the radish and its leaves before chopping. Cut the radish into half circles or quarters. Chop the leaves finely. You will need 2 cups of each.

2. For the tadka, heat the oil in a pan on medium-high heat. (If using mustard oil, heat the oil until it turns smoky. Turn off the heat. After 3 minutes, reheat the oil).

3. Add hing, ajwain and mustard. As the mustard crackles, add radish and radish greens and cook for a minute.

4. Add salt and turmeric and cook for a minute. Cover and cook for 8–10 minutes, or until the leaves wilt and the radish becomes tender. Stir a few times. Add chilli powder and coriander powder and cook for a minute.

5. Add amchur and jaggery, mix well and cook for another minute.

Serve hot with any roti of your choice; ideally with any Sogra (p. 128) and Jaipuri Kadhi (p. 109).

Ask Chef Sameer
Pratibha: Why is the oil heated up and then cooled down?
Sameer: Raw mustard oil lends a strong, pungent flavour. Heating it until it turns smoky decreases its smell, thus preventing the oil from overpowering the dish. Once it turns smoky, the oil must be cooled down otherwise the hing and cumin may burn.

 HALDI KI SABZI   *Fresh Turmeric Root Curry*

Our elders consumed a good amount of fresh turmeric, especially during the winter and rainy seasons. It would protect them from the onslaught of colds and coughs, and boost their immunity to deal with water-borne diseases during the monsoon. Dishes such as this were a good way to convert healing, medicinal ingredients into incredibly tasty preparations.

Serves 4 to 6

2 cups fresh turmeric root, see
  Step 1
1 cup ghee
2 bay leaves
1 tsp cumin seeds
½ cup coarse garlic paste
1½ tsp salt
3 tsp red chilli powder
1 cup fresh curd, beaten

1. Wash and peel the turmeric root. Julienne into thin matchsticks, then cut into 1-cm bits. Alternatively, grate using the large holes of a grater.

2. In a pan, add ghee and bay leaves on medium-high heat. As the ghee warms up, add cumin seeds. As the seeds crackle, add garlic paste and cook for 4–5 minutes on low heat.

3. Add the chopped turmeric root and cook for 4 minutes on medium-high heat and 4 minutes on low heat.

4. Whisk the salt and chilli powder into the curd and add to the pan. Stir continuously and cook for another 5–7 minutes on medium-high heat, or until the ghee separates and floats to the surface.

Serve warm or at room temperature, in small quantities like a pickle, with any roti of your choice.

Shelf life: This sabzi can be preserved for up to a month in the refrigerator.

Chef Sameer says
My thanks to Madhu-ji Birani, a wonderful homemaker and Rajasthani food specialist, for sharing this recipe with me. I have served this globally to people from different cultures, and it has always been a raging success. I would like to highlight the quantity of ghee required in this recipe. Turmeric has heating properties, so it takes the stated amount of ghee to both balance the heating quality of fresh turmeric, as well as to cook it well. Once the ghee floats to the top, you can remove it and use it as rangat (p. 196) in some other preparation. If you intend to store this sabzi for later use, then let the ghee remain as it will help in preservation.

PHALI KACHRI KI SABZI   *Cluster Beans with Fresh Berry*

Here is a delectable combination of two summer vegetables—cluster beans and wild berry. The berry in this recipe is a small, sour berry from the melon family, used both in its fresh and dried form. This recipe provides a foolproof guide to a basic tadka and the addition of simple spices. Follow each step precisely to get the perfect taste, before you experiment with your own creations.

Serves 4

3 cups tender cluster beans, chopped, see Step 1
6 small, fresh kachri (wild berry, about 1 inch each)*

For tadka
2–3 tbsp oil
¼ tsp hing (asafoetida powder)
1 tsp cumin seeds
1 tsp mustard seeds

Basic spices
1 tsp salt
1 tsp turmeric powder
2 tsp red chilli powder
3 tsp coriander powder
1 tsp rai-saunf masala (p. 192)

1. Wash cluster beans, trim off the ends and cut into small bits. Wash the kachri, remove any hard seeds and cut into medium pieces with the peel intact.

2. For the tadka, add oil and hing in a pan on medium-high heat. As the oil warms up, add cumin, and after a few seconds, add mustard.

3. As the seeds crackle, add cluster beans along with salt and turmeric. Cook on high heat for a minute. Reduce the heat to medium, cover and allow the cluster beans to simmer in their own juice for 3 minutes. (If the cluster beans are not very tender, you may need to cook them for a few more minutes.)

4. Add chilli powder and coriander powder, mix well and add ¼ cup of water. Cover and continue to cook for another 2 minutes.

5. Add kachri along with the rai-saunf masala. Mix well and cook for another minute.

Serve with any roti of your choice, ideally Phulka (p. 122) or Sogra (p. 128).

---

* If fresh kachri is not available, substitute it with dry kachri. Soak 5–6 dry kachri in hot water for 30 minutes and then cook in an open pan until tender. Tear them into bits and use in this recipe. Alternatively, you can also use 2 tsp kachri powder or amchur powder.

Ask Chef Sameer

Pratibha: Can you explain the science of cooking in this recipe? Why not add everything together?

Sameer: Since cluster beans take longer to cook than fresh kachri, we allow the cluster beans to initially cook on high heat with salt and turmeric, and then simmer in its own juices on low heat. As we add the remaining spices and kachri, they blend in well without overpowering each other. The gradual addition of ingredients in this recipe brings out the best of these seasonal vegetables and local spices.

KAKDI MIRCH KI SABZI *Summer Cucumber with Bell Pepper*

Summer fruits and vegetables are naturally juicy and are nature's blessings to scorched, thirsty bodies. In Rajasthan, the vegetable vendor would take his produce from one street to another, charming the householders with his poetic descriptions of these summer cucumbers: लैला की अंगुलियाँ, मजनू की पसलियाँ ले लो, ठंडी ठंडी तर ककड़ियाँ ले लो। Sameer says, 'Growing up, even though my mother made this sabzi at least twice a week, my siblings and I never tired of it.'

Serves 4

3 cups cucumber, see Step 1
½ cup capsicum, see Step 1

Basic spices
1 tsp salt
1 tsp turmeric powder
2 tsp red chilli powder
3 tsp coriander powder

For tadka
4 tbsp ghee preferably, or oil
¼ tsp hing (asafoetida powder)
½ tsp cumin seeds
½ tsp mustard seeds
1 green chilli, chopped

Other ingredients
½ tsp dried ginger powder
1 tsp rai-saunf masala (p. 192)
½ tsp Marwadi garam masala (p. 193)
1 tsp amchur (dried mango) powder
or lemon juice

1. Chop the cucumber into 1-cm chunks. Remove the stalk and seeds of capsicum and chop into 1-cm bits. Set aside.

2. Mix the basic spices in ¼ cup water and set aside for 5–10 minutes.

3. For the tadka, add ghee and hing in a pan on medium-high heat. As the ghee warms up, add cumin, and after a few seconds, add mustard.

4. As the seeds crackle, add chopped chilli and the spices mixed in water. Cook for 1–2 minutes on medium heat, or until the ghee separates.

5. Add cucumber and capsicum, cover and cook on medium heat for 5 minutes. (If at any point you feel that the masala may burn, add 1–2 tbsp water.)

6. Add the final ingredients, mix gently for a minute and turn off the heat. Set aside for a few minutes before serving so the flavours are well infused.

Serve with any roti of your choice, ideally hot Phulka (p. 122).

Variation

Grape and Cucumber Curry
Add ½ cup green sliced grapes while adding cucumber and capsicum in this recipe. You will like the sour sweet taste of grapes in this sabzi.

Tip: If using the thin, light-green variety of cucumbers, keep the peel intact. For other cucumber varieties, remove the peel.

🪷 JODHPURI SABUT BHUTTE KI SABZI *Corn on the Cob Curry* (pic on p. 77)

Undoubtedly, this dish is the most versatile gem in this collection. Whether you serve it as a starter, a snack, a sabzi with roti or sogra, or even as a gravy with rice, it never fails to impress. You might think this is an exaggeration, but once you try it, you'll see for yourself. This sabzi stands out for its spicy flavours, luscious gravy, striking appearance and, above all, its easy preparation.

Serves 4

2 to 3 tender cobs of corn (must yield 12 roundels of 1 inch)

For tadka

4–6 tbsp ghee preferably, or oil
¼ tsp hing (asafoetida powder)
2 bay leaves
½ tsp cumin seeds
½ inch piece of mace
1-inch cinnamon stick
2 black cardamoms

For gravy

1 cup thinly sliced onions
2 tbsp ginger-garlic paste
1 tbsp green chilli paste
1 tsp salt
1 tsp turmeric powder
3 tsp red chilli powder
3 tsp coriander powder
1 cup freshly made tomato puree
1 tsp besan (gram flour)
½ cup curd

Other ingredients

3 green chillies, cut into 1-inch pieces
1 tsp Marwadi garam masala (p. 193)
2 tsp kasuri methi (dried fenugreek leaves), lightly roasted
1 sprig of coriander leaves, chopped

1. Steam the corn cobs in a steamer (or a cooker container for about 2 whistles) and cut each cob into roundels of 1-inch chunks. Set aside.

2. For the tadka, add ghee, hing and bay leaves in a pan on medium heat. As the ghee warms up, add cumin, mace, cinnamon and black cardamoms, and sauté for a few seconds.

3. As the seeds crackle, add the sliced onions. Cook for 4–5 minutes, or until they turn golden brown. Add the ginger-garlic paste and green chilli paste, and cook for a minute.

4. Add salt, turmeric, chilli powder, coriander powder and ¼ cup water, and cook for a minute. Add tomato puree and cook for 2–3 minutes.

5. Whisk besan and curd and add to the pan, stirring continuously to prevent curdling. Add ¼ cup water and cook for about 5 minutes, or until the ghee separates.

6. Add the steamed corn chunks and cook for a minute. Add green chillies, garam masala and kasuri methi, and cook for another minute. Turn off the heat. Remove the cinnamon and black cardamoms, and discard them. Garnish with coriander leaves.

Serve hot with steamed rice or any roti of your choice.

Jodhpuri Sabut Bhutte p.76

77

Chanakya Special p.69

Home-style Gatta p.89, variation

RUSTIC SABZI

With Peels, Preserves and More

The desert state of Rajasthan is a dry, sometimes harsh environment, with summers and winters often seeing extreme temperatures. Generations of Rajasthanis have ingeniously adapted to the limited availability of fresh fruits and vegetables by creating delicious meals with sun-dried vegetables such as dried sprouts of moong beans or moth beans known as biri, wafers known as khelra, and nuggets such as wadi, papad and rabodi. Made from lentils and flours, stashed in kitchens round the year, these are now easily available in Rajasthani grocery stores. However, many households still prefer to make them from scratch, especially biri and rabodi.

These dried preserves are used when vegetables are scarce or off-season, and during religious festivals when fresh vegetables are not used. Every year, the Jain festival of Paryushan restricts the use of all fresh vegetables, including greens and root vegetables, for eight whole days! What amazes me is how we never run out of dishes to make despite the restrictions. Look up 'Paryushan recipes' online and see for yourself the endless ideas and recipes available.

Ensure your kitchen is well stocked with these versatile preserves and follow the recipes provided to make wholesome, tasty dishes. Sameer rightly calls them the unsung heroes of Rajasthani cuisine.

RABODI KI SABZI BIKANERI   *Curry with Maize Flour Wafers*

Rabodi refers to sun-dried wafers made from maize flour, which are stocked round the year in Rajasthani kitchens. Although readily available in stores, these wafers are easy to make during the hot summer months. Rabodi can be transformed in a jiffy into a sabzi or raita when combined with the right spices.

Serves 6

2 cups rabodi (about 100 gm)

For paste
½ cup onions, chopped
1 tbsp ginger, chopped
1 tbsp garlic, chopped
1 tbsp green chillies, chopped

For curd mix
1 cup curd
1 tsp besan (gram flour)
1 tsp salt
1 tsp turmeric powder
2 tsp red chilli powder
3 tsp coriander powder

For tadka
4 tbsp ghee preferably, or oil
1 bay leaf
½ tsp cumin seeds
½ inch piece of mace, crushed

Other ingredients
1 tsp saunf (fennel) powder
½ tsp Marwadi garam masala (p. 193)
2 tsp kasuri methi (dried fenugreek leaves), lightly roasted
1 sprig of coriander leaves, chopped
2 green chillies, cut diagonally and lightly sautéed in ghee or oil

1. Wash rabodi and boil in hot water for 8–10 minutes, or until fork-tender. Drain the water.

2. Grind the ingredients for paste with 2 tbsp water and set aside.

3. Whisk the ingredients of curd mix in a bowl and set aside for 5–10 minutes.

4. For the tadka, add ghee and bay leaf in a pan on medium-high heat. As the ghee warms up, add cumin and mace.

5. As the cumin crackles, add the paste and sauté for 3–4 minutes. Add the curd mix and cook for 5–7 minutes, or until the ghee separates, stirring continuously.

6. Add the rabodi along with ½ cup water and cook for 2 minutes. (Many families make this sabzi with more gravy. For that, add up to one extra cup of water or buttermilk.)

7. Add the saunf powder, garam masala and kasuri methi, mix and cook for 1 minute. Garnish with coriander leaves and sautéed chillies.

Serve hot along with any roti of your choice, or with steamed rice.

 Variations

- **Rabodi in Curd Gravy**
  For a Jain version, omit onion, ginger and garlic. Follow the rest of the recipe.

- **Dried Potato Chips in Curd Gravy**
  Substitute rabodi with dried potato chips for an interesting twist. Known as 'aloo ka khelra', these are readily available in the market.

❧ SEV TAMATAR KI SABZI   *Instant Curry from Roadside Dhabas*

If you have eaten at any dhaba, or roadside eatery, on the highway connecting Rajasthan with Gujarat, you will be familiar with this dish. What is interesting is that the dhaba boy will ask you if you want it made in ghee or oil. Jain and Gujarati travellers always opt for ghee and we recommend you do the same. As part of communities that typically follow several food restrictions, they also relish this dish made without onion, garlic or other root vegetables. Ratlami sev is the base for this instant sabzi. Most Rajasthani homes will always have packets of sev in varying thickness and different flavours in their pantry.

Note: Prepare this quick-to-make dish just before serving as it will thicken if kept for some time.

Serves 4

2 cups sev (preferably thicker
   variety known as Ratlami sev)

For tadka
4 tbsp oil
¼ tsp hing (asafoetida powder)
1 tsp cumin seeds
2 green chillies, cut into 1-inch bits

For gravy
1 cup chopped tomatoes
2 tsp ginger paste
½ tsp salt
1 tsp turmeric powder
1 tsp raw cumin powder
2 tsp red chilli powder
3 tsp coriander powder

Other ingredients
½ cup buttermilk
½ tsp Marwadi garam masala (p. 193)
½ tsp chaat masala
2 tsp kasuri methi (dried fenugreek
   leaves), lightly roasted
2 tbsp ghee
1 sprig of coriander leaves,
   chopped

1. For the tadka, add oil and hing to a pan on medium-high heat. As the oil warms up, add cumin, and as it crackles, add green chillies and sauté for a few seconds.

2. Add the ingredients for the gravy, mix well and cook for about 5 minutes, or until the tomatoes turn mushy and are well cooked.

3. Add the buttermilk and cook for 2–3 minutes, or until the mixture begins to boil. Add the sev and cook for a minute.

4. Add garam masala, chaat masala and kasuri methi, and cook for a minute. Add ghee and turn off the heat.

Garnish with coriander leaves and serve immediately with steamed rice or any type of roti, especially hot Phulka (p. 122).

JODHPURI CHAKKI KI SABZI *Curry with Wheat Gluten Squares*

The word 'chakki' means square; hence the word is popularly used to describe dishes cut into that shape, whether sweet or savoury. This recipe refers to the squares made from seitan, or wheat gluten. It can be traced back to the royal kitchens of Jodhpur.

Serves 4

For chakki
6 cups wheat flour
Oil for deep-frying

For onion paste
1 cup onions, chopped
½ cup tomatoes, chopped
2 tbsp ginger, chopped
2 tbsp garlic, chopped
2 tbsp green chillies, chopped

For cashew paste
2 tbsp cashew nuts
2 tbsp watermelon seeds

For curd mix
1 cup curd
1 tsp salt
1 tsp turmeric powder
2 tsp red chilli powder
3 tsp coriander powder

For tadka
½ cup ghee preferably, or oil
½ tsp cumin seeds
½ tsp black cumin seeds
1-inch cinnamon stick
4 green cardamoms, crushed
½ inch piece of mace, crushed

Other ingredients
1 tsp Marwadi garam masala (p. 193)
1 tsp kasuri methi (dried fenugreek
    leaves), lightly roasted
2 sprigs of coriander leaves
2 green chillies

Making the chakki
1. Knead the flour into a semi-stiff dough with water. Immerse this dough in a vessel of water for 1–2 hours (to develop the gluten). Ensure that the water level is 2–3 inches above the dough.

2. Drain the water in which the dough is soaked. Add fresh water to the bowl and knead the dough by stretching and folding it repeatedly. As you knead, the dough will reduce in size as some starch will start to release in the water. The dough may also tend to break apart, but keep gathering and kneading it. Change the water 2–3 times until the dough reduces to less than a quarter and becomes rubbery in texture. Place this gluten in a sieve and wash it under running water, binding it into a round shape.

3. Flatten the gluten dough by patting it into a disk that is roughly 5 inches in diameter and 1 inch thick. Steam it in a pressure cooker or pan (or steamer) for 10–12 minutes, and cool down to room temperature. Cut the dough into 1-inch squares.

4. Heat the oil for frying in a pan. Fry the cut squares on medium heat until golden. These fried squares are known as chakki. Immerse them in a bowl of water for 10 minutes. Then squeeze out the water by gently pressing the chakki between your palms.

Other preparations
5. For the onion paste, grind all its ingredients with ¼ cup water.

6. For the cashew paste, soak cashew nuts and watermelon seeds in water for 15 minutes. Strain and grind into a fine paste with ¼ cup of water.

7. Whisk the ingredients of curd mix in a bowl and set aside for 5–10 minutes.

Making the gravy

8. For the tadka, heat ghee in a pan on medium-high heat. Add the ingredients for tadka and sauté for about 10 seconds.

9. Add the onion paste and cook for about 5–6 minutes, or until the oil separates. Add the cashew paste and cook for another 5 minutes. Add the curd mix and cook for 3 minutes.

10. Add the fried chakki, garam masala and kasuri methi, and cook for 5–7 minutes on medium heat. Garnish with chopped coriander leaves and diagonally cut green chillies.

Serve hot with steamed rice or any roti of your choice, especially Bejhad Roti (p. 126) or any Sogra (p. 128).

Chef Sameer says

In royal palaces and affluent homes, the maharaj—the north Indian term for the main chef—had the responsibility of catering to the diverse needs of the guests, requiring expertise in both vegetarian and non-vegetarian cuisine. This famous delicacy was invented to replicate the texture and appearance of meat by carefully washing the starch out of wheat dough until all that remained was the rubber-like gluten. Try this traditional gluten-based dish instead of store-bought soya nuggets for a sabzi truly fit for royalty.

RASILA PITOD   *Curry with Fresh Besan Pasta*

To make this dish, you will first need to perfect the art of making pitod, which can be best described as a homemade pasta with besan. Although the recipe for making pitod looks simple, you may need a few tries to get it just right. The resulting smooth texture and golden colour of this sabzi will make the effort worthwhile, as this is a dish you can confidently serve to the most discerning guests.

Note: For this dish, keep in mind that you have to prepare the pitod beforehand.

Serves 4

3 cups pitod (p. 201)

For curd mix

1 cup curd, beaten
1 tsp besan (gram flour)
1 tsp salt
1 tsp turmeric powder
2 tsp red chilli powder
3 tsp coriander powder

For tadka

2 to 3 tbsp oil
¼ tsp hing (asafoetida powder)
1 bay leaf
½ tsp cumin seeds

Other ingredients

1 tsp kasuri methi (dried fenugreek
   leaves), lightly roasted
1 tsp Marwadi garam masala (p. 193)
1 sprig of coriander leaves,
   chopped

1. Whisk the ingredients of the curd mix in a bowl and set aside for 5–10 minutes.
2. For the tadka, add oil, hing and bay leaf in a pan on medium-high heat. As the oil warms up, add cumin.
3. Once the cumin begins to crackle, add the curd mix to the pan, stirring continuously. Cook for 3–4 minutes, or until the oil separates.
4. Add pitod pieces and continue to cook for 2 more minutes. Add about ¾ cup warm water and bring to a boil.
5. Finally, mix in the garam masala and kasuri methi, and cook for a minute. Turn off the heat and garnish with coriander leaves.

Serve hot with any of the Basic Rajasthani Rotis (p. 122).

Ask Chef Sameer

Pratibha: Since pitod itself is made with besan, why do you add besan while making the gravy?
Sameer: My grandmother would smile whenever someone asked this. "Add a little besan so the curd doesn't curdle," she'd say. A small trick passed down through generations—that bit of besan keeps the curd smooth and the gravy perfect, no matter how hot the flame.

KHAARAK METHI KI SABZI   *Dried Dates and Fenugreek Curry*

This is a sabzi with dried dates, known as khaarak or chhuara, as its main ingredient. Even though this dish requires some preparation as outlined, the recipe is straightforward and the final taste is perfect. It is inspired by Kanchan-ji Ridhkaran Chopda of Jaipur, whom Sameer calls mamisa and to whom he always turns for des ka khana.

Serves 4

For soaking
20 dried dates
½ cup fenugreek seeds
4 amchur (dried mango) slices, about 1 inch each
2 dried, long red chillies

Basic spices
½ tsp salt
1 tsp black salt
1 tsp turmeric powder
2 tsp red chilli powder
3 tsp coriander powder

For tadka
4 tbsp oil
½ tsp hing (asafoetida powder)
2 bay leaves
1 tsp cumin seeds
1 tsp saunf (fennel) seeds
1 tsp mustard seeds

Other ingredients
½ cup lemon-soaked raisins (p. 209)
2 tsp amchur (dried mango) powder
1 tbsp jaggery or sugar (optional)

1. Start with the ingredients for soaking. Wash them separately and immerse in water, each one in a separate bowl, for about 5 hours.

2. Rinse the dates, amchur slices and red chillies once again, tear them into small bits, and leave them together in a colander to drain. Cook them in 2 cups boiling water for 8–10 minutes. Return them to the colander.

3. Place fenugreek seeds in a sieve and wash under running water to remove the bitterness. Cook them in 2 cups boiling water for 5 minutes. Drain the water and add the seeds to the same colander.

4. Mix the basic spices in ½ cup water and set aside for 5–10 minutes.

5. For the tadka, add oil, hing and bay leaves in a pan on medium-high heat. As the oil warms up, add cumin, saunf and mustard seeds.

6. As the seeds crackle, add the spices mixed in water and cook for a minute. Add all the ingredients from the colander and the lemon-soaked raisins. Mix and cook for 2–3 minutes.

7. Mix in amchur powder and jaggery and turn off the heat. Set aside for about 30 minutes so the flavours are well infused.

Serve at room temperature with Besan ki Tawa Poodi (p. 133) or any of the Basic Rajasthani Rotis (p. 122).

Shelf life: This sabzi can be refrigerated for up to a week.

 Variations

This recipe can be simplified to prepare two traditional sabzis:

🌿 **Amchur Daakh Daana Methi**
Prepare this version by omitting the dried dates.

🌿 **Daakh Daana Methi**
In this all-time favourite sabzi, omit both the dried dates and the amchur slices.

GOVIND GATTA *Curry with Stuffed Besan Nuggets*

Gatta, one of the iconic delicacies in Rajasthani cuisine, are steamed or fried nuggets made with besan. In this recipe, they are lavishly stuffed with khoya. Legend has it that they were offered as prasad to Govind Dev, the resident deity of Jaipur, giving the dish its unique name: Govind Gatta.

Serves 4

For dough

1 cup besan (gram flour)
2 pinches soda bicarbonate
½ tsp salt
½ tsp turmeric powder
½ tsp red chilli powder
2 tbsp curd

For first tadka

1 tbsp oil
¼ tsp hing (asafoetida powder)
1 tsp saunf (fennel) seeds, crushed
1 tsp coriander seeds, crushed
1 tsp kasuri methi

For filling

2 tbsp khoya (reduced milk)
4 raisins
4 cashew nuts

For second tadka

4 tbsp oil (or ghee)
¼ tsp hing (asafoetida powder)
½ tsp cumin seeds
¼ tsp mustard seeds
2 tbsp chilli-ginger paste

For gravy

1½ cup curd, beaten
1 tsp salt
1 tsp turmeric powder
2 tsp red chilli powder
3 tsp coriander powder
½ tsp Marwadi garam masala (p. 193)
1 to 2 tsp kasuri methi
2 sprigs of coriander leaves

Making the dough

1. To prepare the dough, mix besan, soda bicarbonate, salt, turmeric, chilli powder and curd in a bowl.

2. For the first tadka, heat oil in a pan on medium heat. Add a pinch of hing, then the crushed saunf and coriander seeds. As they begin to crackle, add 1 tsp kasuri methi.

3. Immediately pour this tadka over the besan mixture and mix well. Knead into a soft dough using very little water. Divide into 4 equal portions and shape each into a ball.

Making the gatta

4. For the filling, chop the cashews and raisins into tiny bits. Crumble the khoya and mix well with cashews and raisins. Divide this mixture into 4 equal portions and shape into balls. Pat one ball of dough into a small circle and place one ball of filling in the centre of the circle. Close the circle from all sides and shape it carefully into a roll of about 3 inches long. Repeat with the remaining dough and filling.

5. Alongside, boil ½ litre water in a pan. Add the rolls and cook them on medium heat for about 7–8 minutes. They will almost double in size and tiny bubbles will appear on the surface. Strain in a colander and reserve the water. When cool enough to handle, cut each roll into 3–4 pieces and set these gatta aside.

Making the gravy

6. For the second tadka, add 4 tbsp oil and hing to a pan on medium-high heat. As the oil warms, add cumin and mustard. As the seeds crackle, add ginger and chilli paste and cook for 30 seconds.

7. Whisk the ingredients of curd mix and add to the pan, stirring continuously. Cook for 3–4 minutes, or until the oil separates.

8. Add gatta pieces and cook for 2–3 minutes. Adjust thickness of the gravy by adding the reserved water from the rolls. Cook for 1–2 minutes.

9. Add garam masala and kasuri methi, and cook for a minute. Garnish with chopped coriander leaves.

Serve hot with steamed rice or any roti.

 Variations

Mirchi ka Gatta
Coat the gatta dough over whole green chillies (large, non-spicy variety) and shape into rolls. Follow the rest of the recipe.

Home-style Gatta ki Sabzi (pic on p. 80)
Make gatta without the filling, shaping the dough into long rolls of 1 cm thickness. Follow the rest of the recipe.

Chef Sameer says

In order to prevent the gatta from getting mushy, especially when the dish is made in large quantities or repeatedly reheated, traditional chefs often boil and then fry the gatta. You can do the same at home. Many families make very small gatta, almost the diameter of a small coin, and refer to the sabzi as Taka Paisa Gatta. This was inspired by a small brass coin used in India a few decades ago.

PAPAD BADI KI SABZI *Papad Curry with Lentil Nuggets*

Like chips, papads are usually a roasted or fried accompaniment in a meal. In this book, you will find many avatars of the Rajasthani papad: as a fried snack (p. 31), a crushed savoury (p. 203) and, in this recipe, as a sabzi.

Serves 4

2 unroasted Bikaneri papads
1 cup badi (lentil nuggets)*
4 tbsp ghee

Basic spices
1 tsp salt
1 tsp turmeric powder
2 tsp red chilli powder
3 tsp coriander powder

For tadka
¼ tsp hing (asafoetida powder)
1 bay leaf
½ tsp cumin seeds
½ tsp mustard seeds
1 tsp kasuri methi (dried fenugreek leaves)

Other ingredients
1 tbsp green chillies, chopped
½ tsp Marwadi garam masala (p. 193)
1 tbsp fresh coriander leaves, chopped

1. Tear the papad into small bits (about 1 inch).

2. Roast badi in 1 tbsp ghee on low heat until it turns light brown. Boil 2 cups water in a pan, add roasted badi and cook for 5–7 minutes, or until it becomes soft but not mushy.

3. Mix the basic spices in ½ cup water and set aside for 5–10 minutes.

4. For the tadka, add 3 tbsp ghee in a pan on medium-high heat. Add hing and bay leaf. As the ghee warms up, add cumin, and after a few seconds, add mustard. As the seeds crackle, add kasuri methi.

5. Immediately, add the spices mixed in water. Cook for 2 minutes on medium-high heat.

6. Add 1 cup water and bring to a boil. Add the torn papads and cook for 2 minutes. (For a slightly sour flavour, you can add buttermilk or beaten curd instead of water.)

7. Add green chillies, garam masala and the cooked badi, and cook for a minute. Turn off the heat and garnish with coriander leaves.

Serve at once with any roti of your choice. If serving after a while, you may need to add some hot water as this sabzi tends to dry up in some time.

*Available in online stores as Marwadi badi or mangodi.

 Variations

 Papad Methi ki Sabzi
Substitute badi with boiled fenugreek seeds (see point 4, p. 208). Omit Step 2 and follow the rest of the recipe.

 Papad Sev ki Sabzi
Substitute badi with lahsuni sev or masala boondi to enjoy the versatile quality of papad and its possibilities. Omit Step 2 and add sev or boondi directly in Step 7.

BESAN KA PITHLA   *Instant Curry with Gram Flour*

Pithla, a beloved sabzi in Rajasthani cuisine, is a side dish made with gram flour. It serves as the perfect go-to option in many Jain households on days when fresh vegetables are avoided for religious reasons. Despite being traditionally prepared without onions, tomatoes or garlic, it maintains an equally delightful taste. Elevated by the Chilli Ghee as a final glaze and flavour, this dish is freshly prepared just before serving dinner, meant to be savoured piping hot!

Serves 4

1 cup besan (gram flour)

For tadka
4 tbsp oil
¼ tsp hing (asafoetida powder)
½ tsp cumin seeds
½ tsp mustard seeds
10–12 curry leaves

Other ingredients
¼ cup onions, finely chopped
5–6 garlic cloves, finely chopped
1 tbsp green chillies, finely chopped
¼ cup tomatoes, finely chopped
1 tsp salt
1 tsp turmeric powder
2 tsp red chilli powder
2 tbsp chopped coriander leaves

For Chilli Ghee
2 tbsp ghee
1 tsp chilli powder

1. Whisk besan in 2 cups water using a hand blender.

2. For the tadka, add oil and hing in a non-stick (or heavy-bottomed) pan on medium-high heat. As the oil warms up, add cumin, mustard and curry leaves.

3. As the seeds crackle, add onions and garlic, and fry for 2–3 minutes. Add green chillies, tomatoes, salt, turmeric and chilli powder, and cook for 2 minutes.

4. Add the whisked besan and cook for 10–15 minutes, stirring continuously so that no lumps are formed. You may need to add another ½ cup water if the mixture is too thick. The consistency must be like cake batter. When the mixture begins to leave the sides of the pan, turn off the heat. Garnish this pithla with coriander leaves.

5. For Chilli Ghee, heat ghee in a small pan. As the ghee warms up, switch off the flame and add the chilli powder. Immediately, drizzle this chilli ghee over the pithla.

Serve hot or at room temperature with any of the Basic Rajasthani Rotis (p. 122), preferably Kadahi Poodi. If kept for a few hours, it tends to thicken. Add some hot water, mix well, and cook for a few minutes before serving.

Chef Sameer says
Add finely chopped capsicum while adding the tomatoes for a lovely crunch. You can sprinkle Jeeravan Masala (p. 195) and enjoy it as a snack too.

KER SANGRI   *Wild Bean and Berry Curry*

(pic on p. 97)

For those of you unfamiliar with Rajasthani cuisine, this recipe mentions local ingredients such as sangri, ker and kachri. In earlier times, these sun-dried desert vegetables were staples on our summer shopping list, as they were only available only during the hot months of the year. Today, however, they are easily accessible year-round in most cities and can also be purchased online with ease.

Sameer enjoys this curry for its ability to retain the rustic, earthy flavours of the desert. At parties, he gives it a refined twist with his signature fusion touch, making it ideal for contemporary Indian plating or festive menus.

We encourage you to try the variations provided at the end of this recipe and discover more about these hardy desert ingredients.

Serves 8

For soaking
½ cup ker (dried desert capers)

1 cup sangri (thin, wild beans from Khejari tree)

15 amchur (dried mango) slices, about 1 cm each*

3 dried, long red chillies, broken into 1-inch pieces

Basic spices
1 tsp salt

1 tsp turmeric powder

2 tsp red chilli powder

3 tsp coriander powder

For tadka
½ cup oil

¼ tsp hing (asafoetida powder)

1 tsp cumin seeds

1 tsp mustard seeds

1 tsp saunf (fennel) seeds

Final ingredient
2 tsp rai-saunf masala (p. 192)

---

* Instead of amchur slices, you can add ¼ cup of dried kachri crushed into bits. If neither is available, add 1–2 tsp amchur powder at the end.

1. Wash ker and sangri 3–4 times until water appears clean. Soak them in a bowl of water for 5 hours. Wash amchur slices and dried red chillies, and soak them in another bowl of water. Wash again and boil them all together with ½ tsp salt and ½ tsp turmeric powder for about 10–15 minutes, or until the ker and sangri turn tender. Drain the water.

2. Mix the basic spices in ½ cup water and set aside for 5–10 minutes. This is known as kaccha masala (p. 208).

3. For the tadka, add oil and hing in a pan on medium-high heat. As the oil warms up, add cumin and saunf, and after a few seconds, add mustard.

4. As the seeds crackle, add the spices mixed in water. Cook for 2 minutes, or until the oil separates.

5. Add the ker-sangri mixture and mix well to coat the spices. Add rai-saunf masala and cook for 3 minutes, or until the liquid dries up.

6. Turn off the heat and set aside for about 2 hours so the flavours are well infused.

Serve at room temperature with any of the Basic Rajasthani Rotis (p. 122).

Shelf life: Typically, this dish is prepared in generous quantities since it can be refrigerated and enjoyed for up to a week. It's essential not to skimp on the amount of oil used, as it plays a crucial role in preserving the dish. If refrigerated, remember to bring it to room temperature before serving and avoid reheating for the best flavour.

Variations

 Ker Kaju
Omit sangri and double the quantity of ker. Add 2 tbsp whole or broken cashews in the tadka.

Ker Kishmish
Omit sangri and double the quantity of ker. Add ½ cup raisins (preferably lemon-soaked, p. 209) in the tadka.

Pachkoota
A favourite of most Rajasthanis, this sabzi combines five kinds of dried beans and berries, namely ker, sangri, kumatiya, goonda and kachri. Mix them all to add up to 2 cups and follow the recipe.

Ask Chef Sameer

Pratibha: Why do you discard the water in which the ingredients are soaked?

Sameer: Soaking certain ingredients help release any grit into the water. Therefore, be sure to drain the water for lentils, amchur (dried mango), and dried vegetables such as ker, sangri and rabodi.

TURAI KE CHHILKE KI SABZI *Curry with Ridge Gourd Peels*

Here is a sabzi that brings back childhood memories and the forgotten flavours of Rajasthan. Sameer stumbled upon this dish, made with the peels of ridge gourd, a few years ago at Rashmi-ji Chatur's place. It was so delicious that he decided to include it in this collection.

Serves 4, as a side dish

2 cups peels of tender ridge gourd, see Step 1

For tadka
4 tbsp oil
¼ tsp hing (asafoetida powder)
½ tsp cumin seeds
½ tsp mustard seeds

Basic spices
1 tsp salt
1 tsp turmeric powder
2 tsp red chilli powder
3 tsp coriander powder

Other ingredients
2 tbsp besan (gram flour), roasted
½ tsp amchur (dried mango) powder or kachri (wild berry) powder
½ tsp Marwadi garam masala (p. 193)
2 sprigs of coriander leaves, chopped
1 tsp lemon juice (optional)

1. Wash ridge gourds, cut away the ends and remove spiky edges from the skin. Now, peel the green skin off the gourd and chop the peels into small pieces. (Set aside the ridge gourd to use in some other preparation.)

2. For the tadka, add oil and hing in a pan on medium-high heat. As the oil warms up, add cumin, and after a few seconds, add mustard.

3. As the seeds crackle, add chopped peels and salt. Lower the heat, cover and cook for 5 minutes. Add turmeric, chilli powder and coriander powder. Stir for a minute and add 1–2 tbsp water to prevent the spices from burning. Mix well, cover and cook for about 3 minutes.

4. Increase to medium heat, add the besan and cook for about 2 minutes, stirring gently, until any liquid in the ridge gourd dries up.

5. Mix in amchur and garam masala, and turn off the heat. Garnish with coriander leaves. Serve at room temperature with a dash of lemon juice.

Serve with steamed rice or Phulka (p. 122).

 Variation

 Curry with Green Pea Peels
Omit the besan. Use peels of tender green peas. Snip away the ends as well as threads on the sides, then peel away the flimsy skin. You will now have just the succulent part of the peels. Tear them into bits and follow the rest of the recipe.

AAM KE CHHILKE KI SABZI *Curry with Ripe Mango Peels*

Mango lovers have created innovative recipes using every part of the fruit, including a delicious sabzi made with the peels. While you can use peels from any mango variety, we recommend those of Kesar or Alphonso mangoes to bring out the best taste of this sabzi.

Serves 4, as a side dish

2 cups peels of ripe mangoes, see
   Step 1

For tadka
4 tbsp oil
¼ tsp hing (asafoetida powder)
½ tsp cumin seeds
½ tsp mustard seeds

Basic spices
1 tsp salt
1 tsp turmeric powder
2 tsp red chilli powder
3 tsp coriander powder

Other ingredients
1 tsp amchur (dried mango) powder
   or kachri (wild berry) powder
½ tsp Marwadi garam masala (p. 193)
1 sprig of coriander leaves,
   chopped
1 tsp lemon juice (optional)

1. Wash and peel the mangoes, and chop the peels into 1-inch pieces. (Enjoy the mango flesh separately.)

2. For the tadka, add oil and hing in a pan on medium-high heat. As the oil warms up, add cumin, and after a few seconds, add mustard.

3. As the seeds crackle, add the chopped peels and salt. Reduce to medium heat, cover and cook for 5 minutes.

4. Add turmeric, chilli powder and coriander powder. Stir for a minute and add 2 tbsp water to prevent the spices from burning. Mix well, cover and cook for about a minute.

5. Add amchur powder and garam masala, stir to mix and turn off the heat. Garnish with coriander leaves and set aside for about 10 minutes. Add lemon juice just before serving.

Serve with steamed rice or any roti of your choice, especially Phulka (p. 122) or Bejhad Roti (p. 126).

 Variation

 Curry with Dried Mango Peels
Instead of fresh peels, use dried peels of mangoes. Soak 2 cups of dried peels for 10 minutes, then boil them for 5-6 minutes. Drain and follow the rest of the recipe.

Chef Sameer says
Growing up, I used to enjoy watching mango peels being dried and preserved under the hot sun. When you cut a ripe mango, do not discard the peels. Chop them into neat squares, sprinkle salt to avoid discolouration and sun-dry for a few days. In the summer, the sun is so fierce that the peels dry within a day or two. Once dried, they can be preserved and stored in an airtight container for months.

LAUKI KE CHHILKE KI SANGRI   *Curry with Bottle Gourd Peels*

This lauki dish masquerades as sangri, with the peels julienned to look like the famous dry beans of Rajasthan. We recommend cooking it in an iron kadahi which will lend a deep blackish-brown colour to the sabzi. Choose a bottle gourd that is tender. Sameer learnt this recipe in New York from Rupa Bari, the efficient kitchen and house caretaker of his sister, Dr Manjula Bansal.

Serves 4, as a side dish

2 cups peels of bottle gourd, see Step 1

Spice mix
½ tsp black salt
½ tsp salt (and ½ tsp for boiling peels)
1 tsp turmeric powder (and ½ tsp for boiling peels)
2 tsp red chilli powder
3 tsp coriander powder
2 tsp rai-saunf masala (p. 192)
1 tsp amchur (dried mango) powder

For tadka
2 tbsp oil
¼ tsp hing (asafoetida powder)
½ tsp cumin seeds
½ tsp mustard seeds
3 dried, long red chillies, broken

Final ingredient
2 tsp oil (preferably the excess oil from home-made mango pickle)

1. Wash and julienne the bottle gourd peels into thin matchsticks. Boil them with ½ tsp salt and ½ tsp turmeric for 5–7 minutes, or until tender. Drain the water and set aside to cool.

2. Add all the ingredients listed under spice mix to the cooked peels. Rub lightly so the spices blend into the peels.

3. For the tadka, add oil and hing in a pan on medium-high heat. As the oil warms up, add cumin, and after a few seconds, add mustard. As the seeds crackle, add dried chillies and stir for a few seconds.

4. Add the peels, stir and cook for 2–3 minutes.

5. Add pickle oil and turn off the heat. Set aside for at least 30 minutes so the flavours are well infused.

Serve with any roti of your choice or mix it into plain steamed rice and savour the unique flavour.

Ker Sangri p.92

Instant Churma p.8

Besan ka Churma p.8,
variation

Shekhawati Kaanji Vada p.34

Awla ki Kadhi p.115

DAL AND KADHI

Lentil and Yogurt Stews

Though dal and kadhi are different kinds of dishes, they share one commonality: both are liquid, whether like a broth or stew. During most mealtimes, a dal or a kadhi is a must on the menu. They go well with rice and roti, with any randheen, and even dhokla.

It is always a matter of debate to find the correct translation of local terms, and this is something Sameer and I enjoyed exploring through recipe conversations. For instance, kadhi. We can describe this as a 'stew' of curd and gram flour. A stew is a slow-cooked broth of thick or thin consistency, almost soupy, found in almost every part of the world. One origin of the word 'kadhi' comes from Ayurvedic literature, which describes a broth of grain, flour and vegetable as 'kwatitha'. Another etymology shows the origin of kadhi from the word 'kadhna', meaning slow-cooking. Kadhi is best cooked in an iron vessel on low heat for a long period.

If you are just starting to explore Rajasthani cooking, we suggest you start with Moong Chana Dal, which is delicious despite no fresh ingredients. The maandiya is a must-try either as a soup or as a full-fledged meal with Kathi Dal and steamed rice. The ambariya is simple to make and has a distinct taste while the Jaipuri Kadhi is an exercise in tempering spices the right way. Sameer also recommends you stock up on the special dal masala (p. 194), which adds a magic touch to any dal.

ROZ KI DAL *Home-style Everyday Dal*

A comfort meal for the entire family, this everyday dal is loved for its simplicity, ease of preparation and nourishing warmth.

Serves 4

For dal
1 cup tuvar dal
4 tomatoes, halved
¼ tsp turmeric powder

For tadka
3 tbsp ghee
½ tsp mustard seeds
1 tsp white urad dal
¼ tsp hing (asafoetida powder)
½ tsp cumin seeds
7–8 curry leaves
½ tsp cumin seeds
½ tsp red chilli powder

Other ingredients
1 tsp salt
1 tsp sugar
2 tbsp coriander leaves, chopped

1. Wash and soak the dal in water for 30 minutes. Drain and pressure-cook with the whole tomatoes and 3 cups of water for 3 whistles.

2. Once cooked, remove the tomatoes, strain the pulp into the dal, and discard the peels and seeds. Mash the dal and set aside.

3. Heat ghee in a pan over medium heat. Add mustard seeds and urad dal. As the dal turns golden, add hing and immediately switch off the flame.

4. Immediately, add cumin seeds, curry leaves and chilli powder to the hot ghee.

5. Switch on the flame again and pour in the cooked dal. Add about 2 cups water to adjust the consistency, along with salt and sugar. Bring to a gentle boil and simmer for a few minutes. Garnish with coriander leaves.

Serve hot with steamed rice or as part of a wholesome meal.

PANCHMEL DAL *Popular Mix of Five Lentils*

A traditional favourite, this dal is made by blending five different types of lentils, complemented by the addition of tadka in pure desi ghee, and topped off with a sprinkle of dal masala. At weddings, this dal is served at live counters, where it undergoes a fresh frying process with onions, garlic and spices, or is served alongside Garlic Chutney. For those following a strict Jain diet, the live counters also provide a more simple tadka with just hing and cumin seeds. While this dal can be enjoyed with rice or roti, it is the perfect accompaniment to Baati, especially during the rainy season. For an authentic and earthy flavour, prepare this dal in an earthen pot and serve in leaf bowls.

Serves 6 to 8

For dal
¼ cup yellow moong dal
¼ cup white urad dal
¼ cup chana dal
¼ cup tuvar dal or masoor dal
¼ cup chawli dal (split cow peas)
1 tsp salt
1 tsp turmeric powder

For tadka
4–6 tbsp ghee
¼ tsp hing (asafoetida powder)
2 bay leaves
½ tsp cumin seeds
3 cloves
1½ tsp red chilli powder
1 tbsp coriander leaves, chopped

Other ingredients
½ cup tomatoes, finely chopped
1 tbsp fresh ginger, finely chopped
1 tbsp green chillies, finely chopped
1 tsp dal masala (p. 194)
1–2 tbsp lemon juice
2 tbsp coriander leaves

1. Wash all the five varieties of dal and soak in water for about 30 minutes. Drain the water and pressure-cook all of them with 6 cups of water, salt and turmeric for up to 3 whistles. Once the steam has cooled down, open the cooker and mash the dal partially.

2. Turn on the heat again and add the chopped tomatoes, ginger and green chillies to the cooked dal. Simmer for a few more minutes.

3. For the tadka, add ghee, hing and bay leaves in a small pan on medium-high heat. As the ghee warms up, add cumin and cloves. As the seeds crackle, add chilli powder and 1 tbsp coriander leaves. Pour this tadka into the simmering dal. Turn off the heat.

4. Add dal masala and lemon juice, and garnish with the remaining coriander leaves.

Serve hot with steamed rice or any roti of your choice. For a special treat, serve with Baati (p. 134).

Chef Sameer says
I grew up knowing this as 'theekri wali dal', named after the broken shard of earthen pot used to flavour it. In the old days, cooks would heat a piece of clay pot or a roasted leaf bowl (donna) and infuse it into the dal with ghee or a pinch of hing. Such culinary artistry transcends cultures—Bengalis steam paturi in plantain leaves, and the Japanese roast seaweed to elevate flavour. Artistic innovations in food history!

DAL CHANDNI *Moonlight White Lentil with Malai*

On full moon nights during the winter months, members of Jaipur's royal families would dress in white and eat special meals in large silver plates, arranged on low tables known as bajots. The menu would always include this white dal, earning it the tag of 'chandni' meaning 'moonlight'. Do not compromise on the malai in this recipe. Use the thick layer of cream on top of boiled milk; also available as milk malai in the market. This ingredient makes this dal perfectly buttery.

Serves 4 to 6

For dal
1 cup white urad dal
½ cup malai (milk cream), beaten
¾ tsp salt
¾ tsp Marwadi garam masala (p. 193)
    or 1 tsp dal masala (p. 194)
¼ tsp dried ginger powder

For tadka
4 to 6 tbsp ghee
¼ tsp hing (asafoetida powder)
¼ tsp cumin seeds
¼ tsp black cumin seeds
½ inch piece of mace, crushed
½ cup onions, thinly sliced
10 garlic cloves, finely chopped
1 green chilli, finely chopped

For garnish
2 dried, long chillies, broken into
    1-inch bits and fried in 1 tsp ghee
10–12 juliennes of fresh ginger
1 sprig of coriander leaves, chopped

1. Wash the urad dal and soak in water for about 30 minutes. Wash again and drain. Then pressure-cook with 4 cups water for up to 2 whistles. Once the steam has settled down, open the cooker, add malai and salt into the dal, and mix well. Transfer the dal to a serving bowl. Sprinkle garam masala and ginger powder over the cooked dal. Set aside.

2. For the tadka, add ghee and hing in a small pan on medium-high heat. As the ghee warms up, add cumin, black cumin and mace.

3. As the seeds crackle, add onions and sauté until golden brown. Add chopped garlic and green chillies, and cook for a minute. Pour this mix over the dal.

4. Garnish the dal with fried red chillies, sliced ginger and coriander leaves.

Serve hot with steamed rice or any roti of your choice.

Ask Chef Sameer
Pratibha: If I need to serve the dal at different times to different people instead of all at once, what is the best way to do so?

Sameer: Ideally, the dal is presented in a party style, where all the food is set out at the same time for people to help themselves. If you want to serve it individually at different times, you will have to prepare the tadka and toppings individually just before serving, so that the dish retains its fresh flavour and topping textures.

# MOONG CHANA DAL *Spicy Dal from the Jain Kitchens*

A specialty of Jain families, this home-style mix of two lentils is crafted without any fresh ingredients, since many from this community avoid eating fresh fruit and vegetables on certain days of the month. Keep an earthen pot (handi) at home for cooking any dal to capture an earthy flavour.

Serves 6

For dal
½ cup green moong dal
½ cup chana dal

For tadka
4–6 tbsp ghee
¼ tsp hing (asafoetida powder)
2 bay leaves
½ tsp cumin seeds
1½ tsp red chilli powder

Other spices
1 tsp salt
1 tsp turmeric powder
1 tbsp coriander powder
½ tsp dried ginger powder
1 tsp amchur (dried mango) powder
½ tsp kachri (wild berry) powder
   (optional)
½ tsp Marwadi garam masala (p. 193)

1. Wash both the varieties of dal and soak in water for about 30 minutes. Wash again and drain. Then pressure-cook with 3 cups of water for up to 3 whistles. Once the steam has cooled down, open the cooker, add 1 cup hot water and mash the dal.

2. For the tadka, add ghee, hing and bay leaves in a deep pan on medium-high heat. As the ghee warms up, add cumin seeds. As the seeds crackle, add chilli powder.

3. Immediately, add the cooked dal along with salt, turmeric, coriander powder and dried ginger powder. Bring to a boil and simmer for 3 minutes.

4. Add amchur, kachri and garam masala, mix well, and turn off the heat.

Serve hot with steamed rice or any roti of your choice.

❀ SHEKHAWATI MOGAR   *Dry Lentil Curry*

The term 'mogar' generally refers to green gram, which is split and husked, and hence looks yellow. However, Rajasthanis refer to any lentil cooked in a specific dry style as mogar. In the Shekhawati region, this dry lentil preparation is popular at breakfast. For Sameer, this protein-packed dish holds memories of his sister Rani jiji, and her 'haath ka swaad'.

Serves 4 to 6

1¼ cups yellow moong dal

For tadka
3 tbsp ghee (and 2 tbsp ghee for topping)
¼ tsp hing (asafoetida powder)
½ tsp cumin seeds
¼ tsp mustard seeds
½ tsp kuti mirch (coarse chilli powder)

Basic spices
¾ tsp salt
¼ tsp black salt
1 tsp turmeric powder
2 tsp red chilli powder
3 tsp coriander powder

Other spices
1 tbsp fresh ginger, finely chopped
1 tbsp green chillies, finely chopped
1 tsp kasuri methi (dried fenugreek leaves), lightly roasted
½ tsp dried mint powder
½ tsp amchur (dried mango) powder
½ tsp Marwadi garam masala (p. 193) or dal masala (p. 194)

For garnish
1 sprig of coriander leaves, chopped
1 lemon, cut into wedges

1. Wash the dal and soak it in water for about an hour. Drain the water.

2. For the tadka, add 3 tbsp ghee and hing in a pan on medium-high heat. As the ghee warms up, add cumin and mustard. As the seeds crackle, add kuti mirch.

3. Immediately, add the dal and cook for a minute, stirring continuously.

4. Add 3 tbsp water and continue to cook for 3 minutes, or until the water dries up. Repeat this step three to four times until the dal is cooked. Cooking it this way will keep each grain separate and not turn mushy.

5. Add the basic spices along with 2 tbsp of water. Cover partly and cook on low heat for another 4–5 minutes, stirring a couple of times.

6. Add all the ingredients listed under other spices. Cover and cook for another 3 minutes.

7. Mix in 2 tbsp ghee and turn off the flame. Garnish with coriander leaves and serve with lemon wedges.

Serve hot with steamed rice or any roti of your choice. It also makes a delightful breakfast when paired with khankra—a crisp, roasted cracker.

For something more indulgent, enjoy it with roasted papad brushed generously with melted ghee, followed by a sweet bite of Badam Katli (p. 9) or Kaju Katli. This dish is also served as a sabzi during lunch or dinner.

> **Variations**
>
> **Mogar with Dried Sprouts**
> Substitute the dal with dried sprouts of moong beans or moth beans.
>
> **Mogar with Other Lentils**
> Substitute the dal with lentils such as cowpeas, brown chickpeas, moth beans, moong beans and black masoor. Soak these overnight (except masoor). Cook them and follow the above recipe but reduce the cooking time in Step 4 since the lentils have already been cooked.

Ask Chef Sameer

Pratibha: What does 'cover partly' mean?

Sameer: It means placing a lid in a way that it covers only half of the top of the vessel. This allows some heat to be retained while keeping each grain separate.

Pratibha: Why do you add coarse chilli powder instead of fine chilli powder in tadka?

Sameer: In this dish, the coarse chilli powder in the tadka lends a mild smoky flavour. If you add chilli powder, it tends to burn, hence it is added later.

KATHI DAL MAANDIYA *Thick Dal with Spicy Rice Water Soup* (pic on p. 118)

Also known as 'kath' and 'khatta', maandiya is a thin soup of spiced rice water. On cool evenings in Rajasthan, many families enjoy a meal of Dal Chawal Maandiya, followed by a cup or two of just the soup. For Sameer, preparing it is always a nostalgic experience. He says, 'Maandiya reminds me of the Daga family in California. Their kitchen is filled with the flavours of traditional Indian food, and their deep connection to their roots remains strong even after decades abroad. Dal Chawal Maandiya is a weekly feature at their home. Last year, during my stay with them, Asha Daga taught me the perfect recipe.'

Serves 4

For kathi dal

1 cup tuvar dal
½ tsp salt
½ tsp turmeric powder
4 tbsp ghee

For maandiya

3 amchur (dried mango) slices,
    about 2 inch each
2 cups maand (rice water)*
2 tbsp wheat flour

For tadka

2 tbsp ghee
2 bay leaves
¼ tsp hing (asafoetida powder)
½ tsp cumin seeds
2 cinnamon sticks of 1 inch each
2 cloves
1 black cardamom
2 green cardamoms
2 dried, long red chillies, broken
    into 1-inch pieces

Basic spices

1 tsp salt
¼ tsp turmeric powder
½ tsp red chilli powder
¼ tsp pepper powder

For serving

2 tsp warm, melted ghee, per
    serving

1. Wash the amchur slices and soak in water for about 2 hours. Wash again, drain and set aside.

2. To make the kathi dal, wash the dal and soak in water for 30 minutes. Drain and pressure-cook the dal with salt, turmeric and 3 cups water for 3 whistles. Mash, mix in 4 tbsp of ghee and set aside.

3. To make the maandiya, start with the tadka. Add 2 tbsp ghee, hing and bay leaves in a pan on medium-high heat. As the ghee warms up, add cumin seeds. As the seeds crackle, add cinnamon, cloves and cardamoms, and sauté for a few seconds, and then add red chillies.

4. Immediately, add wheat flour and sauté for 10–15 seconds. Pour in the rice water and 4 cups water.

5. Add the basic spices along with soaked amchur. Bring to a boil, reduce the heat and simmer for 30–40 minutes. Remove red chillies and amchur before serving.

To serve, place a mound of 1 cup steamed rice on a plate. Top it with ½ cup kathi dal, drizzle 2 tsp ghee on top, and serve maandiya in a bowl alongside.

Among Oswal Jains, Kathi Dal Maandiya with rice is relished as a complete comfort meal. It is served along with papad, green chutney, kachumbar and a wedge of juicy lemon.

---

* To make maand, cook 1 cup of rice in 1½ litres boiling water with ½ tsp salt and 1 tsp ghee. Once the rice is cooked, strain and reserve the water, known as maand. You should get about 2 cups of maand this way. You can use the cooked rice for serving along with maandiya.

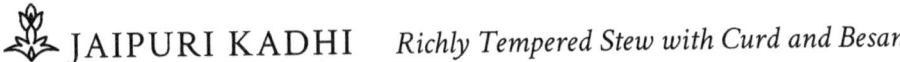 JAIPURI KADHI   *Richly Tempered Stew with Curd and Besan*

The term 'kadhi' means something that has been kadhna, or slow-cooked. The elders would say that a perfect kadhi should have gone through 'chattees ukaal', meaning thirty-six boils. To some of you, 45 minutes may seem a long simmering time, but the end result is a flavour that cannot be achieved by a short cut. When well made, it is no surprise to find people drinking this kadhi one cup after another, relishing its soothing flavours.

Serves 4 to 6

For batter
2 tbsp besan (gram flour)
2 cups curd
1 tsp salt
2 tsp red chilli powder

For tadka
2 to 4 tbsp ghee preferably, or oil
¼ tsp hing (asafoetida powder)
2 bay leaves
¼ tsp cumin seeds
¼ tsp mustard seeds
½ tsp fenugreek seeds
4 cloves
4 green cardamoms

Other ingredients
2 green chillies, slit
1 sprig curry leaves

1. Whisk the ingredients for batter with 8 cups of water into a smooth paste.
2. For the tadka, add ghee, hing and bay leaves in a pan on medium-high heat. As the ghee warms up, add cumin, and after a few seconds, add mustard, fenugreek, cloves and cardamoms. Sauté for a few seconds.
3. As the seeds crackle, pour in the batter mix and cook, stirring continuously. Bring to a boil, and add green chillies and curry leaves. Now allow the kadhi to simmer on low heat for about 45 minutes. Gradually, the ghee will rise to the surface. Turn off the heat and discard the green chillies.

Serve hot with steamed rice or any roti of your choice. Also a preferred accompaniment to rice dishes and randheen varieties.

Tip: You can spike up this kadhi further by adding readily available fried boondi, or any variety of sev, such as 'laung (cloves) ki sev' or 'lahsun (garlic) ki sev' just 5 minutes before turning off the heat.

Chef Sameer says
On a lighter note, I have seen many head cooks strain the prepared kadhi and discard the whole spices used in the tadka. They then add a fresh tadka of ghee, hing and cumin, and when they receive compliments for the taste, they say, 'Oh, this is just a simple kadhi!' The guests are left wondering where the exotic flavours come from. I learnt this recipe from Sumer-ji Bothra, aka Sena Bhabhi. Take my word and try it.

JODHPURI HAVEJI   *Home-style Stew with Curd and Chana Dal*

Hailing from the royal cities of Jodhpur and Udaipur, this dish holds a special place as a staple on any wedding menu. Over time, it has disappeared from the menus, but it deserves to be revived, considering its distinct flavour compared to regular chana dal preparations. What sets it apart is the curry-style taste and texture achieved through the use of curd or chhaach in the recipe. The culinary journey of this dish holds a heartwarming touch, as Sameer learnt it from his beloved masi from Jodhpur, whom he called Chhoti Munni. Originally crafted without tomatoes, Sameer added his creative touch by incorporating the tricolour combination of yellow dal, red tomatoes, and green chillies.

Serves 4

For dal
1 cup chana dal
½ tsp salt
½ tsp turmeric powder

For tadka
2 to 4 tbsp ghee preferably, or oil
¼ tsp hing (asafoetida powder)
2 bay leaves
½ tsp cumin seeds

Other ingredients
½ cup thinly sliced onions
4 green chillies, finely chopped
1 tbsp ginger paste
1 tbsp garlic paste
½ cup chopped tomatoes
½ tsp salt
½ tsp turmeric powder
2 tsp red chilli powder
1 cup curd, beaten
1 tsp Marwadi garam masala (p. 193)
    or dal masala (p. 194)
Coriander leaves, for garnish

1. Wash the chana dal and soak in water for 30 minutes. Wash again and drain. Then pressure-cook with 3 cups water, ½ tsp salt and ½ tsp turmeric for up to 1 whistle on high heat, and 1 whistle on low heat. Turn off the heat, and within 2–3 minutes, release the steam to prevent the dal from getting mushy. Ideally, each grain must be cooked, yet remain separate. Strain the water and reserve. Mash some of the cooked chana dal with a spoon.

2. For the tadka, add ghee, hing and bay leaves in a pan on medium-high heat. As the ghee warms up, add cumin and sauté for a few seconds.

3. As the cumin crackles, add sliced onions and cook for 2–3 minutes, or until they turn light golden. Add green chillies, ginger, garlic and tomatoes and cook for 3 minutes.

4. Add salt and turmeric. Add chilli powder and continue to cook. If required, add some of the reserved water to prevent the masala from burning. Cook for about 2 minutes, or until the ghee begins to float on top. Remove half of the floating ghee with a spoon and reserve to use as rangat (p. 196).

5. Add beaten curd and cook for 3 minutes, stirring continuously. Add cooked chana dal and some of the reserved dal water. Check consistency and add up to 1 cup of hot water, depending on the consistency you prefer.

6. Finally, add in the garam masala, sprinkle coriander leaves and drizzle the reserved rangat on top.

Serve hot with steamed rice or any roti of your choice.

Ask Chef Sameer
Pratibha: Can we reduce the ghee in the tadka?
Sameer: To digest protein, you need fat. Therefore, this haveji with chana dal is richly tempered in ghee.

PAANSI KI KADHI *Curd and Besan Stew with Chickpea Leaves*

During the month of December in Rajasthan, the tender shoots of the chickpea plant start germinating. These soft leaves are a little sour, yet deeply flavourful and add their zing to many Rajasthani dishes such as dal, kadhi and even roti. They are referred to as paansi because of their comparability in flavour to the paan, meaning betel leaf. Kadhi made with paansi leaves is also known by the same name. Sameer enjoys making microgreens from chickpeas round the year, and these are often available fresh on his kitchen counter. When either fresh or dried paansi leaves are not available, adapt this healthy recipe for other greens such as amaranth, fenugreek or spinach.

Serves 4

200 gm fresh (or 50 gm dried)
   chickpea leaves*

For batter
2 tbsp besan (gram flour)
2 cups curd
1 tsp salt
½ tsp turmeric powder
1 tsp red chilli powder

For tadka
4–6 tbsp ghee
¼ tsp hing (asafoetida powder)
¼ tsp cumin seeds
½ tsp mustard seeds
½ tsp fenugreek seeds
4 cloves
4 green cardamoms
2 dried, long red chillies, broken
   into 1-inch pieces

1. Clean, wash and finely chop the chickpea leaves.

2. Whisk the batter ingredients with 6 cups of water, so it becomes a smooth, lump-free mix.

3. For the tadka, add ghee and hing in a pan on medium-high heat. As the ghee warms up, add cumin, and after a few seconds, add mustard, fenugreek, cloves and cardamoms. As the seeds crackle, add red chillies.

4. Immediately, add chickpea leaves and sauté for 3 minutes.

5. Add the batter mix and stir continuously until it comes to a boil. Simmer for about 45 minutes, stirring a few times.

Serve hot with steamed rice or any roti of your choice, especially Khoba Roti (p. 136) or Sogra varieties (p. 128).

* When chickpea leaves are available in season, add fresh chickpea leaves to any dal or kadhi, or even to the dough of roti while kneading. To enjoy the leaves round the year, you can dry and store them in an airtight container (see p. 210).

KALA CHANA KI KADHI *Vegan Stew with Chickpeas and Besan*

In this kadhi from the Jodhpur-Udaipur belt, brown chana is cooked and the reserved boiling liquid whisked with besan to form the base of this curd-less kadhi. Besan has the property of absorbing large quantities of oil and ghee, so some of the oil from the tadka is set aside and added in the end. Such traditional tips show us the wisdom of elders who used less ghee or oil without losing the colour of the dish. Cook this dish in an iron kadahi for perfect colour and taste. If you are not a vegan, make this kadhi in ghee to capture the original flavours.

Serves 4

1 cup kala chana (brown chickpeas)
1½ tbsp besan (gram flour)

For tadka
4 tbsp oil
¼ tsp hing (asafoetida powder)
½ tsp cumin seeds
½ tsp fenugreek seeds

Other spices
½ tsp turmeric powder
1½ tsp red chilli powder
1 tsp salt
1 tsp kachri (wild berry) powder
½ tsp Marwadi garam masala (p.193)

1. Wash the kala chana and soak overnight. In the morning, wash again and pressure-cook until well cooked. Strain and retain the water.

2. Whisk besan with 1 cup of the strained water and 4 cups plain water into a smooth, lump-free mix.

3. For the tadka, add oil and hing in an iron pan on medium-high heat. As the oil warms up, add cumin and fenugreek seeds, and sauté for a few seconds.

4. Add turmeric and chilli powder along with ½ cup water. Cook for 2–3 minutes, or until the oil floats to the top. Remove half of the oil with a spoon and reserve to use as rangat (p. 196).

5. Add the cooked chana and boil for 2–3 minutes. Next, add the besan batter, reduce the heat and simmer for 10 minutes.

6. Add salt and kachri powder and simmer for 3 minutes.

7. Add garam masala and turn off the heat. Cover and set aside for 10 minutes, and then drizzle the reserved rangat.

Serve hot with steamed rice or any roti of your choice.

 Variation

 Moth ki Kadhi
Soak ¾ cup whole moth beans overnight. Substitute them for the brown chickpeas and follow the remaining steps of the recipe.

❧ RAJWADI PAKODA KADHI   *Curd and Besan Stew with Pan-fried Fritters*
(pic on p. 119)

Enlivened with tawa-roasted pakodas, tempered with whole spices, and cooked with onion and garlic, this kadhi can be summed up in one word: exotic.

Serves 4 to 6

For pakodas
1 cup besan (gram flour)
2 tbsp finely chopped onions (or spinach or kasuri methi)
½ tsp salt
½ tsp red chilli powder
½ tsp turmeric powder
1 tbsp hot oil (and 2–3 tbsp oil for roasting)

For kadhi
3 tbsp besan (gram flour)
1½ cups curd

For tadka
4 tbsp ghee (or double it, for the traditional flavour)
¼ tsp cumin seeds
¼ tsp fenugreek seeds
1-inch cinnamon stick
1 black cardamom
4 green cardamoms
4 cloves

Other ingredients
2 dried, long red chillies, broken
1 large onion, finely chopped
1 tbsp fresh ginger, finely chopped
8–10 garlic cloves, finely chopped
1 tsp salt
1 tsp turmeric powder
2 tsp red chilli powder
3 tsp coriander powder
½ tsp Marwadi garam masala (p. 193)

1. Mix the ingredients for pakodas (including 1 tbsp hot oil) with about ½ cup water to form a batter of dropping consistency. You can make about 12 flat pakodas with this batter.

2. Heat a tawa, preferably nonstick, and brush with oil. Drop spoonsful of the pakoda mixture, leaving space in between. Drizzle oil, cover and cook for 2–3 minutes on medium heat. Flip and drizzle oil, cover and cook for another 2–3 minutes, or until they swell up and look well roasted. Set aside. Make the remaining pakodas.

3. For the kadhi, whisk the besan and curd in 6 cups of water to make a smooth mixture, and set aside.

4. For the tadka, heat the ghee in a pan on medium-high heat and add the ingredients for tadka.

5. As the seeds crackle, add red chillies, onions, ginger and garlic. Sauté for 30 seconds.

6. Add salt, turmeric, chilli powder and coriander powder along with ¼ cup water. Cook for 3 minutes, or until the ghee begins to float on top.

7. Add the besan-curd mixture and stir continuously until it comes to a boil. Reduce the heat and simmer for 20 minutes. Add the pakodas and simmer for 10 minutes. Add garam masala, mix and turn off the heat.

Serve hot with any roti or steamed rice, along with a fresh seasonal sabzi. Before serving, drizzle a few drops of rangat (p. 196) on top.

🌿 JAIN BADI KI KADHI   *Curd and Wheat Flour Stew with Lentil Nuggets*

Most Rajasthani kadhis use besan (gram flour) to create a thick, creamy stew. Besan, however, can be heavy to digest, so some thoughtful elders substituted it with wheat flour, added the goodness of methi and the crunch of badi, to create this kadhi. Eaten with roti, it makes a delightfully light meal.

Serves 6

For batter

2 tbsp wheat flour
2 cups curd
1 tsp salt

For tadka

4 tbsp ghee
¼ tsp hing (asafoetida powder)
1 tsp cumin seeds
½ tsp mustard seeds
2 dried, long red chillies, halved
2 cloves
2 green cardamoms

Other ingredients

¼ cup badi (lentil nuggets)*,
   coarsely crushed
1 tbsp fenugreek seeds
½ tsp red chilli powder

1. Whisk the ingredients for batter with 8 cups water into a smooth paste, set aside.

2. For the tadka, add ghee and hing in a pan on medium-high heat. As the ghee warms up, add cumin, and after a few seconds, add mustard, red chillies, cloves and cardamoms. Sauté for 5 seconds.

3. Lower the heat, add badi and fenugreek seeds, and fry until the badi turns golden brown.

4. Add chilli powder and the prepared batter, stirring continuously until it comes to a boil. Reduce the heat, add salt and continue to simmer for 30 minutes.

Serve hot with steamed rice or any roti of your choice.

* Available in online stores as Marwadi badi or mangodi.

114

 AWLA KI KADHI   *Vegan Stew with Indian Gooseberries and Besan*   (*pic on p. 100*)

Famously referred to as ambariya, this is a nearly overlooked winter recipe from Rajasthan. Elevated by the distinctive essence of Indian gooseberries, this kadhi significantly aids digestion. This recipe should be made in an iron pan to maximise its health benefits. This method will also impart a dark brown hue to the kadhi, enhancing its visual appeal. While ghee can be used for the tadka, oil serves equally well in this recipe, rendering it a delightful option for vegans.

Serves 6

For batter

2 tbsp besan (gram flour)
2 tbsp grated Indian gooseberries
    (or 1 tbsp gooseberry powder)
1 tsp salt
1 tsp turmeric powder
2 tsp red chilli powder

For tadka

4 tbsp oil
¼ tsp hing (asafoetida powder)
½ tsp cumin seeds
½ tsp mustard seeds
½ tsp fenugreek seeds
4 cloves
4 green cardamoms
2 dried, long red chillies, broken
    into 1-inch pieces
2 fresh green chillies, whole

1. Whisk the ingredients for the batter into a smooth paste with 1 litre water, first adding a cup of water and whisking well to remove any lumps, and gradually adding the remaining water. Set aside.

2. For the tadka, add oil and hing in a pan on medium-high heat. As the oil warms up, add cumin seeds, and as they crackle, add mustard, fenugreek, cloves and cardamoms. Sauté for a few seconds. Add the red and green chillies.

3. Add the mixed batter and cook, stirring continuously, until it comes to a boil. Simmer over low heat for 15–20 minutes, or until the oil separates. Turn off the heat and keep covered for a few minutes.

Serve hot with steamed rice. You can also enjoy it as a soup along with a meal.

Chef Sameer says

Add a few spoons of rangat (p. 196) on top of the kadhi to enrich its colour. Ideally, prepare the kadhi in an iron pan, which may give it a deep, almost blackish hue. The reddish golden rangat will enhance its visual appeal beautifully.

Spirit of Simple Abundance

In many Rajasthani homes, cooking with just a handful of ingredients has never meant compromising on warmth or flavour. Even with limited seasonal produce, home cooks find ways to create meals that feel generous and comforting. There is a quiet joy in this kind of everyday abundance—rooted in tradition, care and creativity.

This spirit also lives in the story of Chhappan Bhog—the feast of fifty-six dishes offered to Shri Krishna. When he lifted the Govardhan mountain with his little finger to protect the villagers and animals from torrential rains, he missed his meals for seven days. Once the skies cleared, the villagers prepared a meal to make up for every one he had missed—eight meals a day over seven days, adding up to fifty-six.

The recipes that follow are not grand feasts, but they carry the same intention: to make the everyday feel special and to serve with love what is available.

Clockwise from rice:
Besan Churma p.8 (variation)
Instant Churma p.8
Mirch ke Tipore p.170
Panchmel Dal p.103
Home-style Gatta p.89 (variation)
Baati p.134

Maandiya p.108

Kathi Dal with Rice p.108

Awla ki Kadhi p.115

Rajwadi Pakoda Kadhi p.113

119

Khoba Roti p.136

120

ROTI

Flatbreads and Baati

On my first visit to Sameer's home in Jaipur, he treated me to a different roti at every meal of my week-long stay. Rajasthan is famous for its vast repertoire of rotis, including Phulka (thin roti), Sogra (millet roti), Khoba Roti (thick roti with indents) and Poodi (fried roti). Poodi can be deep-fried or shallow-fried, known respectively as Kadahi Poodi and Tawa Poodi. I was especially delighted with Sameer's demystified version of Khoba Roti and have pleased my guests with this ever since.

Once you know the basics of roti-making, you can allow your creativity to run wild. You can experiment with different flours and millets; include seeds such as cumin, carom, nigella or sesame; add fresh or dried herbs and greens; and knead the dough using milk, buttermilk, leftover whey from paneer, or even orange juice.

Rotis are the foundation of pretty much every Rajasthani meal and are considered comfort food in most parts of north India. Served with dal and sabzi, they make a complete meal, whether for lunch or dinner. Most of the rotis in this section can also be enjoyed as a light breakfast or tea-time snack when served simply with plain curd or a pickle. Many, children and elders alike, even enjoy having roti with chopped seasonal fruits such as mangoes, musk melon or ripe plantain.

Any roti is at its tastiest when it is hot, crisp and fresh off the tawa. However, most of the rotis in this section can be prepared beforehand and eaten at room temperature.

❦ BASIC RAJASTHANI ROTIS   *One Dough, Countless Creations*

We are clubbing a group of rotis under one recipe because they are all made from the same basic dough of wheat flour. What distinguishes them are small tweaks in shape, size and thickness.

PHULKA: A thin, round roti that puffs up when roasted.

BAATIYA: A shallow-fried round roti that is thick and flaky.

TAWA POODI: A shallow-fried triangular roti, also known as 'tikda' or 'paratha'.

KADAHI POODI: A smaller, round roti deep-fried in ghee or oil.

Serves 4

(Irrespective of the size and thickness, rotis made with 2 cups of wheat flour serve 4)

Ingredients
2 cups wheat flour

1 tsp salt

Ghee preferably, or oil (as much needed for each kind of roti)

STEP 1: PREPARING THE DOUGH

Except for Kadahi Poodi, others require a soft dough. Kadahi Poodi is made from a stiff dough since it is deep-fried.

1. For the dough, mix wheat flour and salt in a paraat (wide-rim plate). Add water, little by little, to knead into a dough. Cover with a damp cloth and set aside for at least 15 minutes.

2. Apply a few dots of ghee or oil on the dough and knead again, punching it well. Place some dry flour beside the dough for dusting.

3. Depending on which roti you are making, divide the dough into following portions and roll into balls:

    8 for Phulka
    4 for Baatiya
    6 for Tawa Poodi
    10 for Kadahi Poodi

4. Gently flatten a ball of dough and dust with some dry flour. Use a rolling pin to get the desired size. You will need to dip it in the dry flour once or twice to make the rolling easier. Each time, dust off all excess flour. Since the dough of Kadahi Poodi is stiffer, you don't require dry flour for rolling.

STEP 2: ROLLING AND COOKING THE ROTI

To make Phulka

1. Roll out a ball of dough into a 6-inch round roti. Heat a tawa on medium-high heat and place the roti on it.

2. Within 10–15 seconds, as small bubbles appear on the surface, flip the roti using a pair of tongs. In about 20 seconds, as larger air bubbles appear, flip the roti directly on the flame. As it puffs up, take it off the flame.

3. Transfer to a plate, brush with ghee or oil, and serve hot.

To make Baatiya

1. Roll out a ball of dough into a 4-inch round roti. Apply 1 tbsp ghee on top and sprinkle ½ tsp dry flour over it. Fold the roti like a rolled carpet and then into a round coil. Dust it with the dry flour and roll out again into a 6-inch roti.

2. Transfer the roti to a preheated tawa and cook on medium-high heat. Press gently with a small, wooden press, flip over and press again. It takes about 3–4 minutes to cook each roti.

3. Transfer to a plate, and brush with ghee liberally, for traditional flavour.

To make Tawa Poodi

1. Roll out a ball of dough into a 4-inch round roti. Apply ½ tbsp ghee on top, fold once into a semi-circle and again into a triangle. Dust with the dry flour and roll out to about 6 inches (on all the three sides), maintaining the triangular shape.

2. Transfer the roti to a preheated tawa and cook on medium-high heat. Cook on both sides with 1 tbsp ghee per side, pressing gently with a small wooden press until light golden. It takes 2–3 minutes to cook each poodi. Transfer to a plate.

To make Kadahi Poodi

1. Apply a few dots of oil on the balls of dough and also on the rolling pin and board so that the dough will not stick to it. Without dusting with the dry flour, roll out a ball of dough into a 4-inch circle.

2. Fry the poodi in hot ghee or oil on medium-high heat, flipping once or twice. You can fry 2–3 poodis at a time. Transfer to a plate lined with a kitchen towel.

All these varieties of rotis can be served hot or at room temperature. Make rotis with the remaining balls and stack them to keep them soft.

MOTH KI ROTI   *A Shekhawati Breakfast Classic*

A rustic Shekhawati staple made with minimal ingredients, this comforting roti is prepared using moth bean flour and shaped into small, cracker-sized discs. Traditionally dried in baskets and stored in pantries, these rotis are always ready to serve.

Makes 10 rotis

2 cups moth (dew beans) flour
2 tbsp oil
1 tsp salt

1. In a bowl, mix moth bean flour, salt and oil. Gradually add boiling hot water, stir with a spoon and then knead into a semi-tight dough with your palms.

2. Divide the dough into 10 equal portions. Roll each portion into a thin roti, approximately 3 inches in diameter.

3. Cook each roti on a medium-heated tawa, pressing gently with a wooden press or a cloth pad, until both sides turn golden brown and crisp.

4. Place the cooked rotis in a basket for about half an hour to dry completely—like a khakhra or cracker.

Serve at room temperature with alunya makkhan (unsalted butter), Pyaaz ka Achaar (p. 171) and Garlic Chutney (p. 165).

Shelf life: Stays good for 3–4 weeks in an airtight container.

Chef Sameer says

I've always found Moth ki Roti deeply comforting—a glimpse into a time when simplicity was wisdom. Made from the earthy flour of moth beans, these small, crisp discs were shaped by hand, cooked on an iron skillet and laid out in the 'chhika' to dry—a quiet ritual that filled the courtyard with the scent of grain.

A chhika is a hanging net or basket made from bamboo, coir or iron, suspended from the ceiling with ropes. It kept food safe from ants, insects, and the family cat. I still remember Dadi placing milk to cool or setting curd to ferment in it. And how, at any time, anyone feeling hungry could reach up and take out a roti or two from the chhika—such a homely rhythm of life.

 JUNGLI ROTI *Innovative Flatbread with Desert Greens* (*pic on p. 138*)

We feature a roti inspired by the famous Rajasthani poem 'Arre Ghaas Ri Roti!' (The Roti of Grass). This poem by Kanhaiyalal Sethia captures the valour of Maharana Pratap, the great king of Mewar. After his defeat by Akbar's army in 1576, Maharana Pratap and his people took refuge in the forests, where they struggled with scarce rations and were forced to eat rotis made from grass. One day, a wild cat snatched a grass roti from his son Amar Singh, leaving the child in tears—a moment that deeply pained the king and is immortalised in the poem, recited by generations of Rajasthanis.

As a tribute to Rajasthan's enduring spirit, this recipe features regional desert greens.

Makes 8 rotis

For dough

1 cup chopped greens*
¾ cup besan (gram flour)
¾ cup jau flour (barley)
¾ cup regular wheat flour (and
   more for dusting)
¾ cup coarse wheat flour or sooji
   (semolina)
1 tsp green chillies, finely chopped
1 tsp fresh ginger, finely chopped
1 tsp garlic, finely chopped
   (optional)
1 tbsp coriander seeds, coarsely
   crushed
1 tbsp saunf (fennel) seeds, coarsely
   crushed
1 tsp salt
2 tsp oil (and few drops to knead
   again)

For brushing

½ to 1 tbsp ghee or butter or oil,
   per roti

1. Mix the ingredients for dough in a paraat (wide-rim plate). Knead into a semi-soft dough with water. Cover with a damp cloth and set aside for at least 15 minutes. Apply a few drops of oil and knead again for 1–2 minutes. Place some dry wheat flour beside the dough for dusting.

2. Divide the dough into 8 equal portions and roll into balls. Gently flatten one ball and dust with some dry flour. Use a rolling pin to make a round roti of about 6-inch diameter, dusting with the dry flour a couple of times.

3. Transfer the roti to a preheated tawa (iron skillet) and cook on both sides over medium heat. It takes about 2–3 minutes to cook each roti. Transfer to a plate and brush on the top side with melted ghee.

4. Make the remaining rotis.

Serve hot or at room temperature with any chutney, pickle, raita or sabzi of your choice.

 Variation

 Tawa-fried Jungli Poodi
Cook on both sides, brushing 1 tbsp ghee on each side and pressing gently with a small wooden press, until light golden.

* Add a combination of 2–3 seasonal greens to the dough. Choose from amaranth, dill greens, fenugreek greens, mustard greens, onion greens, garlic greens, mint leaves or spinach.

BEJHAD ROTI   *Everyday Flatbread with Healthy Flour Mix*

This roti is known by different names across Rajasthan. Referred to as tikkad in Jaipur, and sogra or bejhad roti in villages, it is a thick roti traditionally cooked over firewood or charcoal. The main ingredient is a readily available nutritional flour made with barley and brown chickpeas. The roti requires some skill to make as it breaks easily; hence some wheat flour is added to the dough for easier rolling.

Makes 6 rotis

For dough

2 cups jau (barley) flour

½ cup kala chana (brown chickpeas) flour*

½ cup wheat flour (and more for dusting)

1 tsp salt

For brushing

½ to 1 tbsp ghee or butter or oil, per roti

---

* You can use besan instead of kala chana flour in this recipe.

1. Mix all the flours and salt in a paraat (wide-rim plate). Knead into a semi-soft dough with water. Cover with a damp cloth and set aside for at least 15 minutes. Apply a few drops of ghee or oil, and knead again for 1–2 minutes. Place some dry wheat flour beside the dough for dusting.

2. Divide the dough into 6 equal portions and roll into balls. Gently flatten one ball and dust with some dry flour. Use a rolling pin to make a round roti of about 6–8-inch diameter, dusting with flour a couple of times.

3. Transfer the roti to a preheated tawa and cook on both sides over medium heat. You can also cook it partially on the tawa and then on the flame. It takes about 3–4 minutes to cook each roti. Transfer to a plate and brush on the top side with melted ghee.

4. Make the remaining rotis.

Serve hot or at room temperature with any sabzi, dal or kadhi, or even a pickle.

 MISSI ROTI   *Popular Flatbread with Besan and Spices*

Missi Roti is made in many regions across India, with each region favouring its own combination
of grains and lentils. The Rajasthani Missi Roti is different from the Murshidabadi Missa or Punjabi
Missi Roti. Rajasthanis bring a unique flavour to their Missi Roti with besan, and flavour it with dried
fenugreek leaves, fennel seeds and spices, making it a true signature dish from the desert land.

Makes 8 rotis

For dough

2 cups besan (gram flour)

1 cup wheat flour (and more for
   dusting)

2 tbsp kasuri methi (dried
   fenugreek leaves)

½ tbsp coriander seeds, coarsely
   crushed

½ tbsp saunf (fennel) seeds, coarsely
   crushed

¼ tsp hing (asafoetida powder)

1 tsp red chilli powder

1 tsp turmeric powder

1 tsp salt

2 tbsp oil (and a few drops to knead
   again)

For topping

½ to 1 tbsp ghee or butter or oil,
   per roti

1. Mix the ingredients for dough in a broad-rimmed dish.
    Knead into a semi-soft dough with water. Cover with a
    damp cloth and set aside for at least 15 minutes. Apply a
    few drops of oil and knead again for 1–2 minutes. Place
    some dry wheat flour beside the dough for dusting.

2. Divide the dough into 8 equal portions and roll into balls.
    Gently flatten one ball and dust with some dry flour. Use a
    rolling pin to make a round roti of about 6-inch diameter,
    dusting with the dry flour a couple of times.

3. Transfer the roti to a preheated tawa (iron skillet) and
    cook on both sides over medium heat. You can also cook
    it partially on the tawa and then on the flame. It takes 2–3
    minutes to cook each roti as besan takes longer to cook.
    Transfer to a plate and brush on the top side with melted
    ghee.

4. Make the remaining rotis.

Serve hot or at room temperature with any chutney, pickle,
raita or sabzi of your choice.

Variation

 Tawa-fried Missi Poodi
Cook on both sides, brushing 1 tbsp ghee on each side
and pressing gently with a small wooden press, until it
turns light golden.

🌱 SATNAJIYA SOGRA   *Rustic Flatbread with Seven Grains*

The gluten-free diet is gaining popularity these days, and there is much demand for multigrain roti. This dough cannot be kept for long after kneading, so prepare small portions at a time. Tweak the combination of grains and lentils to try out variations of this roti, based on your personal preference or health requirement.

Makes 6 sogra

For dough
½ cup besan (gram flour)
½ cup jau (barley) flour
½ cup makki (maize) flour
½ cup bajri (pearl millet) flour
½ cup jowar (sorghum) flour
½ cup moth (dew beans) flour
½ cup soya bean or ragi (finger millet) flour
1 tsp salt

For topping
1 tbsp ghee or butter or oil, per sogra

1. In a bowl, mix the ingredients for the dough. Transfer one-third of this mix to a paraat (wide-rim plate) and knead with water into a soft dough. (Since this dough tends to dry up, knead just enough flour to make 1 or 2 roti at a time.) Set aside some dry flour for dusting.

2. Divide the dough into two portions and roll each into a ball. Gently flatten one ball and dust with some dry flour. Pat the ball with your palms or use a rolling pin to make a round roti of about 6-inch diameter, dusting with the dry flour a couple of times.

3. Heat an iron or earthen skillet, brush with ghee or oil, and place the roti on it. Cook for 30 seconds on one side and for a minute on the other. Flip over again and cook on medium heat for 2 more minutes, or until golden blackish spots appear. You can also roast on a roasting net. The sogra is now ready.

4. Repeat with the other ball. Once two sogras are done, knead some more dough and make the remaining sogras. Brush each sogra with ghee.

Serve hot or at room temperature with any sabzi, dal or kadhi of your choice. Leftover sogra tastes delicious with ghee and boora sugar, or even a fresh chutney or pickle.

🌱 **Variations**

 Bajri ka Sogra | Jowar ka Sogra | Makki ka Sogra
Make more gluten-free rotis using the same method. Simply replace the multigrain flour with any millet flour, such as bajri (pearl millet), jowar (sorghum), makki (maize) or ragi (finger millet) to make this much-loved recipe from the desert state.

AWLA KA BAATIYA *Flaky Flatbread with Indian Gooseberry*

Indian gooseberries, known as amrit phal (nectar fruit), are packed with Vitamin C, fibre and antioxidants. One of the most frequently used ingredients in Ayurveda, awla is believed to balance and rejuvenate the body. This roti made with a dash of Indian gooseberry is popularly eaten during winters in Rajasthan. Ideally, cook this roti on an iron pan, keeping in mind that the roti may turn blackish due to a reaction of iron with the vitamin C from the awla.

Makes 6 baatiya

For dough

3 cups wheat flour (and more for dusting)

2 tbsp grated gooseberries (or 2 tsp gooseberry powder)

¼ tsp pepper powder

1 tsp salt

2 tbsp oil (and few drops to knead again)

For brushing

1 tbsp ghee preferably (or butter or oil), per baatiya

1. Mix the ingredients for dough in a paraat (wide-rim plate). Knead into a soft dough with water. Cover with a damp cloth and set aside for at least 15 minutes. Apply a few drops of oil and knead again for 1–2 minutes. Set aside some dry wheat flour for dusting.

2. Divide the dough into 6 equal portions and roll into balls. Gently flatten one ball and dust with some dry flour. Use a rolling pin to make a round roti of 4-inch diameter. Apply 2–3 tsp ghee on the top side and sprinkle ½ tsp dry flour over it. Fold the roti like a rolled carpet and then into a round coil. Dust it with the dry flour and roll out again into a 6-inch roti. These thick rotis rolled with ghee are known as baatiya.

3. Transfer the baatiya to a preheated tawa and cook on medium-high heat. Press on both sides gently with a small wooden press. It takes about 3–4 minutes to cook each baatiya. Transfer to a plate and brush on the top side with melted ghee.

4. Make the remaining baatiya.

Serve the baatiya hot or at room temperature with any sabzi, dal or kadhi of your choice, or even a chutney or pickle.

> **Variation**
>
> **Tawa-fried Awla ka Baatiya**
> Cook on both sides, brushing 1 tbsp ghee on each side and pressing gently with a small wooden press, until it turns light golden.

KORMA KI TAWA POODI   *Shallow-fried Flatbread with Coarse Lentil Flour*

The word 'korma' in today's anglicised world brings to mind a thick, rich, south Indian gravy made from grinding nuts and spices together, referred to as kurma. However, in the Rajasthani kitchen, korma, also known as koruyu, refers to a coarse powder of leftover lentil skins. Traditionally, seasonal lentils would be ground at home in the chakki or stone grinder, and meticulously stored in earthen pots. Any residual skin or powder would be added into the making of papad, badi, roti, and even halwa and kheer by thrifty grandmas, unwilling to allow the slightest waste. Nowadays, with modern conveniences, grinding lentils or grains at home is rare. You can find coarse lentil flour in stores, which can be used as korma. This crisp Korma Poodi is very popular in Rajasthan and an ideal travel food served with pickle.

Makes 8 poodis

For dough

1 tbsp curd

2–3 tbsp oil (and few drops to
    knead again)

¼ tsp hing (asafoetida powder)

2 cups wheat flour (and more for
    dusting)

1 cup coarse flour of green moong
    dal

2 tsp red chilli powder

1 tsp turmeric powder

1 tsp cumin seeds

1–1½ tsp salt

For roasting

2 tbsp ghee or butter or oil, per
    poodi

1. In a broad-rimmed dish, start by mixing curd, oil and hing. Now add the remaining ingredients for the dough. Knead with water into a semi-soft dough. Cover with a damp cloth and set aside for at least 30 minutes. Apply a few drops of oil and knead again for 1–2 minutes. Place some dry wheat flour beside the dough for dusting.

2. Divide the dough into 8 equal portions and roll into balls. Gently flatten one ball and dust with some dry flour. Use a rolling pin to make a round roti of about 6-inch diameter, dusting with flour a couple of times.

3. Transfer the roti to a preheated tawa (iron skillet) and cook on medium-high heat. Cook on both sides with 1 tbsp ghee per side, pressing gently with a small wooden press, until it turns light golden. It takes 2–3 minutes to cook each Tawa Poodi. Transfer to a plate.

4. Make the remaining poodis.

Serve hot or at room temperature with any raita, chutney or pickle of your choice.

GWARPATHA KI ROTI *Soft Flatbread with Aloe Vera*

Every state in India uses local produce in its cooking. In the desert state of Rajasthan, aloe vera is available in plenty and is often used in pickles, curries and sweet dishes. Here is one more delicacy made from the succulent, nutritious aloe vera. Enjoy this soft roti and its health benefits. Remember that the addition of aloe vera will keep the roti soft and not allow it to become crisp.

Makes 8 rotis

For dough

½ cup aloe vera pulp, see Step 1

1 tsp salt

2 cups wheat flour (and more for
   dusting)

1 cup coarse wheat flour or sooji
   (semolina)

2 tbsp besan (gram flour)

1 tsp kuti mirch (coarse chilli
   powder)

1 tsp cumin seeds

For serving

1–2 tbsp ghee preferably (or butter
   or oil)

1. Rinse the aloe vera leaves a couple of times. Cut about an inch of the leaves from the tail end and place them straight up in a tumbler or narrow container for a couple of hours. The yellow sap-like liquid from the aloe vera will collect at the bottom of the container. Discard the liquid and wash the aloe vera leaves 2–3 times. Cut away the sharp spikes. Now, remove the skin and mash the pulp with a fork into a creamy paste.

2. Mix aloe vera pulp with ½ tsp salt and set aside for 15 minutes. Place the pulp in a fine sieve and allow the salty water to drip out. Discard that water.

3. Mix the pulp with all three flours, rubbing it nicely. Add ½ tsp salt, kuti mirch and cumin seeds, and knead with water into a soft, pliable dough. Cover with a damp cloth and set aside for a minimum of 10 minutes. Using just a few drops of ghee, knead again for 1–2 minutes. Place some dry wheat flour beside the dough for dusting.

4. Divide the dough into 8 equal portions and roll into balls. Gently flatten one ball and dust with some dry flour. Use a rolling pin to make a round roti of about 6–8-inch diameter, dusting with wheat flour a couple of times.

5. Transfer the roti to a preheated tawa on medium heat and cook on both sides. It takes about 2 minutes to cook each roti. Transfer to a plate and brush on the top side with melted ghee.

6. Make the remaining rotis.

Serve hot or at room temperature with any sabzi of your choice, or even a raita, chutney or pickle.

When the Fire Rests

Recipes such as Besan ki Tawa Poodi—which can be enjoyed cold too—have a connection with the festival of Basoda when no food is cooked. It comes quietly, when winter has not fully left and summer has not yet arrived. On this day, no fire is lit in the home. Food is cooked the day before and savoured cold—auliya, pua, poodi, kanji vada, ker sangri, raabdi...

Children walk with elders to Sheetala Mata's temple, carrying this feast of silence and simplicity. No one calls it stale. It is sacred and delicious—offered to the Goddess with this prayer: 'Sheetala Maa, protect this home. Keep the children safe. Keep us well.' An innocent trust in the divine.

Perhaps the body, too, listens when seasons shift. Perhaps that's why these ancient customs arose—not just for worship but also for well-being. The fire outside extinguished... so the fire within can stay steady.

BESAN KI TAWA POODI   *Shallow-fried Roti with Gram Flour Filling*

A flavourful, spiced flatbread made with a simple yet aromatic filling of besan (gram flour) and spices, encased in whole wheat dough and tawa-fried to perfection. Crisp on the outside and soft inside, it has a satisfying texture and a rich, earthy taste–a wholesome, fuss-free meal on the go.

Makes 6 poodis

For dough

2 cups wheat flour (and more for
    dusting)
2 tbsp oil
1 tsp salt

For filling

1 tbsp oil
½ cup besan (gram flour)
1 tsp dried mint powder
1 tsp kasuri methi (dried fenugreek
    leaves)
½ tsp salt
1 tsp red chilli powder
½ tsp Marwadi garam masala (p. 193)
½ tsp amchur (dried mango)
    powder
1 tsp cumin seeds, coarsely crushed
1 tsp crushed saunf (fennel) seeds,
    coarsely crushed
1 tsp coriander seeds, coarsely
    crushed

For roasting

2 tbsp oil, per poodi

1. For the dough, mix the flour, oil and salt in a broad, rimmed dish. Knead into a semi-soft dough using as much water as required. Cover with a damp cloth and set aside for about 15 minutes. Apply a few dots of oil on the dough and knead again, punching it well. Place some dry wheat flour beside the dough for dusting.

2. For the filling, heat 1 tbsp oil and roast the besan for 1–2 minutes on medium heat, or until it turns light golden and aromatic. Add the remaining ingredients for the filling and roast for about 15 seconds. Set aside to cool to room temperature. Then, sprinkle a few drops of water to moisten the filling and divide into 6 parts.

3. Divide the dough into 6 portions and roll into balls. Flatten one ball, dust it with dry flour and roll into a disk of 3-inch diameter. Place one portion of filling on the disk and pack it in by pulling the edges together over it. Once sealed, dip into the dry flour and roll out again into a 6-inch disk. Rolling lightly and evenly ensures the even spreading of the filling inside the poodi.

4. Transfer the roti to a preheated tawa, (iron skillet), and cook on both sides over medium heat, applying 1 tbsp oil per side. Press gently with a small wooden press and cook until it turns light golden. It takes about 3–4 minutes to cook each poodi. Transfer to a plate.

5. Make the remaining poodis.

Serve warm or at room temperature, on its own, or with any chutney or pickle.

Shelf life: It stays fresh for a couple of days without refrigeration, making it an excellent choice for travel, picnics or tiffins.

BAATI *Baked Crispy Balls of Wheat Dough*

(pic on p. 117)

The beloved baati, central to the iconic menu of Dal Baati Churma, is a roasted or baked ball of wheat dough. While many now fry baati in ghee or oil, it was traditionally roasted over hot ashes of cow dung cakes, a method still used at large functions.

The original version used a firm dough which required much pressure to knead and roll. Sameer, ever sympathetic to the novice cook in the kitchen, suggests a mix of coarse and regular flour. This not only adds a delightful nuttiness but also makes the dough easier to shape into smooth baatis.

With this simple tweak, making perfect baatis has never been easier. They can be baked in a gas tandoor or even in a paniyaram or aape pan. An oven, however, ensures even roasting without flipping.

Makes 6 baatis

1 cup regular wheat flour
1 cup coarse wheat flour*
½ tsp soda bicarbonate
1 tsp salt
1 tsp ajwain (carom) seeds, lightly crushed
3 tbsp ghee

For soaking baati
1 cup ghee

* Coarse wheat flour, or mota aata, can be store-bought, or you can grind wheat grains in a mixer-grinder into a coarse flour.

1. For the dough, mix all the ingredients in a broad-rimmed dish, rubbing the ghee well into the flour. Knead into a soft dough using as much water as required. Knead well, cover with a damp cloth and set aside for about 30 minutes.

2. Apply a few dots of ghee on the dough and knead again, punching it well for 30 seconds. Divide the dough into 6 portions and shape into round balls. Shape well so that the ball has a smooth surface without any cracks.

3. Bake all the baatis in a preheated oven at 280°C by placing directly on the grill in the centre slot. Bake for 10 minutes. Reduce the oven temperature to 250°C and bake for a further 5–7 minutes. The baatis will evenly roast to golden brown and also develop cracks which is the sign of a perfect baati.

4. Remove all the baatis from the oven and transfer to a bowl. Pour about a cup of ghee over them. While serving, remove each baati carefully with a slotted spoon to drain off excess ghee. (You can strain and transfer the excess ghee back into its container.)

Serve hot with Panchmel Dal (p. 103); it also pairs well with Garlic Chutney (p. 165) and a tangy pickle.

 Variations

Masala Baati
Stuff the dough with a spiced filling of your choice—potatoes, peas or paneer—before shaping into balls. Proceed with the recipe

Sweet Baati
Stuff the dough with a sweet filling of khoya, chopped almonds and pistachios, and boora sugar—before shaping into balls. Proceed with the recipe.

Bejhad Baati
Replace both the wheat flours with the flours of Bejhad Roti (p. 126). Add crushed fennel, coriander seeds, chilli powder, ginger and green chillies to the dough. Shape into balls and continue with the recipe.

MEETHI POODI   *Sweet Paratha with Nuts*

In Rajasthani homes, Meethi Poodi is a life-saver for several reasons: it serves as a filling and satisfying dish, appeases even the fussiest of children, and is an instant fix for unexpected guests or when Dadisa craves for something sweet during her meal. Traditionally, Meethi Poodi is made by incorporating sugar and ghee into the dough while rolling out rotis. However, the ever-generous chef, Sameer couldn't resist adding an exotic touch to it. Embracing temptation, he introduced saffron, cardamom and nuts, which lend an unusual hue and crunch to this dish. What makes a Meethi Poodi extra special is when the sugar melts and caramelises in certain spots, creating a delightful crispy texture.

Makes 4 thick poodis

¾ cup ghee

For dough
1 cup wheat flour (and more for dusting)
½ cup sooji (semolina)
½ cup maida (all-purpose flour)
¼ tsp salt

Other ingredients
1 tsp saffron strands
8 tbsp sugar
¼ tsp nutmeg powder
1 tsp cardamom powder
2 tbsp almond slivers
2 tbsp pistachio slivers

1. Mix the ingredients for dough in a paraat (wide-rim plate). Rub in 2 tbsp ghee, then knead with water into a soft dough. Cover with a damp cloth and set aside for at least 15 minutes. Apply a few drops of ghee and knead again for 1–2 minutes. Keep aside some dry wheat flour for dusting.

2. Mix the saffron and sugar with nutmeg, cardamom, and almond and pistachio slivers. Divide this filling into 4 equal portions and set aside.

3. Divide the dough into 4 equal portions and roll into balls. Gently flatten one ball and dust with some dry flour. Using a rolling pin, roll it out into a 4-inch disk. Spread 2 tsp ghee on the disk, sprinkle 1 tsp dry flour and place one portion of filling in the centre. Pack it in by pulling the edges of the rolled disk together and over it. Once sealed, dip lightly into the dry flour and roll out to a 6-inch poodi, maintaining the round shape.

4. Transfer the poodi to a preheated tawa (iron skillet) and cook on medium heat. Flip and cook on both sides with 1 tbsp ghee per side, pressing gently with a small wooden press, until it turns light golden. It takes 2–3 minutes to cook each poodi. Add more ghee at every stage if you want it crisper and tastier. Make the remaining poodis.

Serve at once as it tastes best when it is hot and crisp.

KHOBA ROTI   *Thick, Decorative Flatbread with Deep Indents*   *(pic on p. 120)*

Khoba means indents—designed to soak in ghee and more ghee! This special roti is also known as Mandkya Roti, rooted in 'mandna', meaning decorative pattern. Skilled hands craft intricate designs like concentric circles and stars, by making indents in the roti.

Sameer fondly recalls his father-in-law Shyam Sundar-ji, a perfectionist in making Khoba Roti. 'Watching him create those beautiful patterns is a joy,' says Sameer's wife, Sudha. 'His enthusiasm grows when he makes it for his son-in-law and grandchildren.'

Makes 4 thick rotis

For dough

2 cups wheat flour (and more for dusting)

2 cups coarse wheat flour or sooji (semolina)

½ cup maida (all-purpose flour)

1 tsp ajwain (carom) seeds, hand-crushed

¼ tsp hing (asafoetida powder)

1 tsp salt

5–6 tbsp melted ghee

For topping

2–3 tbsp ghee or butter or oil, per roti

1. In a broad-rimmed dish, mix the dough ingredients with 5 tbsp melted ghee. Check if the mixture holds when pressed in your fist—if it crumbles, add more ghee. Knead with warm water into a semi-soft dough. Knead for 2 minutes more, cover with a damp cloth, and rest for at least 30 minutes.

2. Before rolling, smear 1 tsp ghee over the dough and knead for a minute. Divide into 4 portions and roll into balls. Dust lightly with flour, and roll into a thick 6-inch roti.

3. Heat a skillet and a roasting net on separate burners over medium heat. Cook the roti on the skillet for 1 minute on each side, then transfer to a plate. Now, create the indents by pinching the roti, as shown in the image (p. 137). (Nowadays, many chefs make the indents with tweezers.)

4. Return the roti to the skillet, indent side up. After 2–3 minutes, flip the roti onto the roasting net. Keep adjusting the position of the net so that the roti cooks evenly. Flip again and cook the other side too. It takes 2–3 minutes on each side to turn the roti a beautiful golden colour.

5. Place the cooked roti on a plate, indents facing up. Smear 2–3 tbsp ghee on top, allowing the indents to soak in the ghee. As one roti cooks on the net, start the next one on the skillet. Each roti takes about 8–10 minutes, so plan accordingly.

Serve hot with any sabzi, dal or kadhi of your choice.

Shelf life: These rotis can be preserved for 4–5 days without refrigeration.

Ker Sangri p.92

Khoba Roti p.136

Jodhpuri Chakki
ki Sabzi p.84

Gauri Moth ka Pulav p.146

137

Jungli Roti p.125

Sabut Bhutte ki
Sabzi p.76

Aloo Pyaaz Jaipuri p.63

Singhada ka Pulav p.147

Jodhpuri Kabuli p.144

RICE

Simple to Layered Pulavs

Rice is the most common staple food with over 40,000 varieties grown across the globe. In India alone, hundreds of rice varieties were grown, many of which have been lost over time. Mrs Prema Srinivasan, a Chennai-based scholar and author, introduced Sameer to many of them in one memorable conversation. Lakshmi bhog, Raj bhog, Indra bhog, Kamini, Rajahamsa, Gandhashala, Champa, Annapoorna, Bhutmuri and Sonamasoori were some of the varieties she described, respectfully and lovingly unveiling the history and culture behind each type. We salute Mrs Srinivasan for her vast treasure of knowledge and feel grateful that she shared it so generously.

Like most chefs, amongst all the varieties of rice, Sameer prefers the popular long-grained Basmati. Its rich flavour and texture are unmatchable, and it is the perfect go-to choice when you want to add a royal touch to a meal. This section includes many kinds of pulav from the simple Gauri Moth ka Pulav to the skilled Gatta ka Pulav. On a day when you are willing to spend that extra time in the kitchen, make the unmatchable Kabuli—follow the recipe perfectly and you will win everyone's heart! Refer to p. 208 to learn the perfect method to cook rice.

KESARIYA MEETHA CHAWAL   *Saffron-flavoured Sweet Rice*

Also known by other names such as Binaj or Saloni Khichdi, this delicacy is prepared during feasts and festivals. In many families, it is prepared as part of the Suhaag Thaal (the bride's first meal at her new home) as well as Kanwar Kaleva (the groom's first meal at the bride's home). Borrowing golden hues from saffron and sweetness from sugar, this rice dish is abundant with spices and nuts.

Serves 4 to 6

3 cups cooked Basmati rice (see tip
   to cook rice perfectly, p. 208)
3 tbsp ghee
2 tbsp (about 25) raisins
1 cinnamon stick
2 cloves, coarsely crushed
1 cup sugar
¼ tsp nutmeg powder
½ tsp (15–20) saffron strands

For garnish
½ tsp cardamom powder
2 tbsp almond slivers
2 tbsp pistachio slivers

1. Spread the cooked rice on a plate to cool.

2. Heat ghee in a pan on medium heat. Add raisins, cinnamon and cloves.

3. As the raisins puff up, add ¼ cup of water along with sugar, nutmeg powder and saffron. Cook for about 2 minutes on medium-high heat, or until the sugar dissolves and turns into a syrup.

4. Add the cooled rice and mix well. Cover and simmer on low heat for 5–8 minutes. Turn off the heat.

5. Sprinkle cardamom powder and garnish with almond and pistachio slivers.

Serve hot as a sweet dish at the beginning of a meal. Popularly served in a festive meal along with Gatta ka Pulav (p. 143). This combination is referred to as Meetha Charka Chawal, meaning sweet rice and spicy rice.

Tip: Good quality saffron turns the rice into a rich yellow colour. Add a pinch of turmeric or a drop of yellow food colouring while cooking the rice if the saffron is not up to the mark.

Ask Chef Sameer

Pratibha: Can we add nutmeg along with cloves in this recipe?

Sameer: Hot ghee brings out the flavour of cloves but is too strong for nutmeg, causing it to release an acrid smell. To prevent this, nutmeg is added later along with water.

GATTA KA PULAV   *Rice with Besan Dumplings*

What is commonly known as pulav in Indian cuisine is referred to as khichdi or tyaari in Rajasthan. Thus, a pulav made with rice and gatta is referred to by different names such as Gatta ka Chawal, Gatta ki Tyaari or Gatta ki Khichdi in different regions of the desert state. It is also known as Ram Khichdi for its divine taste. Gatta or besan dumplings, flavoured with a perfect combination of spices and herbs, bring alive the traditional flavours of this rice dish.

Serves 4

3 cups cooked Basmati rice (see tip to cook rice perfectly, p. 208)

For gatta
¾ cup besan (gram flour)
1 pinch soda bicarbonate
½ tsp salt
½ tsp turmeric powder
1 tsp red chilli powder
1 tsp crushed saunf (fennel) seeds
1 tsp crushed coriander seeds
1 tbsp oil

For tadka
3 tbsp oil
¼ tsp hing (asafoetida powder)
2 small bay leaves
2 cloves, coarsely crushed
½ tsp cumin seeds
½ tsp mustard seeds

For gravy
½ cup curd, beaten
¾ tsp salt
½ tsp black salt
½ tsp turmeric powder
1 tsp red chilli powder
1 tsp kasuri methi (dried fenugreek leaves)
1 tbsp fresh ginger, finely chopped
1 tbsp green chillies, finely chopped

Other ingredients
½ tsp chaat masala
½ tsp Marwadi garam masala (p. 193)
1 tsp dried mint powder
2 tbsp chopped coriander leaves

1. Spread the cooked rice on a plate to cool.

2. Mix the ingredients for gatta in a bowl and knead into a soft dough with 1–2 tbsp water. Divide the dough into 4 equal portions and shape each one into a long cylindrical roll of 6–7 inches.

3. Boil ½ litre water in a pan. Drop the rolls in the boiling water, cover and cook for about 7–8 minutes on medium heat. As they double in size and bubbles appear on the surface, turn off the heat. Remove the rolls with a perforated spoon and set aside on a plate. (You can use the strained liquid in some other preparation.) When they are cool enough to handle, cut them into 1-cm pieces. Set these gattas aside.

4. For the tadka, add oil, hing and bay leaves in a pan on medium-high heat. As the oil warms, add cloves, cumin and mustard.

5. As the seeds crackle, add all the ingredients for the gravy and keep stirring. Cook for 2 minutes and add ¼ cup water. Cook on medium heat for 3 more minutes, or until the oil separates. Add the gattas and mix gently, coating them with the gravy.

6. Add the cooled rice, chaat masala, garam masala and mint powder, and mix well. Cover and cook on low heat for about 3 minutes. Turn off the heat and garnish with coriander leaves. Serve hot.

Serve hot with a drizzle of melted ghee, along with any raita or kadhi, a favourite choice being Jaipuri Kadhi (p. 109).

Tip: For a richer touch, fry 10 cashews and 10 raisins in 1 tbsp ghee and mix into the rice dish.

JODHPURI KABULI   *Rice Delicacy of Royals*   *(pic on p. 140)*

The making of Kabuli in a Rajasthani kitchen is a gourmet experience. A richly layered dish from Jodhpur, it isn't complex to make but does require preparation and patience.

Note: This recipe uses double the quantity of rice compared to others in this cookbook to allow for the intricate layering of an authentic Kabuli.

Serves 8

6 cups cooked Basmati rice, see Step 1
½ cup ghee (for various steps)
1 tbsp lemon juice
1 tsp cardamom powder

For layering
Oil for deep-frying
3 medium-sized potatoes
3 slices of bread
3 medium-sized tomatoes
15–20 fresh mint leaves

For saffron liquid
½ tsp saffron strands
2 tbsp warm milk

For tadka
½ tsp cumin seeds
½ tsp saunf (fennel) seeds
½ tsp coriander seeds
3 cloves
5 peppercorns

For gravy
2 tbsp ginger-garlic paste
1 tbsp green chilli, finely chopped
1 cup freshly made tomato puree
1½ tsp salt
1 tsp turmeric powder
3 tsp red chilli powder
3 tsp coriander powder
1 cup thick curd, beaten

Other ingredients
1 large onion, cut into round slices
1 cup fresh green peas
1 tsp Marwadi garam masala (p. 193)

Preparation for the layers
1. See tip to cook rice perfectly on p. 208.
2. Spread the cooked rice on a plate to cool. Drizzle with 2 tsp ghee and 1 tbsp lemon juice. Sprinkle cardamom powder and set aside.
3. Heat oil in a pan for deep-frying. Peel and slice potatoes into thick chips, soak in ice-cold water for 5 minutes, drain, pat-dry and fry until golden. Transfer them to a plate and sprinkle some salt.
4. Cut bread into 1-inch squares, fry until they are crisp in the same oil and add to the plate. Slice tomatoes into rounds, wash and tear the mint leaves, and place both in the plate.
5. In a small bowl, mix saffron and milk with 2 tbsp melted ghee to prepare the saffron liquid.

Making the gravy
6. Crush the ingredients of tadka coarsely using a pestle and mortar. Heat 5–6 tbsp of ghee in a large pan over medium-high heat. Add the crushed ingredients and stir for 10 seconds.
7. As the seeds crackle, add the gravy ingredients in steps. First add ginger-garlic paste and chopped chillies, and cook for a minute.
8. Add tomato puree along with salt, turmeric, red chilli powder and coriander powder, and cook for 3–4 minutes, or until the ghee separates. Lastly, add beaten curd and cook for 2–3 minutes, stirring continuously.
9. Separate the onion slices into rings and add them to the gravy along with green peas. Continue to cook for about 3 minutes until the onions turn soft. If the gravy seems too thick, add 2–3 tbsp of water, cook for a minute and add garam masala. Turn off the heat.

Layering and baking

10. Preheat the oven to 150°C. Spread one-quarter of the rice over the bottom of an oven-proof dish that is about 8×8 inches in size. Spread one-third of the potatoes, bread, tomatoes and mint leaves on top, covering them with one-third of the gravy. Make two more layers the same way, then finish with the remaining rice.

11. Warm the saffron liquid and drizzle it all over the layered Kabuli. Cover the dish loosely with foil and bake for 15–20 minutes. Lift off the foil and garnish with coriander leaves and lemon slices.

Serve hot with roasted papad. It becomes a complete meal by itself when served with any raita or kadhi, a favourite choice being Jaipuri Kadhi (p. 109).

 Tips and Variations

1. Traditionally, potatoes and bread were fried as suggested in the recipe. But if you want to avoid frying, you can oven-roast them instead.

2. Many families use yam instead of potatoes in this recipe. You can also add vegetables such as carrots, cauliflower and beans besides green peas.

3. For a Jain version, use raw plantain instead of potato, and avoid onion and garlic.

4. For a richer and nutty flavour, add some fried cashews and almonds in the layers or on top.

Chef Sameer says

The origins of Kabuli can be traced to many sources, but the name itself comes from 'qabila', meaning a group or tribe. Some say it draws inspiration from the Persian/Afghani Biranj rice—what we know today as biryani—often made as a meal for a gathering. Others link it to the Gadiya Lohar, a nomadic tribe of Rajasthan, who prepare this as a one-pot wedding dish for their qabila. Regardless of origin, Kabuli remains a celebration of flavour and togetherness.

GAURI MOTH KA PULAV   *Rice with Moth Beans*

Light brown moth beans give this dish a delicate look, aptly named Gauri, meaning a fair maiden. This rice dish is the perfect proof of the concept 'less is more'. The addition of just moth beans adds a flavour that is subtle yet distinct. No overpowering spices are used, not even cumin.

Serves 4

½ cup whole moth (dew beans)
3 cups cooked Basmati rice (see tip
   to cook rice perfectly, p. 208)

For tadka
3–4 tbsp ghee
¼ tsp hing (asafoetida powder)
½ tsp mustard seeds
1 bay leaf

Other ingredients
1 tsp salt
1 tbsp lemon juice

1. Wash the moth beans and soak in water overnight. Strain and rinse once again.

2. Spread the cooked rice on a plate to cool.

3. For the tadka, add ghee, hing and bay leaf in a pan on medium-high heat. As the ghee warms, add mustard seeds.

4. As the seeds crackle, add moth beans and 1 tsp salt. Reduce the heat, cover and cook for about 7–8 minutes, stirring a few times to avoid the beans sticking to the bottom. Check if cooked, otherwise, cook for a few more minutes.

5. Lower the heat, add the cooled rice and cook for 2 more minutes, mixing gently. Turn off the heat and add lemon juice.

Serve hot with the crunch of roasted papad. You can also serve it with any raita or kadhi, a favourite choice being Jaipuri Kadhi (p. 109).

Variation

Biri ka Pulav
Substitute moth beans with dried sprouts of moong beans or moth beans, which can be found in the pantry of many Rajasthani homes. Soak the dried sprouts for 10 minutes. Skip Step 1 and follow the remaining recipe.

Chef Sameer says
For a spicy flavour, add ¼ tsp turmeric powder, 1 tsp chilli powder and ¼ cup curd once the moth beans are cooked. Cook for 2–3 minutes and proceed with the recipe. You can also add 1 tsp garam masala while adding the lemon juice.

SINGHADA KA PULAV *Spiced Rice with Water Chestnuts*   (pic on p. 139)

Seasonal water chestnuts, known as singhada, have inspired the creation of numerous delicacies due to their succulent texture, slightly sweet taste and distinct crunch. This Indian risotto is influenced by Sheherwali (Jain Oswal) cuisine, who call it Paniphal ki Khichdi. It is an amalgamation of rich flavours, which is surprisingly simple to prepare. Water chestnuts are low in calories and high in antioxidants, making them a healthy choice. When making this recipe, choose ones that are fleshy, fresh and tender.

Serves 4

For rice

3 cups cooked Basmati rice (see tip
   to cook rice perfectly, p. 208)
½ tsp Marwadi garam masala (p. 193)
2 cups water chestnuts
20 almonds
½ cup milk preferably, or water

For tadka

2 tbsp ghee (plus 1 tbsp to sauté
   water chestnuts)
1 pinch hing (asafoetida powder)
½ tsp cumin seeds
½ tsp mustard seeds
½ tsp fenugreek seeds
½ inch cinnamon stick
4 cloves
4 green cardamoms

For curd mix

1 cup curd
1 tsp besan (gram flour)
1 tsp salt to taste
2 tsp red chilli powder
1 tsp sugar

For chilli ghee

(This step is optional, but imparts
   a festive colour)
2 tbsp ghee (or double it, for the
   traditional richness)
1 tsp red chilli powder

1. Spread the cooked rice on a plate, sprinkle the garam masala and set aside.

2. Peel the water chestnuts, cut into quarters and sauté in 1 tbsp ghee for 5 minutes. Set aside.

3. Blanch the almonds, peel and grind into a fine paste with ½ cup milk. Set aside.

4. For the tadka, add 2 tbsp ghee and hing in a pan on medium-high heat. As the ghee warms up, add cumin, and after a few seconds, add mustard, fenugreek, cinnamon, cloves and cardamoms. Sauté for 8–10 seconds.

5. Add the ingredients of curd mix and cook, stirring until the first boil. Reduce to medium heat and continue to cook for 4–5 minutes. (For those of you who do not prefer whole spices while eating, you can strain the gravy at this point and discard the spices.)

6. Add almond paste and cook for 2–3 minutes. If the consistency looks very thick, add 2–3 tbsp of hot water or milk.

7. Add the cooled rice and water chestnuts. Mix well and turn off the heat.

8. For chilli ghee, heat ghee in a small pan. As the ghee warms up, switch off the flame and add the chilli powder. Immediately, drizzle this chilli ghee over the rice and mix gently.

Serve hot with melted ghee and the crunch of roasted papad.

🌱 **Variations**

🍥 **Spiced Rice with Green Peas**
Substitute water chestnuts with tender green peas in this recipe.

🍥 **Spiced Rice with Lotus Stem**
Substitute water chestnuts with kamal kakdi (lotus stem). Chop and boil the lotus stem until tender, sauté in ghee or oil for a few minutes and follow the recipe.

NAMKEEN AULIYA   *Fermented Mustard Rice with Curd*

This probiotic rice dish fermented with various ingredients keeps your digestive system healthy and balanced. Easy to prepare and often eaten as breakfast, pretty much every region in India has its own equivalent, such as kanji in south India and panta bhaat in Bengal. Cast your net a little wider and you will find this dish echoing back as chao in Vietnam, jook in China, okayu in Japan and hsan pyok in Burma.

Serves 4

¾ cup raw rice
3 cups curd

For spices

1 tsp salt
1 tsp mustard powder*
2 tsp green chillies, chopped (optional)
¼ tsp red chilli powder
¾ tsp cumin seeds, roasted and crushed

1. Wash the rice and soak for about 30 minutes. In an open pan, bring 1 litre water to a boil. Add the rice and cook until it turns soft and slightly mushy. Strain and discard the water to remove starch. This will speed up the fermentation process. Set aside for about 30 minutes.

2. Mix rice and curd together, and mash well. Add the salt, mustard powder, chopped chillies and chilli powder. Allow the mix to ferment overnight.

3. Next morning, mix well and check if you need to add some curd or water. Sprinkle the crushed cumin on top.

Serve this comforting, cooling dish at lunch time.

* To make mustard powder, grind mustard with salt in a mortar and pestle. The salt will absorb the oil in the mustard seeds, preventing the powder from tasting bitter.

 Variation

Sweet Auliya

To make the sweet variation, substitute the spices with ¼ cup sugar, ½ tsp cardamom powder, 1 tbsp each chopped pistachios and almonds, and a few saffron strands. Except saffron, mix everything else together and leave to ferment overnight. Sprinkle the saffron strands on top before serving.

RAITA

Cooling off with Yogurt

No cookbook from the desert state would be complete without the curd-based dishes known as raita. Though curd dishes are common across Indian cuisines, often featuring a wide variety of raita made with fruit and vegetables, this section will certainly surprise you with something new. Try mixing fox nut with stewed pineapple in one recipe or mashing fresh cluster beans with a hint of charcoal smoke in another. Sample the subtle sweetness of the sugar candy raita, or let the mango raita bring a burst of flavour to your palate.

A couple of old and forgotten recipes use the word 'chhachita', a term we have retained as a tribute to the language of the state. It means mixed with chhaach or buttermilk. Add these raitas to your menu for a simple, flavourful way to impress your guests. Sameer has delighted visitors from around the globe by serving these raitas as dips with an assortment of vegetable dippers and crackers, earning rave reviews every time.

An Ode to Batasha (Sugar Candy)

Amidst the colour and celebrations, the golds, the reds, the laughter
The batashas lie quietly, glistening pristine white
Presented with gratitude to those who grace the occasion
Carried home in soft bags of cotton and velvet

The star attraction to little hands waiting in anticipation
They are counted out and distributed, equally, fairly
Carefully carried to the top of the staircase or under the tree
To be enjoyed in solitude, slowly, crunched one by one

Many eyes watch as the last few are stored away
Reappearing to revive weary visitors
Hot and dusty from the harsh desert sun
Finding relief in water sweetened with the white gems

बताशा

आज के वर्तमान परिप्रेक्ष्य में शादी विवाह व अन्य शुभ अवसरों पर खूबसूरत डब्बों में बन्द, नफ़ासत से सजे और महँगे काग़ज़ और सुनहरी डोरी में बंधे लड्डू, मिठाई व चॉकलेट भी मुझे इतना नहीं लुभाते जितना कि बचपन के बताशे। सूती या मख़मली थैली में किसी मांगलिक निमंत्रण के साथ आए मीठे बताशे, किसी धार्मिक उत्सव से आयी काग़ज़ की भूरी थैली में भरे बताशे, या पड़ोस के किसी घर से सौहर गाकर लौटी माँ या दादी के आँचल में बंधे बताशे हमें ख़ूब लुभाते थे।

हम भाई बहनों के बीच चार-चार पाँच-पाँच समान रूप से बाँटे बताशों के बाद बचे बताशे पहुँच जाते थे मिट्टी की किसी हांडी में, जहाँ माँ या दादी उन्हें सहेज कर रखती थी। किसी भी मेहमान के आते ही उन्हें पानी के साथ कटोरी में एक या दो बताशे दिए जाते थे। उस समय लगता था कि बच्चों की मानिंद ये बताशे उन्हें क्यों दे रही हैं? पर आज जब उस बात पर गौर करता हूँ तब विस्मय होता है कि कैसे उन गृहणियों को इतनी समझ थी कि दूर से आए उस पाहुने की क्षीण होती ऊर्जा को त्वरित ताज़गी मिल पाए।

समीर

KESAR BATASHA DAHI   *Sweet Curd with Saffron and Sugar Candy*

(pic on p. 157)

Serves 4

3 to 4 batashas (sugar candy),
   coarsely crushed
½ tsp (15–20) saffron strands
½ cup chilled milk or fresh cream
¼ tsp cardamom powder
2 cups hung curd, beaten

1. Reserve half the batasha and saffron. In a bowl, soak the remaining batashas and saffron in milk. Add cardamom powder and set aside for 8–10 minutes.

2. Add curd to the soaked mixture and stir it once. Sprinkle the remaining saffron on top and place it in the refrigerator for about 30 minutes.

3. Just before serving, sprinkle the remaining batashas on top for an added crunch.

Serve in any meal as a cooling, sweet yogurt.

 ## MAKHANA BATASHA RAITA   *Sweet Curd with Fox Nut and Sugar Candy*

Serves 4

2 tsp ghee
2 cups makhana (fox nuts)
7–8 batashas (sugar candy), coarsely
   crushed (or 2 tbsp sugar)
2 cups curd, beaten
½ cup milk or cream
½ tsp salt
½ tsp black salt
½ tsp cumin seeds, roasted and
   crushed
½ green chilli, finely chopped
1 tsp kuti mirch (coarse chilli
   powder)

1. Heat ghee in a pan and roast the makhanas on medium heat for 5–7 minutes, stirring continuously so they evenly turn light golden. Cool down to room temperature and crush them roughly. (You can do this easily by putting them in a thick plastic bag and crushing them with a heavy spoon or rolling pin.)

2. In a bowl, mix together the crushed makhana with all the remaining ingredients, except kuti mirch.

3. To chill it, place it in the refrigerator.

Serve chilled, topped with kuti mirch, any time of the day.

AAM KA RAITA   *Spiced Curd with Ripe Mango*

Serves 4

1½ cups chopped ripe mango
¼ cup mango pulp
2 cups curd, beaten
1 tbsp sugar
1 tsp salt
1½ to 2 tsp red chilli powder
1 tsp raw cumin powder
1 tbsp green chillies, finely chopped
1 tbsp coriander leaves, finely
 chopped
2 tsp lemon juice
1 tbsp any neutral oil (except
 mustard oil)

1.   Mix all the ingredients in a mixing bowl. Refrigerate for 30 minutes to 1 hour.

Serve chilled or at room temperature in a meal.

 PYAAZ KA RAITA   *Spiced Curd with Roasted Onion*

Serves 4

4 medium-sized onions
2 tsp oil (preferably mustard oil)
2 cups curd, beaten
½ tsp salt
½ tsp black salt
½ tsp cumin seeds, roasted and
 crushed
1 tsp red chilli powder
1 tsp rai-saunf masala (p. 192)
1½ tsp sugar (optional)

1.   Roast whole onions in a gas tandoor or oven at 180 °C for about 7–10 minutes, or until they are soft. Set aside to cool. Peel and chop them roughly and transfer to a serving bowl.

2.   Mix oil into the chopped onions. Add the curd and remaining spices and mix well.

Serve chilled or at room temperature in a meal.

TANATAN RAITA   *Spiced Curd with Bhujia*

Serves 4

1 cup aloo bhujia or Bikaneri
   bhujia*
2 tbsp milk
2 cups curd, beaten
¼ tsp salt
½ tsp black salt
½ tsp red chilli powder
½ tsp cumin seeds, roasted and
   crushed
½ tsp dried mint leaves, crushed
1 tsp sugar
3–4 fresh mint leaves

1. Set aside 1–2 tbsp bhujia for garnishing. Add the remaining bhujia to a mixing bowl. Pour in the milk and lightly toss together. Set aside for 5–7 minutes.

2. In a serving bowl, mix the remaining ingredients (except the mint). Add the bhujia soaked with milk and mix well. Set aside for 5–7 minutes. Add some milk or water if the mixture seems too dry (as bhujia tends to soak up the moisture).

3. Garnish with fresh mint leaves and reserved bhujia.

Serve chilled or at room temperature in a meal.

* Available in Indian stores and many online sites.

FOGLA KA RAITA   *Spiced Curd with Wild Desert Flower*

Fogla, the wild desert flower, is quite an adaptable ingredient. Used in a comforting dhokla on p. 46, it is also put to good use here in a cooling raita.

Serves 4

½ cup fogla (a desert shrub)
2 cups curd, beaten
1½ tsp green chilli, chopped
1½ tsp fresh ginger, chopped
½ tsp salt
½ tsp black salt
½ tsp red chilli powder
½ to 1 tsp jeeravan masala (p. 195)

1. Clean the fogla and soak in hot water for 10 minutes. (See p. 46 for tip to clean fogla.)

2. Boil the fogla in the soaked water for 5 minutes so it turns soft. Wash well in a fine sieve, drain and transfer to a serving bowl.

3. Mix in the remaining ingredients.

Serve chilled or at room temperature in a meal.

✤ DHUNGAARI CHHACHITA   *Spiced Curd with Smoked Cluster Beans*

(pic on p. 157)

This dish captures the very essence of Rajasthani cooking—minimal, resourceful, and full of character. Nothing compares to the taste of tender, seasonal gwarphali (cluster beans), whose gentle bitterness melds beautifully with the creaminess of curd, the warmth of spices, and that magical hint of smoke—creating a flavour that is both surprising and comforting.

Serves 4

1 small piece of charcoal (about
    1×1 inch)
2 cups cluster beans
½ tsp cumin seeds, freshly crushed
1 tsp kuti mirch (coarse chilli
    powder)
1 tsp salt
1 tsp sugar
2 tsp oil (preferably mustard oil)
½ tsp ghee
¼ tsp hing (asafoetida powder)
2 cups beaten curd (or 4 cups
    buttermilk)

1. Clean, wash and chop off the ends of cluster beans. Boil in water until they are tender or pressure-cook for up to 1 whistle. Drain the water and place the cluster beans in a colander, cooling them down to room temperature. Squeeze them to remove any excess water, then mash them gently with your hands or a spoon. Transfer to a bowl.

2. Alongside, heat the charcoal directly on high flame. It would take 2–4 minutes for the charcoal to burn and become fiery hot.

3. Add crushed cumin, kuti mirch, salt, sugar and oil to the cluster beans. Mix well and make some space in the centre to place a small earthen or steel bowl.

4. Place the burnt charcoal in the small bowl. Add ghee and hing on the charcoal. Quickly cover with a lid for 3–4 minutes. Take off the lid and remove the bowl of charcoal.

5. Add beaten curd (or buttermilk) into the cluster beans and mix well.

Serve chilled or at room temperature in a meal.

Note: For more on the distinctive smoky 'Dhungaar' effect and some easy recipes, turn to p. 202.

PITOD KA RAITA   *Spiced Curd with Fresh Besan Pasta*

For those who love pitod—those soft, besan-rich sheets, almost like our desi pasta—it's no surprise that it appears in many sections in this book: as a snack in Kapura Pitod (p. 28), as a curry in Rasila Pitod (p. 86), and here, as a cooling raita. Another delicacy with pitod, this dish carries all the signature flavours of Rajasthan.

Note: Keep in mind that you have to make the pitod beforehand.

Serves 4

2 cups pitod (p. 201)
2 cups beaten curd
½ tsp salt
½ tsp black salt
1 tsp red chilli powder
½ tsp dried mint powder
½ tsp roasted cumin powder
½ green chilli, finely chopped
1 tbsp fresh mint leaves

For tadka
1 tsp oil
1 pinch hing (asafoetida powder)
¼ tsp mustard seeds
1 pinch turmeric powder

1. In a serving bowl, mix the curd with salt, black salt, chilli powder, mint powder, cumin powder and chopped green chilli. Add pitod pieces and gently stir them in.

2. For the tadka, heat oil and hing in a pan. As the oil warms up, add the mustard. As the mustard crackles, add turmeric, and pour this tadka over the curd-pitod mixture.

3. Garnish with chopped mint leaves.

Serve chilled or at room temperature in a meal.

Chef Sameer says
My grandmother would often ask for Pitod ka Raita on sweltering afternoons, saying it brought 'thandak' to the body and peace to the mind. Watching her enjoy each spoonful of the cool curd, the soft pitod and that fragrant tadka taught us that true comfort lies in simple, soulful food.

ANANAS MAKHANA RAITA   *Sweet Curd with Pineapple and Fox Nut*

(pic on p. 157)

Serves 4

1 cup makhana (fox nuts)

4 slices of canned (or fresh, stewed) pineapple

7–8 batashas (sugar candy), coarsely crushed (or 2 tbsp sugar)

2 cups hung curd, beaten

½ cup milk

½ tsp black salt

¼ to ½ tsp pepper powder

1. Soak the makhanas in warm water for 10 minutes. Squeeze out the water well and transfer them to a serving bowl.

2. Cut the pineapple slices into small bits and add to the bowl. Add the remaining ingredients and stir once.

Serve chilled, any time of the day.

 ## RAI MIRCH KA CHHACHITA   *Spiced Curd with Mustard and Chillies*

Serves 4

8 large green chillies (long, thick variety that is not very spicy)

1½ tsp salt

1½ tsp sugar

1½ tsp mustard seeds

2 tsp oil

2 cups beaten curd (or 4 cups buttermilk)

1. Slit the green chillies and boil them in sufficient water along with ½ tsp salt and ½ tsp sugar for 2 minutes. Drain the water and allow the chillies to cool. Remove the seeds and the stalks. Pound the chillies roughly.

2. Pound the mustard seeds with the remaining salt and sugar until the seeds crack into a coarse powder. Add to the pounded chillies and mix in oil. If you like, add a smoky flavour to the chillies using the dhungaar method on p. 202.

3. Keep covered for a day or two. You can refrigerate these pickled chillies for 2–3 days. When required, mix them into curd.

Serve chilled or at room temperature in a meal.

Dhungaari Chhachita p.154

Kesar Batasha Dahi p.151

Ananas Makhana Raita p.156

Green Chutney p.162

Pyaaz ka Achaar p.171

Amrood ki Dilawari p.169

Mirchi ke Tipore p.170

Hari Mirch ka Koota p.170

Angoor ki Launji p.167

Kairi ka Achaar p.173

Bharwan Nimbu ka Achaar p.172

Lahsun ka Achaar p.174

Tamarind Chutney p.163

Lahsun Kachri ki Chutney p.165

Nimbu ki Chutney p.166

Bharwan Nimbu ka Achaar p.172

160

CHUTNEY AND PICKLE

Palate Changers and Side-kicks

If you ever attend a Rajasthani wedding, you will be enveloped by the enchanting melodies of folk songs sung for each occasion. One of the most loved folk songs, titled 'Chutney', depicts a romance between a young couple, where the act of making chutney becomes a heartfelt conversation about their deep love for each other.

छेलो आवे आधी रात बटावे चटनी,

छेलो खावे रोटी एक बनवावे दस जी।

चटनी बाटे तो गोरी, पोदीना री बाट दे,

नहीं तो सो जा म्हारी गोरी, मैं खा ल्यूँ रोटी कोरी।

When her love arrives at midnight's hush, she grinds the chutney fresh,

And rolls out rotis—a dozen, though he savours but one.

Grind the chutney, O lovely one, with the fragrance of mint,

Else, slumber sweetly, my dearest, while I eat the plain, bland roti.

In a nutshell, this was the heart of grinding a fresh chutney. In large joint families of earlier generations, grinding chutney was a daily ritual. While some women were busy cooking the main meal, someone else would be making a chutney on the grinding stone. Unlike dal or vegetables, which required more resources and time, a chutney was a quick fix, adding vibrant flavour to any meal.

No Rajasthani cookbook can ever be complete without a range of chutneys and pickles, some prepared instantly and others made to last for years. These not only add extra zing to a meal but also help cleanse your palate in between courses. A fresh chutney is always finger-licking delicious and usually made minutes before being served to preserve freshness. Pickles use ancient preservation techniques and are stored in cool, dark cupboards, remaining flavourful and unctuous throughout the year. The range of condiments also includes relishes known as launji made with seasonal fruits or vegetables. Cooked with the right combination of spices, it has a shelf life in between a chutney and a pickle, lasting up to a week.

In this section, you will find a wide range of these spicy accompaniments from the freshly pounded chilli relish to the artfully stuffed lemon pickle. Some of them may even remind you of salsa or pesto.

❧ HARA DHANIYA KI CHUTNEY   *Green Chutney*

Serves 4

1 cup coriander leaves
1 small green chilli
1 inch piece of ginger
1 tbsp lemon juice
1 tbsp curd
½ tsp salt
½ tsp black salt
1 tsp chaat masala
2 ice cubes

Grind all the ingredients along with ice cubes into a fine paste. The ice cubes and curd will help to retain a fresh green colour. Serve this all-time dip with any snack, and in a meal.

Shelf life: Best when served fresh, but can be refrigerated for up to 2 days.

Tip: For a richer texture and taste, add 2 tbsp aloo bhujia or Bikaneri bhujia while grinding.

❧ KAIRI PODINA KI CHUTNEY   *Raw Mango and Mint Chutney*

The simple list of ingredients in this recipe lends a flavour so subtle and delicate that adding any other ingredient such as ginger or garlic, or even cumin, seems an excess. For an authentic Shekhawati taste, grind this chutney on a stone grinder or crush it in a wooden mortar and pestle, preferably using sea salt or crystal salt.

Serves 4

1 cup grated raw mango
2 cups mint leaves
3 green chillies, roughly chopped
½ tsp black salt
1 tsp salt
1 tbsp roasted chana (brown
   chickpeas, without skin)
2 small ice cubes

Grind all the ingredients along with ice cubes to a coarse paste. Transfer to a bowl. Serve as a spicy-tangy dip in a meal.

Shelf life: Best when served fresh, but can be refrigerated for a day.

KACHHI IMLI KI CHUTNEY   *Raw Tamarind Chutney*

Serves 4

½ cup thick tamarind pulp
½ cup jaggery or sugar
1 tsp salt
1 tsp black salt
1 tsp dried ginger powder
1 tsp roasted cumin powder
2 tsp red chilli powder
2 tsp chaat masala
4 tbsp lemon juice

Mix all the ingredients and transfer to a jar. Serve with snacks like kachori and dahi vada as a sweet-spicy dip.

Shelf life: Can be refrigerated for 2 weeks.

 Variation

Cooked Tamarind Chutney
Omit the lemon juice from the recipe. Add ½ cup water to the remaining ingredients and cook on medium heat for about 10 minutes until the mixture thickens. Transfer to a jar; it can be refrigerated and used for up to 6 months.

BANJARA CHUTNEY   *Gypsy-Style Onion Tomato Chutney*

For those who like the sharp flavours of raw onion and garlic, this is an instant treat.

Serves 4

1 medium-sized onion, cut into
  chunks
1 medium-sized tomato, cut into
  chunks
6 garlic cloves, peeled
¼ tsp black salt
1 tsp salt
1 tbsp red chilli powder
1 tbsp sugar
2 tbsp lemon juice (or vinegar)

Grind all the ingredients with ¼ cup water into a coarse paste. Transfer to a serving bowl. Serve as a spicy dip in a meal.

Shelf life: Serve fresh, or within a couple of hours.

❦ HING MIRCH KI CHUTNEY   *Raw Spicy Sandwich Chutney*

With its burst of raw, rustic and spicy flavours, this dip is a perfect accompaniment to any meal. Mix it into steamed rice or pair it with warm rotis. Elevate the flavour of sandwiches and vada pav by using this dip as a spread, and also try mixing it into lahsunia bhel. A simple recipe that involves no cooking; follow it precisely to enjoy the zesty flavours.

Serves 4 to 6

1 medium onion, cut into chunks
   (about ½ cup onions)
2 tbsp raw mango, grated
8–10 garlic cloves, peeled
½ tsp hing (asafoetida powder)
¾ tsp salt
2 tsp cumin seeds
3 tsp red chilli powder

Grind all the ingredients into a coarse paste with 2 tbsp water. Grind with quick turns, to maintain the coarse texture. Transfer to a bowl and serve as a spicy dip in a meal.

Shelf life: Serve fresh, or within a couple of hours. If refrigerated, it can be consumed within a day.

❦ KACHRI MIRCH KI CHUTNEY   *Spicy Chutney with Wild Berry*

The combination of kachri and chillies lends a delicious tangy-spicy flavour to this chutney. In season, it is common to see this chutney prepared with fresh kachri and fresh red chillies in Rajasthan.

Serves 6

10–12 dried kachris (a wild berry)
10–12 dried, long red chillies,
   de-seeded
2 tsp cumin seeds
1½ tsp salt
2 tbsp lemon juice
2 tbsp oil

1. Tear the kachri into 2 or 3 pieces, and soak along with red chillies in warm water overnight. Discard the water and rinse a couple of times. Grind the kachri and chillies with cumin seeds into a fine paste using very little water. The consistency should be like tomato sauce.

2. Transfer to a jar or serving bowl and mix in salt, lemon juice and oil. Serve as a spicy-tangy dip in a meal.

Shelf life: Best eaten fresh but can be refrigerated for 2 weeks.

❧ LAHSUN KACHRI KI CHUTNEY   *Garlic Chutney with Wild Berry*

Enhance any dal or sabzi for a party, and even pav bhaji with a dash of this chutney for a rich colour and a magical touch. In season, make this chutney with fresh kachri and fresh red chillies.

Serves 8 to 10

10 dried kachris (a wild berry)
20 dried, long red chillies, de-seeded
1 cup garlic cloves, peeled (about 200 gm)
6 tbsp ghee preferably, or oil
½ tsp cumin seeds
1 tsp turmeric powder
2 tsp salt

1. Tear kachri into 2 or 3 pieces and soak along with red chillies in warm water overnight. Discard the water and rinse a couple of times. Grind the soaked kachri and chillies with garlic into a fine paste with ½ cup water.

2. Heat ghee in a pan and add cumin seeds. As the seeds crackle, add the ground paste, turmeric and salt. Mix and cook on medium heat for about 10 minutes, or until the ghee separates. The consistency should be like tomato sauce. If it is too thick, add a little hot water.

3. Cool to room temperature and transfer to a jar or serving bowl. Serve as a spicy-tangy dip in a meal.

Shelf life: Can be refrigerated for a couple of weeks.

❧ LAHSUN TAMATAR KI CHUTNEY   *Garlic Chutney with Tomatoes*

Serves 8 to 10

1 cup garlic cloves, peeled (about 200 gm)
20 dried, long red chillies, de-seeded
6 tbsp ghee preferably, or oil
½ tsp cumin seeds
1 tsp turmeric powder
2 tsp salt
½ cup freshly made tomato puree

1. Soak the red chillies in warm water for a couple of hours. Strain and grind with garlic to a fine paste using ½ cup water.

2. Heat ghee in a pan and add cumin seeds. As the seeds crackle, add the garlic and chilli paste. Add turmeric and salt, and cook on medium heat for about 10 minutes, or until the ghee separates.

3. Add tomato puree and cook for 5 more minutes. Cool and transfer to a jar or serving bowl. Serve as a spicy-tangy dip in a meal.

Shelf life: Can be refrigerated for a couple of weeks.

❧ NIMBU KI CHUTNEY *Spicy Relish with Lemons*

Makes about 750 gm chutney

10–12 medium-sized lemons (about
    500 gm)
2 cups sugar
1½ tbsp salt
1½ tbsp black salt
3 tbsp red chilli powder
3 tbsp cumin seeds, roasted and
    crushed
1 tbsp Marwadi garam masala (p. 193)

1. Wash, wipe and halve the lemons, discarding the seeds. Extract the lemon juice and set it aside in a bowl. Chop the lemon peels finely and grind them into a smooth paste. You can add up to 1 cup sugar along with the lemon peels to help with the grinding process.

2. Mix lemon juice with the lemon peel paste and the remaining ingredients in a bowl. Cover and set aside for an hour.

3. Cook the mixture on low heat for 7–10 minutes, or until it thickens slightly. Turn off the heat and set aside to cool down. Transfer to an airtight jar.

Serve as a pickle or palate cleanser in a meal. Transform into a salad dressing by diluting it with water. Additionally, explore its potential as a creative topping for crackers.

Shelf life: Store in a dry, cool place for up to six months (without refrigeration).

❧ KATHODI KI CHUTNEY *Sour and Spicy Wood Apple Chutney*

Kathodi is a sour fruit with a lot of seeds, similar to wood apple. It is packed with fibre and its powder is available online and in Indian grocery stores.

Serves 4

4 tbsp kathodi powder
½ tsp salt
½ tsp black salt
1 tsp cumin seeds
4 tbsp crushed jaggery or sugar
1 green chilli, chopped
1 tbsp fresh ginger, grated

Soak the kathodi powder in ½ cup water for 10 minutes. Grind it along with the soaked water and remaining ingredients into a fine paste. Transfer to a serving bowl and serve as a spicy-tangy dip.

Shelf life: Best when served fresh but can be refrigerated for a day.

ANGOOR KI LAUNJI *Green Grape Relish*

A seasonal delight, grape relish captures the juiciness of fresh grapes enhanced by a rich Rajasthani tempering of spices. This exotic treat stands out, even on the most lavish spread.

Serves 10 to 12

4 cups seedless green grapes

For tadka
4 tbsp oil (preferably mustard oil)
1 pinch hing (asafoetida powder)
½ tsp cumin seeds
½ tsp mustard seeds
½ tsp fenugreek seeds
½ tsp kalonji (nigella) seeds
½ tsp saunf (fennel) seeds
½ tsp coriander seeds, coarsely crushed
2 dried, long red chillies (broken into 1-inch bits)

Other ingredients
½ cup crushed jaggery or sugar
½ tsp salt
1 tsp black salt
4 tsp chaat masala
2 tbsp white vinegar

1. Wash the grapes and remove any stems. If the grapes are round, you can cut them in half, but long thin grapes are fine to use as they are.

2. For the tadka, heat oil in a pan on medium-high heat. (If using mustard oil, heat the oil until it turns smoky. Turn off the heat. After 3 minutes, reheat the oil). Add all the ingredients for the tadka.

3. As the seeds crackle, add grapes and cook for 5–7 minutes, or until the grapes become soft and start to wrinkle.

4. Finally, add the items listed under other ingredients and cook for 10 minutes, or until the mixture thickens. Turn off the heat. Cool to room temperature and transfer to a jar.

Serve as a spicy-sweet palate cleanser in a meal.

Shelf life: Can be refrigerated for up to a month.

❧ HARE TAMATAR KI LAUNJI *Green Tomato Relish*

Serves 4 to 6

4 green tomatoes (about 2 cups),
  see Step 1

For tadka

4 tbsp oil
¼ tsp hing (asafoetida powder)
½ tsp mustard seeds
½ tsp fenugreek seeds
½ tsp kalonji (nigella) seeds
½ tsp cumin seeds, coarsely crushed
½ tsp coriander seeds, coarsely
  crushed
½ tsp saunf (fennel) seeds, coarsely
  crushed
1 dried red chilli, halved

Basic spices

½ tsp salt
½ tsp black salt
½ tsp turmeric
2 tsp red chilli powder

Other ingredients

½ cup jaggery or sugar
2 tbsp amchur (dried mango)
  powder
½ tsp Marwadi garam masala (p. 193)

1. Wash the green tomatoes and chop them into 8 quarters.

2. Heat oil in a pan and add all the ingredients for the tadka. As the seeds crackle, add tomato chunks. Cook on high heat for 2 minutes; this will release the juice in the tomatoes.

3. Add the basic spices along with ¼ cup water. Turn the heat to medium and cook for 5 minutes.

4. Add jaggery and amchur powder along with ¼ cup water. Mix well and cook for 5 more minutes. Add garam masala and turn off the heat. The consistency of this dish is chunky, almost like a juicy salsa. Cool to room temperature and transfer to a jar.

Serve as a spicy pickle in a meal.

Shelf life: Can be refrigerated for a week.

❧ Variations

❀ **Star Fruit Relish**
Substitute green tomatoes with star fruit. Cut into slices and discard any overripe seeds. Reduce the amchur powder to 1 tbsp and follow the rest of the recipe.

❀ **Fresh Green Jujube Relish**
Substitute green tomatoes with fresh ber (jujube). Cut into slices and remove the seed. Follow the rest of the recipe.

❀ **Raw Mango Relish**
Substitute green tomatoes with raw mangoes. Peel and cut raw mango into big chunks. Omit the amchur powder and follow the rest of the recipe.

❁ AMROOD KI DILAWARI *Spicy Guava Salsa*

Also known as guava chutney or guava kachumber, meaning chopped salad, this salsa makes a delicious topping for papad, khichiya, khankra or any cracker. In the hot weather of Rajasthan, many locals use plenty of raw onions to cool down. Therefore, dilawari with its crunch of onions is a preferred summer accompaniment to any meal.

Serves 6 to 8

2 semi-ripe guavas (about 250 gm)
2 tbsp lemon juice
1 tsp salt
1 tsp kuti mirch (coarse chilli powder)
1 tsp cumin seeds, coarsely crushed
1 tbsp sugar
1 tbsp oil
2 tbsp green chillies, finely chopped
2 tbsp coriander leaves, finely chopped
½ cup onions, finely chopped

1. Grate the guava, discarding the seeds as much as possible. Immediately, mix in the lemon juice to prevent discolouration.

2. Add the remaining ingredients and mix well.

Serve chilled or at room temperature. Makes a delicious palate changer in a meal.

❁ Variations

❁ **Smoky Guava Salsa**
Roast the whole guava directly on the flame or in a preheated oven at 180°C, turning it on all sides as you would do for a brinjal bharta. Proceed with the recipe as given here and enjoy a smoky, delicious salsa.

❁ **Ripe Mango Salsa**
Substitute guava with finely chopped ripe, sweet mangoes. Proceed with the recipe as given.

❁ **Star Fruit Salsa**
Substitute guava with a ripe semi-sweet star fruit. Cut the fruit into tiny pieces and discard any seed. Proceed with the recipe as given.

❧ MIRCH KE TIPORE *Spicy Green Chilli Relish*

Serves 4 to 6

8 large green chillies (long, thick
    variety that is not very spicy)

For tadka
4 tbsp oil
½ tsp hing (asafoetida powder)
1 tsp cumin seeds
1 tsp mustard seeds
1 tsp saunf (fennel) seeds

Other ingredients
1 tsp turmeric powder
2 tsp red chilli powder
3 tsp coriander powder
2 tbsp curd, beaten
1 tsp salt
½ tsp black salt
2 tsp sugar
2 tsp amchur (dried mango) powder
2 tsp rai-saunf masala (p. 192)

1. Wash, pat-dry and chop the chillies into 1-cm rings.
2. For the tadka, add oil and hing in a pan on medium-high heat. As the oil warms up, add cumin, mustard and saunf seeds.
3. As the seeds crackle, add turmeric, chilli powder and coriander powder along with 4 tbsp of water. Cook for 1–2 minutes, or until the oil separates. Add beaten curd and cook for one more minute.
4. Add the chopped green chillies along with salt and black salt. Mix and cook for 5 minutes. Add sugar, amchur powder and rai-saunf masala. Mix well and turn off the heat. Cool down to room temperature before serving.

Serve as a spicy pickle in a meal.

Shelf life: Best eaten fresh but can be refrigerated for 2–3 days.

❧ HARI MIRCH KA KOOTA *Instant Green Chilli Salsa*

Serves 4 to 6

8 large green chillies (long, thick
    variety that is not very spicy)
2 garlic cloves (optional)
A fistful of tender coriander stems
    (not the leaves), finely chopped

Basic spices
1 tsp cumin seeds
½ tsp mustard seeds
½ tsp saunf (fennel) seeds
1 tsp salt

Other ingredients
1 tbsp lemon juice
1 tbsp oil (preferably mustard oil)
1 tsp kuti mirch (coarse chilli
    powder, optional)

1. Mince the green chillies, garlic and coriander stems in a chopper, or pound them in a mortar and pestle.
2. Roughly crush cumin, mustard, saunf and salt into a coarse powder.
3. Mix the ingredients of Step 1 and Step 2. Add lemon juice and oil. Mix well and set aside for 1 hour so the spices get absorbed. Transfer to a bowl.

Serve this instant pickle in a meal, sprinkled with kuti mirch.

Shelf life: You can refrigerate and consume this chilli salsa within 2–3 days.

> ❧ **Variation**
>
> **Mooli ki Kuchhi**
> Substitute green chillies with 1 cup chopped or grated tender radish in this recipe.

PYAAZ KA ACHAAR *Pickle with Baby Onions*

Serves 8

400 gm baby onions, about 1-inch
    diameter
4 tbsp oil (preferably mustard oil)
2 tbsp white vinegar

Spices
2 tsp salt
2 tsp red chilli powder
1 tsp kalonji (nigella) seeds
2 tsp fenugreek seeds, powdered
2 tbsp rai-saunf masala (p. 192)

1. Peel onions and wash them well. Wipe them with a kitchen cloth and cut a deep cross in each. Transfer to a mixing bowl and toss with vinegar. Add all the spices and mix gently.

2. Heat oil and then set aside to cool. Pour it over onions and toss well to ensure they are well coated in the oil and spices.

3. Transfer this onion pickle to a wide-mouth glass jar. Tie the mouth of the jar with a muslin cloth and set aside for a day or two so the spices blend in well. Shake occasionally.

Serve this onion pickle to enhance any meal.

Shelf life: Store in an airtight jar in a dry, cool place for up to 2 weeks (without refrigeration). Ideally, this pickle must be eaten after a day, but you can eat it immediately as well.

To add a smoky flavour: Follow the dhungaar method given on p. 202. Infuse the empty jar with charcoal smoke before transferring the pickle into it.

Ask Chef Sameer

Pratibha: Why do you heat and then cool the oil before pouring over the onions?

Sameer: If you add hot oil to onions, they will lose their crispiness and wilt, leaving the end product tasting more like a sabzi than a pickle. Therefore, it is important to cool the oil before adding to the pickle.

❀ BHARWAN NIMBU KA ACHAAR *Stuffed Lemon Pickle* *(pic on p. 160)*

A connoisseur's recipe, here is a delightful way to preserve whole lemon with spices. Sameer says, 'One summer afternoon, over a delicious lunch at Rashmi-ji Chatur's house, I discovered these artistically stuffed lemons. I was so enamoured by the recipe that I replicated it as soon as I got home. I am truly excited to share her recipe with my readers.'

Makes 32 quarter pieces

8 medium-sized lemons (choose
  lemons with thin skin)
2 cups salt (for roasting lemons)
1 cup lemon juice

For filling
8 dried dates
2 tsp garam masala
2 tsp peppercorns, crushed
2 tsp dried ginger flakes, roughly
  crushed
1 tsp salt
1 tsp black salt
2 tsp cumin seeds
2 tsp ajwain (carom) seeds
2–3 pippali (long pepper), crushed

For marinating
6–8 tbsp sugar
½ tsp salt
½ tsp black salt
½ tsp ginger powder

Tip: When the lemons are roasted in salt, they tend to spurt out their juice, sometimes along with the salt. Hence, we recommend you use a flat wire mesh, also available as a splatter guard cover, to protect yourself from the hot juice.

1. For the filling, soak the dried dates in ¼ cup lemon juice overnight. Next morning, strain and reserve the lemon juice. De-seed the dates and chop them finely. Set aside.

2. Add 2 cups salt to an iron wok. Turn on the heat, add the lemons and roast them in the salt for about 10 minutes, stirring gently with a ladle. The lemons will start to change colour, develop cracks and may release some juice. Continue roasting until each lemon turns soft, then transfer it to a plate as it reaches the desired texture.

3. Allow the lemons to cool down and then wipe each one with a cloth or paper towel to remove any excess salt. Find the natural crack in each lemon; if a crack isn't visible, make a small slit. Gently press on the cracked side to extract the pulp, juice and seeds. Discard the seeds, and set the pulp and juice aside in a bowl.

4. Add the chopped dates and the remaining ingredients for the filling to the bowl containing the pulp and juice. Mix well and fill this spice mix into the lemons carefully from the cracked side. You can gently shape the lemons back into shape as you stuff them with the filling.

5. Gently, transfer the lemons to a glass jar. Pour the remaining ¾ cup lemon juice over the lemons. Also, pour the reserved lemon juice from the soaked dates. Shake lightly, cover with a cloth and place the jar in the sun for 2–3 hours every day.

6. After three days, add the marination ingredients and shake gently. Return the jar to the sun for another couple of days. By this time, the lemons will have turned a yellowish-brown colour and regained their original shape. They are now ready to use.

To serve, remove a lemon from the jar and cut into quarters. Enjoy as a pickle, or as a pachak—a traditional digestive.

Shelf life: These stuffed lemons can be stored for years without refrigeration. The salt and sugar act as natural preservatives. With time, the lemons will turn blackish, but they do not spoil.

KAIRI KA ACHAAR *Mango Pickle with the Signature Pickle Masala*

A must-have in the pantry of every Rajasthani kitchen, this pickle is prepared in generous quantities to be savoured all year round. As the summer season dawns and brings the smell of ripe and raw mangoes, it is the perfect time to make this delectable pickle. The Ramkela or Rajapuri variety of raw mangoes, hailing from Uttar Pradesh, are ideal for pickles. To ease the laborious task of chopping, vendors offer pre-chopped raw mango pieces, which many home cooks gladly procure to prepare the pickle at home. To make this pickle, use a stock pot or a deep bowl that is large enough to hold the chopped raw mangoes, masala and oil.

Makes about 1 kg pickle

1 kg raw mangoes, chopped into
    1-inch pieces
1 tbsp salt
1 tsp turmeric powder
2 tbsp dried ginger flakes
200 gm pickle masala (p. 194)
250 ml oil, preferably mustard oil
1 tsp hing (asafoetida powder)

1. Wash the chopped raw mangoes several times until all the grit is removed. Drain away the water completely and wipe them well. Transfer to a large vessel. Add salt and turmeric powder and mix well. Cover the vessel with a muslin cloth and leave it overnight. This process will release the water from the raw mangoes.

2. Next morning, drain away the water from the raw mangoes. (You can use this water for making a pickle with chana, see variation below the recipe.) Spread the raw mangoes on a thick cloth and air-dry for 5–6 hours, or more. Ensure that the mango wedges have dried completely.

3. Transfer the wedges to a broad-rimmed dish. Add the pickle masala and gently massage the raw mango pieces so the spices coat them completely.

4. Heat the oil to a smoky point and then allow it to cool down to room temperature. Add hing to the oil and pour this oil over the pickle. Mix well.

5. Transfer the pickle to a ceramic or glass jar. Tie the mouth of the jar with a muslin cloth and set aside for at least a week. During this time, the oil will rise to the surface, which helps in preserving the pickle.

Shelf life: Stays good for over a year in a dry, cool place. Take care not to touch the pickle with your hands. Always use a dry spoon or a pair of tongs to take out the pickle.

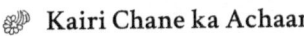 **Variation**

Kairi Chane ka Achaar

For 1 kg raw mangoes, you can add 200 gm of Kabuli chana (white chickpeas). Soak the chana in the discarded water from the raw mangoes for at least 12 hours. Drain away the water and air-dry the chana for 5–6 hours. Mix with the chopped raw mangoes and continue from Step 3 of the recipe.

❧ LAHSUN KA ACHAAR *Garlic Pickle with the Signature Pickle Masala*

Simplicity meets excellence in this garlic pickle, as it effortlessly enhances the flavours of even the humblest of meals. Sameer calls it an absolute lifesaver during busy moments, as the pickle can be conveniently ground into a versatile paste to be used in sabzis, raitas, salsa, dosa topping, crackers, vada pav and even as a sandwich spread. Elevate your culinary adventures!

Makes about 400 gm pickle

250 gm garlic cloves, peeled
100 ml white vinegar
100 gm pickle masala (p. 194)
80 ml oil (preferably mustard oil)

1. Wipe garlic with a damp cloth and air-dry for 10–15 minutes.

2. Boil the garlic in vinegar for 5 minutes. Set aside to cool along with the vinegar.

3. Add pickle masala to the cooled garlic.

4. Heat oil to a smoky point and then allow it to cool down to room temperature. Pour this oil over the garlic pickle. Mix well.

5. Transfer the pickle to a ceramic or glass jar. Tie the mouth of the jar with a muslin cloth and set aside for two days at least.

Serve in a meal and see how it complements any sabzi or dal, enhancing the overall taste.

Shelf life: Stays good for over a year in a dry, cool place. Take care not to touch the pickle with your hand. Always use a dry spoon or a pair of tongs while removing the pickle.

❧ MIRCH KA ATHANA   *Chilli Pickle with the Signature Pickle Masala*

Summer brings with it perfect raw mangoes for creating delectable pickles, and Rajasthani berries like goonda and ker are equally ideal. However, during the winter season, it is the pickling of chillies that takes the spotlight. These chillies are thick, vibrant and bursting with colour, offering a flavourful experience with a hint of sweetness. Whether red or green, both varieties of pickled chillies are equally delicious. Choose fresh red or green chillies that are longer and thicker, and not as fiercely spicy as the thinner ones.

Makes about ½ kg pickle

500 gm green or red chillies (long, thick variety that is not very spicy)
2 tbsp white vinegar
150 gm pickle masala (p. 194)
150 ml oil, preferably mustard oil

1. Wash the chillies, wipe and air-dry for an hour.

2. Keeping the stalks intact, make a slit in each chilli such that it remains whole.

3. Sprinkle vinegar over the chillies to coat them lightly. (Chillies contain moisture and can catch fungus easily. Brushing with vinegar will increase their shelf life.)

4. In a bowl, mix pickle masala with 50 ml oil. Add the filling to the chillies. If any masala remains, sprinkle it over the chillies.

5. Arrange the chillies in a ceramic or glass jar.

6. Heat the remaining oil until it turns smoky. Allow it to cool down until it is just warm. Pour this oil over the chillies. Tie the mouth of the jar with a muslin cloth and set aside for at least one day.

Serve as a pickle in a meal.

Shelf life: Stays good for about 6 months in a dry, cool place. Take care not to touch the pickle with your hand. Always use a dry spoon or a pair of tongs while removing the pickle.

Chef Sameer says
If you do not want large, stuffed chillies, you can discard the stalks and cut the chillies into 1-cm bits. Mix in the masala and add oil.

An Ode to Kadahi ka Doodh

Sophistication, perfection, discernment
These Jaipur traits kept me on my toes
Observed, catered to, understood and finally absorbed
Influencing my palate and the very core of my being

Driving me to mithai shops on late winter nights
Timing my visit perfectly with the magic hour
When the milk is embraced over and over by the boiling iron pot
Thickened and enriched, sweetened with time and love

The last few earthen tumblers, snowy white to the brim
More coveted and precious than antique diamonds at auction
Triumphantly held in the hands of the winners
The rest left with their imaginations to warm themselves on chilly nights

कड़ाही का दूध

जयपुरवालों के नख़रों ने, उनकी अभिजात रुचियों ने, उनकी परिमार्जित सोच ने मुझे भी शायद परवान चढ़ा दिया। उनकी तमाम फ़रमाइशों को पूरा करते-करते मैं भी थोड़ा परिष्कृत हो गया। कड़ाही के दूध से इसका क्या नाता है और मैं क्यों लिख रहा हूँ, यह आगे की बात से स्पष्ट हो जाएगा।

सर्दी की देर रात में कड़ाही में कढ़ते इस दूध के आख़री कुछ सकोरों (earthen glasses) के लिए हलवाई की दुकान पर अक्सर बड़ी विषम स्थितियाँ पैदा हो जाती थी। पकते-पकते यह दूध इतना गाढ़ा और स्वादिष्ट हो जाता था कि उस दूध की दुकान का नज़ारा शेयर बाज़ार में लगती बोलियों का दृश्य लगने लगता था। १० रुपये की क़ीमत का वो दूध कभी-कभी १०० रुपये में भी बिकता और ख़रीदने वाला बड़े ही विजयी भाव से उसका आनंद ले परितृप्त हो जाता था।

यूँ तो ऐसी बातें कहने बैठूँ तो शायद एक पूरा शीतकाल भी कम पड़ जाए, इसीलिए थोड़ा लिखा ही उचित है। बाक़ी आपकी कल्पना के लिए छोड़ दिया है।

समीर

Kadahi ka Doodh p.182

Chhachiti p.188

179

BEVERAGES

Warming Sips and Cooling Gulps

Over the last few decades, much has changed in our eating habits. The kinds of cuisines we have access to are as innumerable as the channels on our television. We like eating out, ordering in and are even reinventing tried and tested recipes with different ingredients and cooking techniques. But if there is one thing that has not changed in Chennai where I live, it is the coffee. Rain or shine, summer or winter, enter any south Indian home and you will surely be offered a tumbler of steaming hot filter coffee.

When I asked Sameer what Rajasthan's equivalent to filter coffee was, he said, 'Depends on the season. This land offers its guests a wide variety of refreshments, keeping pace with the changing weather.' He then reeled off a list of coolers with seasonal fruits and flowers—all chosen to give respite from the scorching summer sun. For winters, he mentioned Raab, which is made with cooked flour and can be consumed as a warm soup. This is also very popular as a cooling summer beverage. Not to be missed is the Kadahi ka Doodh, which is milk simmered and thickened in an iron pan, ideal for the cold winter months.

We are both delighted to share several of these recipes with you in this section. One of my favourites is the Chhachiti, an unusual spiced buttermilk made by churning together curd and vegetables. I am also excited by the perfect Kaanji recipe in which you will enjoy the taste of carrots in fermented mustard water. Take a quick look at the recipes, gather the ingredients and get ready to work some Sameer-style magic!

 KADAHI KA DOODH   *Milk Simmered in Iron Pan*   *(pic on p. 177)*

Nothing compares to this indulgent beverage of patiently simmered, creamy milk. Always cook this in an open, broad kadahi so that the heat from below and cool air from the top allows thick malai to form in layers. The best vessel to use for this is a good quality, heavy-bottomed iron pan, a must in every kitchen, which thickens the milk without it burning or sticking to the bottom. Although this beverage can be enjoyed throughout the year, it is most popular during winters and at weddings.

Serves 4

1½ litres full-fat milk (6 cups)
½ tsp cardamom powder
10–12 saffron strands
2 tbsp almond slivers
2 tbsp pistachio slivers
½ cup sugar (preferably boora
   sugar; add more, as you prefer)

1. Heat 2 tbsp of water in a heavy-bottomed pan, preferably an iron kadahi. Once the water starts boiling, pour in the milk from a height of a foot to create froth. (Adding water to the pan first will prevent the milk from sticking to the bottom.)

2. Boil on medium heat for 30 minutes. Reduce the heat and simmer for further 30 minutes, or until it reduces to two-thirds.

3. Sprinkle cardamom, saffron, and almond and pistachio slivers on top. Turn off the heat and set aside.

4. When a thick layer of malai (milk cream) starts to form on top, carefully skim it off and set aside.

5. Pour the thickened milk in a jug (preferably metal or glass jug) and add sugar. Create a froth by pouring the milk briskly back and forth from the jug into an earthen pot (kulhad) or any tumbler and back into the jug, and so on. Finally, top it with the reserved malai.

Serve hot in earthen cups for an authentic, earthy feel. You can also serve it chilled.

Chef Sameer says
During weddings and special occasions, silver cups are a popular choice for serving this beverage. To make it even more special, stir in a tablespoon of soaked almond paste before serving.

 GOND KI RAYI   *Beverage with Edible Gum*

Made in minutes with just three ingredients—edible gum, ghee and fennel seeds—this drink packs in goodness with every sip. Each ingredient by itself has medicinal properties and in combination, cools and rejuvenates the system. For tiredness or lethargy, a glass of Gond ki Rayi is the perfect homemade remedy.

Serves 4

1 tbsp saunf (fennel) seeds
1 tbsp ghee
1 tbsp gond (edible gum), roughly broken
1 tbsp mishri (rock sugar), powdered

1. Soak saunf in 1½ cups of water overnight. Strain the water and set aside. (Discard the saunf and use in another recipe or simply have it as a mouth freshener.)

2. Heat ghee in a pan and add the broken gond, letting it puff up. Add the strained saunf water and powdered mishri and boil for 2–3 minutes, or until the gum fully dissolves.

Serve hot in winters and chilled in summers. Pour in teacups or fancy glasses, and enjoy sip by sip.

 UKAALI   *Hot Beverage with Healthy Spices*

Also known as dhanagra, this drink will warm your core during winters and soothe a common cold. It is popularly consumed during the Jain paarna (first meal after fasting) as it energises the body and gently restarts the metabolism. Often found brewing at bedtime in Rajasthani homes, Ukaali is also believed to act as a sleep aid.

Serves 4

2 dried dates
1 tbsp ghee
1 tbsp almond slivers
1 tbsp ukaali masala (p. 192)
2 tbsp sugar or jaggery

1. Soak dry dates in hot water for 30 minutes. Wash well to remove any grit or impurities. Chop the dates into tiny bits.

2. In a deep pan, heat ghee on medium heat. Add the chopped dates and almond slivers, and sauté for a few seconds. Add 5 cups of water and ukaali masala and boil for 10–15 minutes, or until it reduces to 4 cups.

Add sugar and boil for 2 more minutes. Turn off the heat. Pour hot in teacups and enjoy sip by sip.

BATASHA KA SHARBAT   *Summer Cooler with Sugar Candy*

A refreshing summertime cooler with divine basil and aromatic cloves, sweetened with sugar candy. In Rajasthan, the drinking water was sometimes brackish and so children were tempted with batasha-sweetened water as a means of hydration. It was also common to serve it to visitors who came in weary and dehydrated by the desert heat. This recipe is a tribute to that childhood memory.

Serves 4

25 to 30 fresh leaves of basil (or mint or lemongrass)
12 batashas (sugar candy)*
8 cloves
2 cups crushed ice

* Batasha can vary in size and sweetness, so measure out the quantity based on your preference for sweetness.

1. Set aside about 8–10 basil leaves for garnishing. Churn the remaining basil leaves with batashas, cloves and ½ cup water in a blender. (Even though the cloves may not get fully crushed, their flavour will seep in.)
2. Add 4 cups water and churn again for a minute. Strain this syrup through a fine sieve and set aside.
3. To serve, fill four glasses with ½ cup crushed ice each. Pour the syrup equally on top in all the glasses.

Garnish with basil leaves and serve immediately.

AAMALVANIYA   *Flavoursome Tamarind Sharbat*

Also known as Imlaana or Imli ki Chhaach, meaning a tamarind-based drink, this simple recipe skilfully blends tamarind with cardamom, clove, rose water and saffron, resulting in a heady and exotic flavour. In Bikaner, this drink is served as the perfect accompaniment to Kheech (p. 52).

Serves 4

1 cup thick tamarind pulp (extracted from 2 large lemon-sized balls of tamarind)
½ cup sugar or jaggery
1 tsp cardamom powder
½ tsp clove powder
1 tsp black salt
1½ tbsp rose water
Few saffron strands

1. Mix all the ingredients (except saffron) in 1 litre water. Set aside for 30 minutes so the flavours are well infused.
2. Stir once and pass through a fine sieve into a pitcher. Add the saffron strands and stir again.

Serve at room temperature or chilled, depending on the weather.

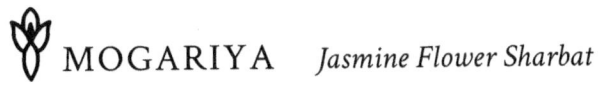 MOGARIYA *Jasmine Flower Sharbat*

A delicate, fragrant sharbat reminiscent of a refreshing breeze tinged with jasmine.

Serves 6

50 jasmine flowers, full bloomed
  (edible variety)
½ cup sugar
2 tbsp lemon juice
3 cups crushed ice, to serve

1. Wash the jasmine flowers and pat them lightly on a thick cloth.

2. Reserve 4–5 flowers for garnishing, and gently mix sugar into the remaining flowers by rubbing them lightly. The sugar will easily dissolve in the flowers and release their essential oils.

3. Boil 1 litre water in a pan. Add the sweetened flowers and boil for 5 minutes. Set aside to cool down, then strain the syrup through a fine sieve. Add lemon juice to the strained syrup. Chill it in the refrigerator for a couple of hours.

4. To serve, take an earthen cup or a tall glass of about 250 ml. Add ½ cup of crushed ice to the glass. Pour the chilled jasmine syrup over the crushed ice, leaving some space at the top. Finally, place the reserved jasmine flower on the surface so it floats.

Serve as a welcome drink or just to cool off during warm days.

Shelf life: Keep this sharbat (without adding the crushed ice) in a dry, cool place and consume within 2–3 days. Refrigerate it to preserve for a few weeks.

Chef Sameer says
For an exotic look, make ice cubes with jasmine flowers. Add a jasmine flower to every section of the ice tray. Now fill the ice tray with hot, but not boiling water. Set in the freezer to make ice cubes. Top the sharbat with these floral ice cubes. Ice cubes are usually opaque but when you make them with hot water, they sparkle like crystals.

KAIRI PANAA   *Raw Mango Sharbat*

Also known as Kairi ki Chhaach, this is a summer drink made from the early summer raw mangoes. This is a refreshing sweet-sour beverage, often used to prevent heat strokes during Rajasthan's intense summer months.

Serves 4 to 6

2 medium-sized raw mangoes
½ cup sugar
1 tsp salt
1 tsp black salt
1 tsp cumin seeds, roasted and
    crushed
1 tsp chaat masala
1 tbsp lemon juice
½ tsp red chilli powder
½ tsp Marwadi garam masala (p. 193)
1 tsp dried mint powder (or fresh
    mint leaves)
About 1 cup crushed ice (and more
    to serve)

1. Wash the raw mangoes and make deep cuts in them (so they cook quickly and evenly). Place them in a pressure cooker with enough water to cover them. Pressure-cook for up to 2 whistles so they turn mushy and the skin splits on its own. Transfer the mangoes to a wide bowl and set aside for 3–4 hours.

2. Rub the mangoes well to slough off the skin and remove the seeds while retaining the pulp and liquid.

3. Blend the mango pulp (along with the liquid) with the remaining ingredients and churn with the crushed ice. Strain through a fine sieve and set aside the sharbat. Discard the fibre which remains on top of the sieve.

To serve, mix this sharbat with equal measure of chilled water. Serve as a summer cooler any time of the day.

Chef Sameer says
Popularly, the word chhaach refers to diluted curd. But it also means a sour drink that might not contain any curd. For example, a drink with raw mangoes is known as Kairi ki Chhaach, just as one with tamarind water is known as Imli ki Chhaach. Also, the word 'panaa' is derived from peya or paan, which means to drink. Hence, many beverages are known as panaa, such as Kairi Panaa (raw mango drink), Imli Panaa (tamarind drink) and Kharbooje ka Panaa (musk melon drink).

GAAJAR KI KAANJI *Carrots in Fermented Mustard Water*

Long considered a year-round elixir, Gaajar ki Kaanji is the big brother of the kefirs and kombuchas of today. A fermented drink, kaanji provides a much-needed dose of probiotics, vitamins, minerals and antioxidants. A traditional staple, it is good for the digestive system and overall health. This recipe requires kaanji masala, which can be made in a jiffy. Try and procure sweet carrots, especially the purple ones because of their beautiful colour and higher nutritional value.

Note: Plan this dish two days in advance as the kaanji fermentation takes 24–36 hours.

Serves 6

4 medium-sized carrots
2 tbsp kaanji masala (p. 195)

1. Chop the carrots into 2-inch sticks (like French fries) and blanch them in boiling water for 3 minutes. Drain and pat dry, then lay them out on a kitchen towel for 30 minutes.

2. Boil 1 litre water and set aside to cool.

3. Transfer the carrots into a glass or earthen jar. Add kaanji masala and toss with a wooden spoon so the carrots are coated with the spices. Pour in the cooled water, stir well and cover tightly with a cloth.

4. Leave the jar in a warm place for 24 hours, stirring occasionally. Check if the liquid has fermented; it must have a sharp, sour flavour. Otherwise, cover again and leave it for another 12 hours. Now, it is ready to use. In winters, allow an extra 12 hours for fermentation.

Serve the carrots along with kaanji, preferably in an earthen glass or leaf bowl. Relish it any time of the day.

Shelf life: You can preserve this kaanji with carrots for up to a week in the refrigerator.

 Variations

Radish Kaanji
Substitute carrots with tender radish and proceed with the recipe. You can also add few beetroot sticks for a beautiful colour.

Sugarcane Kaanji
Spike the Carrot Kaanji or Radish Kaanji with sugarcane juice. Add 1 cup sugarcane juice after the kaanji has fermented for 24 hours. Allow it to ferment for another day, then serve. Enjoy its sweet and sour taste.

CHHACHITI *Buttermilk with Vegetables*   (pic on p. 178)

I remember one summer afternoon in Jaipur when, bothered by the heat, none of us felt like eating any solid food. Sameer went into the kitchen and, within minutes, returned with this delicious buttermilk. It had the perfect combination of vegetables churned with fresh curd and spiked with the right balance of spicy, sweet and astringent rasa.

Serves 4

2 cups fresh curd
1 cup crushed ice
½ cup tomatoes, chopped
½ cup cucumber, chopped
2 tbsp onions, chopped
2 sprigs of coriander leaves,
   chopped
1 tbsp green chillies, chopped
1 tbsp lemon juice
1 tbsp sugar (or jaggery or honey)
1 tsp salt

1. Except the curd and crushed ice, churn the remaining ingredients into a fine paste.
2. Add curd, crushed ice and 3 cups chilled water, and churn again.
3. Strain through a sieve or cheesecloth and pour the liquid into a serving jug.*

Serve at room temperature or chilled.

---

* Many people do not strain the drink as they enjoy the fibrous texture of the vegetables. If you choose to strain it, use the pulp in a salad or raita, or even mix it into roti dough.

DOODH BABCHI SHARBAT   *Milkshake with Basil Seeds*

This milkshake combines nutrient- and fibre-rich basil seeds and leaves with chilled milk, and is an ideal summer morning beverage due to its cooling effect. The seeds of the basil plant are also known as babchi or tukmaria, but more popularly as falooda seeds, after the popular Indian summer dessert, falooda.

Serves 4

500 ml milk
2 tsp basil seeds (falooda seeds)
10–12 fresh holy basil leaves (tulsi)
½ tsp cardamom powder
4 tbsp powdered sugar or crushed
   jaggery
1 cup crushed ice

1. Boil the milk. Cool to room temperature and chill it in the refrigerator for a couple of hours.
2. Soak the basil seeds in ½ cup water for 10 minutes. The seeds will puff up and look as if covered with jelly.
3. Wash and pat-dry the basil leaves. Crush them with cardamom powder using a mortar and pestle. Add to the chilled milk along with sugar. Blend the milk using a blender or cocktail shaker until the sugar dissolves completely.
4. To serve, fill four tall glasses with ¼ cup crushed ice each. Pour equal quantities of milk into each glass and top with the basil seeds (along with the soaked liquid).

An ideal breakfast delicacy, though you can serve it anytime as a welcome drink in shot glasses.

BAJRI KI RAAB   *Cream of Millet Soup*

Here is the simplest of recipes: millet flour slow-cooked in buttermilk and spiked with just cumin and chillies. Raab, also known as raabdi in rural areas, has always been a part of the Rajasthani meal. Rotis with raab and sliced onions is a popular lunch preference, even today. Sameer recommends serving this raab as a warm soup during cool evenings. His guests, especially those from outside Rajasthan, always showered him with praise for the distinctive flavour of this warm, soupy beverage.

Serves 4

For batter

3 tbsp bajri (pearl millet) flour
1½ cups curd
2 whole green chillies, with stalks
1 tsp cumin seeds
1 tsp salt

For serving

1 to 2 cups curd (or buttermilk), to serve
1 tsp cumin seeds, roasted and crushed

1. Whisk the bajri flour and curd with 4 cups of water into a lump-free batter.

2. Cook the batter in a heavy-bottomed pan on high heat, stirring continuously until it comes to a boil.

3. Add green chillies, cumin seeds and salt. Reduce to low heat, cover partly with a lid and simmer for 30–45 minutes, stirring now and then. Add some hot water if it becomes too thick. It should be of a pouring soup consistency. Turn off the heat. Remove the green chillies and discard.

Serve the Raab, sprinkled with crushed cumin on top, at room temperature or chilled, preferably in earthen glasses.

Shelf life: You can preserve the Raab for a day or two in the refrigerator.

 Variations

 Jowar ki Raab | Makki ki Raab | Gehun ki Raab
Customise your Raab by using different flours based on your taste and seasonal availability. Substitute the flour in the recipe with jowar (sorghum), gehun (wheat) or makki (maize) flour.

Chef Sameer says
This Raab tends to thicken over time. If serving it chilled, dilute it with a spoonful of curd or buttermilk. If serving hot, simply dilute with a little water. For an earthy, smoky flavour, finish with a wisp of charcoal smoke using the dhungaar method (see p. 202).

JAU GULI KI RAAB *Thick Barley Soup with Curd and Vegetables*

Barley has therapeutic powers and is used to treat heartburn, acid reflux and even gout. This thick Raab is commonly enjoyed on Shitalashtami, a Hindu festival celebrated after Holi, at the start of the warm season. Traditionally, only salt and roasted cumin were added as seasoning, but Sameer enjoys adding chopped chillies, ginger, onions and tomatoes for a more wholesome treat, along with lots of green coriander, so you can enjoy it as a soothing beverage, or even as a light, satisfying meal.

Serves 4

For batter
¼ cup broken jau (barley)
2 tbsp jau (barley) flour
1½ cups curd

Other ingredients
2 tbsp onions, finely chopped
1 tbsp tomatoes, finely chopped
½ tsp ginger, finely chopped or grated
½ tbsp green chillies, finely chopped
2 sprigs of coriander leaves, finely chopped
1 tsp salt

For serving
1 to 2 cups curd (or buttermilk)
1 tsp cumin seeds, roasted and crushed

1. Whisk the broken jau, jau flour and curd with 4 cups of water into a lump-free batter.

2. Cook the batter in a heavy-bottomed pan on high heat, stirring continuously until it comes to a boil.

3. Reduce to low heat, cover partly with a lid and simmer for 30–45 minutes, stirring now and then. Turn off the heat.

4. Cool down and mix in all the items listed under other ingredients.

Serve the Raab at room temperature or chilled. Since it tends to thicken with time, dilute it with a dollop of curd or buttermilk if you wish to use it after a few hours. Sprinkle crushed cumin on top while serving.

 Variation

 Meethi Raab
For a sweet variation, follow the recipe till Step 3. Add some sugar and 1 tbsp of melted ghee.

MASALAS AND BASICS

Pantry Prep, the Inner Core of Cooking

Most Rajasthani kitchens will have one or two spice boxes, known as hatadi, filled with little bowls of whole and powdered spices. When I entered Sameer's kitchen for the first time, what caught my attention was five identical hatadis stacked on a shelf. Sameer opened each one, explaining, 'These are my spice containers, each having seven sections. I teach my students to organise their spices in this manner. I keep five of these containers in the kitchen, and the sixth one in the fridge.'

He further says, 'What these hatadis do is help me cook with speed and efficiency. Our Indian cooking is rich with spices and herbs. In a simple sabzi, we add more than 5 ingredients in the tempering and 5 spices later on. In a chaat, we add another combination of 7–8 spices. These hatadis allow me a no-compromise system while cooking.'

Spices such as turmeric, coriander, cumin, cloves, cardamom, pepper, fennel and carom seeds have been grown in India for centuries, while others such as red chilli, cinnamon and saffron have been integrated from other cultures. These incredible spices are multifunctional. They protect and nurture us with their medicinal qualities, and lure us with their unique fragrances. Their use extends beyond the kitchen walls. Look closely and you will see them making up the colours of rangolis and even the fabric in our clothes.

In this section, you will find a mixture of different masalas—some that you will always want to keep on hand, and some that are great for a change. Most of them can be made and preserved for months, and are truly worth the effort.

A successful cook is one who learns to combine and balance spices. He enjoys experimenting and never stops learning. Take a leap of faith and make space in your kitchen for some of these spice blends—you will not be disappointed.

UKAALI MASALA *Spice Mix for Healing Drink*

This aromatic spice blend is mainly used to prepare Ukaali, a healing beverage commonly used during the breaking of fasts in Jain homes. You can also incorporate this masala into tea, spicy cakes, and cookies, adding a unique twist to these treats.

2 tsp dried ginger powder
1 tbsp peppercorns
1½ tbsp saunf (fennel) seeds
1½ tbsp coriander seeds
2 cinnamon sticks of 1 inch each
5 cloves
10 green cardamoms
10–12 saffron strands

Mix and grind the ingredients into a fine powder. Sieve to ensure there are no coarse pieces in the masala. Store in an airtight jar in a dry, cool place.

Shelf life: Stored properly, this spice mix can be preserved for up to six months (without refrigeration).

Recipes with Ukaali Masala: Ukaali (p. 183).

Quick Spicy Tea: You can also boil 1 tbsp ukaali masala in 4 cups of water until it reduces to 3 cups. Add sugar and ½ cup hot milk. Strain and serve hot.

RAI-SAUNF MASALA *Spice Mix of Mustard and Fennel*

Combining the pungent mustard with the digestive fennel, this minimalist spice mix serves as a taste enhancer for many dishes. In Rajasthan, many families prefer it over garam masala in various recipes. It complements seasonal vegetables like cluster beans, pointed gourd and apple gourd. Instead of this spice mix, you can add the same proportion of mustard powder and fennel powder to the recipes that call for rai-saunf masala.

¼ cup saunf (fennel) seeds
¼ cup mustard seeds
1 tbsp salt

Mix and grind the ingredients into a fine powder. Store in an airtight jar in a dry, cool place.

Shelf life: Stored properly, this masala can be preserved for up to six months. You can preserve it in the refrigerator for longer.

Recipes with Rai-Saunf Masala: Dahi Wali Turai (p. 70), Phali Kachri ki Sabzi (p. 74), Ker Sangri (p. 92), Pyaaz ka Raita (p. 152) and Pyaaz ka Achaar (p. 171).

MARWADI GARAM MASALA   *Signature Spice Powder*

Around 15 spices, including dried rose petals, come together to make this spice mix. Endowed with the power to transform a simple sabzi or dal into a richly spiced dish, garam masala plays a key role in Rajasthani cooking.

Sameer advises his young students to keep an array of garam masalas in their kitchens. As a wise mentor, he shares this bit of advice: 'Let your pantry boast four distinctive garam masalas: (*i*) a homemade blend, (*ii*) a favourite store-bought option, (*iii*) a treasured recipe handed down from your mother or grandmother and (*iv*) an adventurous blend from different cookbooks. This assortment guarantees each sabzi, dal or pulav you prepare will have its own distinct flavour.'

1 large nutmeg
6–8 mace
4 pippali (long pepper)
6 bay leaves
8 black cardamoms
12 cinnamon sticks (1 inch each)
20 green cardamoms
1 tbsp dried rose petals
2 tbsp cloves
2 tbsp peppercorns
2 tbsp black cumin seeds
½ cup cumin seeds
¼ cup coriander seeds
¼ cup saunf (fennel) seeds

Roughly crush nutmeg and mace in a mortar and pestle (to avoid damaging your grinder blades). Then, grind them with the rest of the ingredients into a fine powder. Sieve to ensure there are no coarse pieces. Store in an airtight jar in a dry, cool place.

Shelf life: Stored properly, this spice powder can be preserved for up to six months. You can preserve it in the refrigerator for even longer.

Chef Sameer says
Almost always added at the end, Marwadi garam masala is like a final touch of perfume—completing the dish with its warm, lingering aroma. It is used in over 30 recipes in this cookbook.

🌸 DAL MASALA   *Spice Powder for Dal Recipes*

This masala adds a tang that elevates any dal preparation. Inspired by the famous 'Chaubejee dal ka masala' from the Agra–Mathura region, Sameer fondly recalls it being called 'bhojan sudhar masala'—a spice mix to fix any dish. A perfect second garam masala for your kitchen!

¼ tsp nutmeg powder
¼ tsp citric acid (optional)
2 tsp black salt
2 tsp ajwain (carom) seeds
2 tsp dried ginger powder
1 tbsp coriander seeds
1 tbsp kasuri methi (dried
    fenugreek leaves), lightly roasted
2 tbsp cumin seeds
2 tbsp amchur (dried mango) powder
2 black cardamoms
2 pippali (long pepper)
8 green cardamoms
10 cloves

Mix and grind all the ingredients into a fine powder. Sieve to ensure there are no coarse pieces in the masala. Store in an airtight jar in a dry, cool place.

Shelf life: Stored properly, this spice powder can be preserved for up to six months. You can preserve it in the refrigerator for a longer duration.

Recipes with Dal Masala: Dal Dhokli (p. 48), Panchmel Dal (p. 103), Dal Chandni (p. 104), Shekhawati Mogar (p. 106) and Jodhpuri Haveji (p. 110).

🌸 PICKLE MASALA   *The Handy Signature Achaar Masala*

A must in every home, this masala is used in instant pickles, preserved pickles and sabzis. The prominent flavour is from split yellow mustard, available in the market as rai ki dal or rai kuria.

1 tbsp cumin seeds
2 tbsp fenugreek seeds
2 tbsp black mustard seeds
4 tbsp saunf (fennel) seeds
2 tbsp oil (preferably mustard oil)
1 tsp hing (asafoetida powder)
1 tbsp turmeric powder
1 tbsp kalonji (nigella) seeds
2 tbsp split yellow mustard
3 tbsp salt
3 tbsp kuti mirch (coarse chilli
    powder)
3 tbsp Kashmiri chilli powder
4 tbsp amchur (dried mango) powder

Lightly, dry-roast the cumin, fenugreek, black mustard seeds and saunf. Crush them roughly using a mortar and pestle. Heat the oil in a pan. Add the crushed seeds and immediately turn off the heat. Allow it to cool and then add the remaining spices. Mix well and transfer to a dry jar.

Shelf life: Store in an airtight jar in a dry, cool place for up to 3 months (without refrigeration). If refrigerated, it can be preserved for up to a year.

Recipes with Pickle Masala: Kairi ka Achaar (p. 173), Lahsun ka Achaar (p. 174), Mirch ka Athana (p. 175), Paneer Papad Kurkure (p. 31) and its variations.

JEERAVAN MASALA   *Spice Powder to Enhance any Snack*

This spicy, tangy masala adds a magical flavour when sprinkled on papad, khichiya (a variety of thick papad), fruit chaat, poha or any fried snack. Popular especially in Udaipur and Indore, it is often used as a substitute for chaat masala and garam masala.

1 tsp turmeric powder
1 tsp yellow chilli powder
2 tsp red chilli powder
2 tsp Kashmiri red chilli powder
2 tsp ajwain (carom) seeds
1 tbsp kachri (wild berry) powder
1 tbsp black salt
2 tbsp salt
2 tbsp kathodi powder (or chaat masala)
4 tbsp cumin seeds
4 tbsp amchur (dried mango) powder

Mix and grind all the ingredients into a fine powder. Sieve to ensure there are no coarse pieces. Store in an airtight jar in a dry, cool place.

Shelf life: Stored properly, this masala can be preserved for up to six months. You can preserve it in the refrigerator for longer.

Recipes with Jeeravan Masala: Kapura Pitod (p. 28), Dahi ki Bhindi (p. 64), Fogla ka Raita (p. 153), and in many toppings.

KAANJI MASALA   *Spice Mix for Probiotic Drink*

A traditional spice blend used in the preparation of kaanji, a fermented drink known for its tangy and spicy flavours, and probiotic properties.

2 tbsp black mustard seeds
1 tbsp split yellow mustard
1 tsp saunf (fennel) seeds
1 tsp red chilli powder
¼ tsp turmeric powder
3 tbsp salt

Mix and grind all the ingredients into a coarse powder. Store in an airtight jar in a dry, cool place.

Shelf life: Stored properly, this spice mix can be preserved for up to six months. You can preserve it in the refrigerator for longer.

Recipes with Kaanji Masala: Shekhawati Kaanji Vada (p. 34) and Gaajar ki Kaanji (p. 187).

Instant Carrot Pickle: Mix the kaanji masala with finely chopped carrots (or radish), a drizzle of oil and a dash of lemon juice.

 RANGAT *The Signature Rajasthani Chilli Glaze* (pic on p. 197)

Rajasthanis are known for enhancing many dishes by glazing them just before serving. Known as rangat, meaning colouring, this glaze is created with hot ghee or oil to which red chilli powder and turmeric powder are added. The ghee or oil takes on the rich colour and flavour of the spices. In this cookbook, many recipes use rangat to enhance the look of the dish.

4 tbsp ghee preferably, or oil
¼ tsp turmeric powder
1 tsp red chilli powder

1. In a small pan, heat the ghee until warm. Add turmeric and chilli powder.

2. As the mixture turns frothy, add 1 tbsp water (or milk) and increase the heat. Within a minute the water will boil and reduce, leaving behind a rich coloured residue, known as rangat. Remove the pan from the heat and set aside.

Drizzle about half a spoon of rangat as glaze on sabzi, dal and kadhi, enriching the colour of the meal. If the ghee solidifies, reheat gently before serving.

Shelf life: Stays good for 2–3 days at room temperature.

 CHILLI GHEE *Chilli-infused Ghee for an Instant Lift*

Another quick tip, similar to Rangat, is Chilli Ghee. Much like chilli oil in Chinese cuisine, Chilli Ghee holds a special place in Rajasthani kitchens. It adds the perfect final flavour to dishes such as Khaariya, Kheech, any rice dish or dal. You can even brush it over rotis for that special touch—try it with Besan ki Tawa Poodi.

4 tbsp ghee, preferably, or oil
2 tsp kuti mirch (coarse chilli powder)

1. In a small bowl, add the kuti mirch.

2. Heat the ghee and pour it over the kuti mirch.

3. Let it infuse for about 3 minutes.

Drizzle about half a spoon over any dish for added spice and a glossy finish. If the ghee solidifies, reheat gently before serving.

Shelf life: Stays good for 2–3 days at room temperature.

Rangat p.196

197

Dhungaar p.202

198

ratlami sev

aloo bhujia

fogla
(desert shrub)

batasha
(sugar candy)

mishri
(rock sugar)

kuti mirch
(coarse chilli powder)

makki
(maize)

bajri
(pearl millet)

dried mango peels

whole turmeric

split yellow mustard

whole yellow mustard

moth dal
(split dew beans)

moth
(whole dew beans)

chawli dal
(split cow peas)

chawli
(whole cow peas)

badi
(lentil nuggets)

ker
(desert capers)

sangri
(wild beans)

rabodi
(maize flour wafers)

BASIC PITOD   *Fresh Rajasthani Pasta with Gram Flour*

This Rajasthani delicacy requires some practice and skill, and this recipe will give you the confidence to get started. The humble yet versatile besan, which forms the base for pitod, is transformed into thin pasta-like layers.

1 cup besan (gram flour)
½ cup curd
1 tsp ginger paste
1 tsp green chilli paste
½ tsp turmeric powder
¾ tsp salt

1. Whisk together (preferably with a hand blender or balloon whisk) the ingredients for pitod in 2½ cups of water to make a smooth, lump-free batter.

2. Cook this batter in a deep, heavy-bottomed pan, stirring continuously on medium-high heat for 5–7 minutes, or until it thickens and starts to leave the sides of the pan.

3. Grease two steel plates larger than 8 inches in diameter and gently wipe with kitchen paper. Spread half of the cooked batter on each plate into a circle that is roughly 8 inches in diameter and ¼ inch thick. Spread it out evenly with a spatula or the back of a ladle. (You can also do this on your kitchen slab.)

Set aside to cool, then cut into shapes of your choice (square, circle or diamond) and use them as required.

Recipes with Pitod: Kapura Pitod (p. 28), Rasila Pitod (p. 86) and Pitod ka Raita (p. 155).

DHUNGAAR

(pic on p. 198)

The Smoky Charcoal Effect

Dhungaar is the technique of infusing a smoky flavour into dishes. Cooking over wood, charcoal or in a tandoor naturally infuses food with this rich smokiness, elevating the flavours and lending the preparation a special touch. Most of us do not have access to these cooking methods, but we can still add a smoky flavour to our dishes by heating charcoal, placing it in the dish and allowing the plumes of smoke to do their magic. In this cookbook, more than a dozen recipes are embellished with this smoky charcoal effect.

You will need:

1 small piece of charcoal (about 1×1 inch)
½ tsp melted ghee
1 pinch hing (asafoetida powder)

Substitute: Instead of hing, use crushed cloves or minced garlic, as you prefer, for each dish.

How to infuse charcoal smoke into solids

Place a tiny earthen or metal bowl on the top of the prepared dish. Heat a piece of charcoal directly on the stove until red hot. Using tongs, carefully place this charcoal in the bowl. Pour the ghee and hing over it, then quickly cover the entire dish with a large plate. Let it sit covered for a minute to allow the dish to absorb the smokiness. For a stronger smoky flavour, keep it covered for 3–4 minutes. Remove the plate and allow the smoke to settle before serving.

How to infuse charcoal smoke into liquids

Place a tiny earthen or metal bowl on the kitchen counter. Heat a piece of charcoal directly on the stove until it turns red hot. Using tongs, place the burnt charcoal in the bowl. Pour the ghee and hing over it, and immediately cover the bowl with the empty jar placed upside down. Let it sit for a few minutes to allow the smoke to fill the jar. Once the jar is well smoked, remove it and quickly pour in the prepared liquid or beverage. Cover the jar so the smoke is sealed in, allowing the flavours to infuse gently before serving.

DHUNGAARI ALOO   *Smoky Mashed Potatoes*

3 potatoes
1 onion, finely chopped
2 green chillies, finely chopped
1 tsp grated ginger
2 sprigs coriander leaves, finely
    chopped
¾ tsp salt
1 tsp kuti mirch (coarse chilli
    powder)
1½ tbsp mustard oil

1. Boil the potatoes and mash them roughly.

2. Mix in all the remaining ingredients and finally drizzle
    mustard oil over it.

3. Flavour with charcoal smoke and serve.

 # DHUNGAARI KER   *Smoky Desert Berries*

½ cup dried ker
1½ tbsp ghee or oil
1 tsp cumin seeds
¾ tsp salt
¼ tsp black salt
1 tsp red chilli powder
½ tsp turmeric powder
2 tsp coriander powder
½ tsp amchur (dried mango) powder

1. Soak the dried ker overnight and cook them the next
    morning (refer to step 1 of Ker Sangri on p. 92). Strain
    away the liquid and mash the ker lightly.

2. Mix in the remaining ingredients, except ghee.

3. Heat the ghee and pour it over the prepared ker.

4. Flavour with charcoal smoke and serve.

 # DHUNGAARI PAPAD CHOORI   *Smoky Crushed Papads*

4 Bikaneri papads
1 tsp red chilli powder
1 tsp crushed cumin seeds
1 tbsp melted ghee

1. Roast the papads directly on the flame. Crush them into
    tiny bits in a large bowl.

2. Mix in the remaining ingredients.

3. Flavour with charcoal smoke and serve. If preparing in
    large quantities, store in an airtight container.

 # DHUNGAARI CHHAACH   *Buttermilk Infused with Charcoal Smoke*

1 cup curd
½ tsp salt
½ tsp black salt
1 tsp roasted cumin powder

1. Mix 1 cup curd with 2 cups water and whisk well to make
    buttermilk.

2. Add the remaining ingredients.

3. Flavour with charcoal smoke and serve chilled or at room
    temperature.

PART 2

BEYOND RECIPES
Essentials and Inspirations

Fusion Food

We often think about how to bring the newer generations closer to our roots, and back to basic cooking habits. Sameer says, 'Even during my classes, I find that very few students are interested in the traditional art of cooking desi food. It is not just true for Rajasthani cuisine … the same holds true for other cuisines as well. This realisation has led me to create some fusion variations with my recipes. Here are a few fusion food ideas that I hope you will enjoy making.'

1. **Fusion lasagna ravioli or cannelloni:** Use Pitod sheets (p. 201) instead of lasagna sheets. Use your favourite pasta sauce with spinach and mushroom filling, and bake with grated cheese on top.

2. **Fusion bruschetta:** Make Bejhad Roti (p. 126) of 2-inch thickness and spread red pasta sauce, basil, olives and cherry tomatoes over the roti. Top with parmesan cheese and olive oil.

3. **Fusion bagel:** Slice Makki ka Dhokla (p. 44) into two, like a bagel, and spread with cream cheese to enjoy.

4. **Fusion gnocchi:** Make desi gnocchi with leftover Bajri ka Khichda (p. 56) or Bajri ki Ghaat (p. 54).

5. **Fusion pizza:** On a thick roti of your choice, spread your favourite sauce, generous amounts of cheese, and top with Ker Sangri (p. 92). Bake it and your wild berry pizza is ready.

6. **Fusion moong beans hummus:** Made with Shekhawati Mogar (p. 106), which is ground with some curd and any Garlic Chutney (p. 165) into a fine paste. Serve with some crispy roti strips as lavash.

7. **Fusion macarons:** Make two Missi Roti (p. 127) of 2-inch diameter. Spread Kesar Batasha Dahi (p. 151) on one roti and cover with another roti. Serve as a fusion dessert.

8. **Fusion baklava:** Make a roll of leftover barfi or laddu. Roll them thickly with crushed Rajasthani pheeni into small logs. Sprinkle honey or syrup and bake for a few minutes until it sets. Cool and enjoy the crispy outer layer with a soft centre.

9. **Fusion cracked wheat cake:** Mix some Maanglik Laapsi (p. 3) with nuts and chocolate chips, and some chocolate sauce to bind. Set in a cake tin, chill, demould on a plate and pour over warm melted butter scotch sauce or Nutella. Cut into triangle slices and enjoy.

10. **Gulgule with a twist:** Sprinkle cinnamon powder or vanilla sugar on hot Meethe Gulgule (p. 10). Alternately, reduce jaggery by half and pour caramel or chocolate sauce on the fried gulgule.

11. **Punjab-inspired hariyala gatta:** Make Home-style Gatta (p. 88, variation) without the filling and add it to a rich spinach gravy.

12. **Besan pitod pasta:** Lasagna or cannelloni with fresh dough pasta sheets or besan pitod pasta sheets (p. 201) filled with baked beans and topped with saffron sauce.

13. **Nachos with kadhi sauce:** Nachos topped with cheese and Kadhi (as sauce) makes an interesting dish. Serve with Smoky Guava Salsa (p. 169, variation).

Menu Planning

JEEMAN □ THE GRAND FEASTS

Rajasthani spreads, crafted for festive gatherings and occasions

MENU 1

Start with:
Dal ki Pakodi • 26
Kairi Panaa • 186

Main course:
Home-style Gatta • 89 (see variation)
Dhungaari Mogri • 66
Panchmel Dal • 103
Jaipuri Kadhi • 109
Baati • 134
Masala Baati • 134 (see variation)
Steamed rice

Accompaniments:
Mirch ke Tipore • 170
Papad

Mithai:
Instant Churma • 8

MENU 2

Start with:
Bajri ki Raab • 189
Mewa Chaat • 33

Main course:
Bajri ka Khichda • 56
Paansi ki Kadhi • 111
Aalan ki Sabzi • 67
Jodhpuri Sabut Bhutte ki Sabzi • 76
Satnajiya Sogra • 128
Phulka • 122

Accompaniments:
Kesar Batasha Dahi • 151
Angoor ki Launji • 167

Mithai:
Matar ka Halwa • 16
Kadahi ka Doodh • 182

MENU 3

Start with:
Gond ki Rayi • 183
Paneer Papad Kurkure • 31

Main course:
Kurkuri Bhindi • 64 (see variation)
Taazi Matar ki Sabzi • 65
Dahi Wale Aloo • 70 (see variation)
Dal Chandni • 104
Awla ki Kadhi • 115
Phulka • 122

Accompaniments:
Shekhawati Kaanji Vada • 34
Banjara Chutney • 163

Mithai:
Aam Ka Kalakand • 11

MENU 4

Start with:
Mogariya • 185
Paneer Roll • 29
Tanatan Kofta • 24

Main course:
Missi Roti • 127
Baatiya • 122
Chanakya Special • 69
Govind Gatta • 88
Haldi ki Sabzi • 73
Kala Chana ki Kadhi • 112
Singhada ka Pulav • 147

Accompaniments:
Rai Mirch ka Chhachita • 156
Green Chutney • 162

Mithai:
Meetha Kheech • 4

CHHOTI BAJOT ☐ LESS IS MORE
Small menu—and still, a feast to remember

MENU 5
Batasha ka Sharbat • 184
Bejhad Roti • 126
Aloo Pyaaz Jaipuri • 63
Ananas Makhana Raita • 156
Lahsun Kachri ki Chutney • 165
Diljani • 12

MENU 6
Jodhpuri Kabuli • 144
Awla ki Kadhi • 115
Kachri Mirch ki Chutney • 164
Jhajhariya • 6

MENU 7
Khoba Roti • 136
Jodhpuri Chakki ki Sabzi • 84
Hari Mirch ka Koota • 170
Aam ka Raita • 152
Instant Mishri Mawa • 7

MENU 8
Gehun ka Kheech • 52
Aamalvaniya • 184
Papad Badi ki Sabzi • 90
Easy Badam Katli • 9

KALEVA ☐ MINI FEASTS
A traditional breakfast or tea-time menu, featuring something sweet and savoury

MENU 9
Instant Dal ka Halwa • 14
Jodhpuri Mirchi Vada • 23
Green Chutney • 162
Tamarind Chutney • 163

MENU 10
Doodh Babchi Sharbat • 188
Pyaaz ki Kachori • 27
Green Chutney • 162
Tamarind Chutney • 163

MENU 11
Chawli ka Bhapiya • 32
Prem Prakash Samosa • 25
Green Chutney • 162

MENU 12
Ukaali • 183
Kapura Pitod • 28
Shekhawati Mogar • 106
Papad
Kankri Mirch • 13

DESI HANDI ☐ ONE-POT MEALS
Choose any of the dhokla or dhokli (p. 41), or randheen (p. 51): each one is a complete and comforting delight.

Basic Preparations

1. Making kaccha masala

Adding spices to a dish is both an art and a science. In most Indian cuisines, spices are typically added directly to the cooking pan, be it sabzi or dal or a rice dish. But many Rajasthani recipes have an interesting twist: the spices are soaked in water or curd for a while before being cooked. This is known as kaccha masala, while the former is known as pakka masala.

When spices such as red chillies, turmeric powder and coriander powder are added to water or curd, they tend to thicken, and add a subtle and distinct flavour as well as texture and colour when added to the dish and further cooked. In this book, you will find many recipes with kaccha masala.

2. Cooking rice perfectly

Wash the rice 2–3 times and soak in water for about 30 minutes. For 1 cup of Basmati rice, heat 1 litre of water in a vessel large enough to hold about 2.5 litres. Cover and bring the water to a rolling boil, then add the rice (after draining the soaked water), ½ tsp salt and 1 tsp ghee. Stir it once gently, but briskly. Cover partly and boil on high heat for 4 minutes and then on medium heat for another 4 minutes, or until cooked. Strain and discard the water. Perfectly boiled rice grains will look like unbloomed jasmine buds—white and tender—cooked yet each grain separate.

3. Cooking dal perfectly

Wash the dal and soak overnight if required in the recipe, or for a minimum of 30 minutes. Soaking the dal allows it to cook fully, making it more easily digestible, so don't be tempted to skip this step. Drain and discard the water, wash the dal again, and pressure-cook in four times the water, infused with a pinch of turmeric powder and salt. The cooking time is mentioned in each recipe, depending upon the dal used.

4. Cooking fenugreek seeds

Wash fenugreek seeds and soak in water for about 5 hours. Place in a sieve and wash again under running water to remove the bitterness. Measure out water in a pan such that it is about 1 inch higher than the fenugreek seeds. Bring the water to a boil and then add the fenugreek seeds. Cook for 3 minutes. Drain and use in the respective preparations.

Many people also soak the fenugreek seeds for just 10 minutes and then cook them for a longer period. But the first method is the ideal way to bring out the best of this healthy seed.

5. Making lemon-soaked raisins

When soaked in lemon juice, raisins turn soft and more flavourful, and enhance the taste of any filling, poha, pulav, green chutney or sweet chutney, or simply behave as a palate changer.

Soak 1 cup raisins in 1 cup of lemon juice. Add ½ tsp salt and 2 tbsp sugar. Cover with a muslin cloth or a wire mesh and leave out in the sun for 2–3 days. The raisins will soak up the juice and swell in size. Store in an airtight bottle and refrigerate for up to a year.

6. Setting curds

Boil milk, preferably full-fat milk, or else, 1% or 2% fat. (Adding about ¼ cup of milk powder to 1 litre of milk while boiling will help the milk set well into thick curd.) Allow it to cool until it is still a little warm; then transfer to an earthen or porcelain vessel for best results. To 1 litre of milk, add 1 tbsp of homemade curd and swirl once. Cover and allow to rest without disturbing it for 4–6 hours in summer, and overnight in winter. The milk should set into curd.

If you do not have access to a homemade culture, you can use store-bought curd too. Be patient as it takes 3–4 three cycles of curd-making to get the perfect flavour and consistency.

In most Indian homes, we always set aside some curd to use as culture. This is known as jaaman, best translated as 'mother curd'. Most of us have grown up watching jaaman travel from one household to another in the neighbourhood. No one ever hesitates while asking for or giving 1 tbsp of jaaman; it is happily shared.

Sameer says, 'Believe it or not, I know families who have jaaman created from an unbroken chain going back more than four decades! What this means is that a very small quantity of curd, such as 1 tbsp, was set aside one day four decades ago to make curd from the next pot of milk, and once that pot of curd was set, a spoonful from that was set aside and so on, without breaking the ritual for even one single day. Families proudly announce their jaaman was made by their great-great-grandmothers, and married daughters happily carry some of this into their new homes. My wife Sudha brought her grandmother's jaaman to our home.'

What a beautiful tradition of heart-warming rituals! These are sweet, simple practices that once bound families and neighbourhoods together.

7. Making hung curd

Pour fresh curd into a sieve with a fine mesh that is placed on another deep bowl to collect the strained liquid. Cover with a lid and refrigerate for a few hours or even overnight. The excess water will slowly drip into the bowl, leaving you with thick, hung curd in the sieve. (If you leave this outside the refrigerator, the curd tends to get sour.)

8. Growing chickpea leaves and microgreens at home

If fresh or dry paansi (chickpea leaves) are not easily available, you can grow your own. Wash a cup of brown chickpeas and soak in water overnight. Strain them and transfer to a basket or utensil which has small holes in the bottom. Place the basket in a shallow-rimmed plate filled with 1–2 inches of water, such that the base of the basket is wet. Cover with a cloth and change the water every day, ensuring the chickpeas are always in contact with water. Within a few days, the chickpeas will sprout and grow leaves. In less than a week, you will have your microgreens ready to cook.

9. Rinsing dried or dehydrated vegetables

This book features many dried vegetables such as ker, sangri, badi and rabodi. Some need to be soaked overnight, while others have to be boiled in water before being added to the gravy. When using dried vegetables, rinse them several times in fresh, cool water, before soaking, after soaking, and even after boiling. Discard any water used for soaking or boiling, so that any remaining grit or mud clinging to the vegetable does not ruin the dish.

10. Making buttermilk

To 1 cup curd, add 2 cups water. Whisk it well until it turns frothy. The buttermilk is ready to drink or to use in recipes. For thin buttermilk, add 3 cups water.

While growing up, most of our homes had a spot where the grandmother would sit with a large pot of curd, which she would churn with water every morning to make butter. The leftover fat-free liquid was known as chhaach, meaning buttermilk. But that tradition is no longer to be seen in urban homes. So now we dilute curd with water and call it buttermilk.

11. Making malai

Malai is the thick layer of milk fat that forms on top of boiled milk. To get malai or milk cream, boil milk and let it cool. Once cooled, a thick layer of cream forms on top, which can be gently skimmed off. For excess malai, use full-fat milk.

Malai is also created by boiling milk for a longer duration. As the milk boils, the creamy layer on top gets thicker and thicker. It is also available in the market as milk malai—not to be confused with fresh cream.

Know These Ingredients

1. Boora Sugar

Boora, also known as tagar, is porous sugar, which has a dry, grainy texture. To make boora, sugar syrup is cooked till it turns dry and reaches a state of crystallisation. Boora is readily available in stores. It is primarily used to make milk sweets because unlike regular sugar, boora allows the milk to retain its thick consistency rather than thinning it down when added.

2. Gond (Edible Gum)

Edible gum is a natural gum made from the sap of the acacia tree. Known for its emulsifying, heating and strengthening properties, it is an ideal ingredient in winter dishes and for postnatal health. Available in varying sizes of translucent yellow and grey crystals, it can be stored for years.

While buying gond, choose clean, golden-coloured crystals almost the size of chickpeas. Before use, ensure that the gum crystals are dry and crisp, otherwise sun-dry or oven-roast them first. When you fry it, the crystals should pop like popcorn. After frying, cool and break into desired size. This is made easy if you seal the gond in a Ziploc bag and gently pound the bag with a heavy spoon or rolling pin.

3. Bhujia (Sev)

Another all-time favourite is bhujia (also known as sev). These are lentil-based fried munchies, which originally hail from Bikaner in different sizes, flavours and base ingredients. The thickness of bhujia can range from delicate nylon threads to finger-like. Made in diverse flavours, for instance, with potato (aloo bhujia, also known as Tanatan bhujia), with cloves (laung ki sev), with garlic (lahsun ki sev) or with asafoetida (hing ki sev).

Specialised bhujia makers use secret ingredients that have stayed guarded across generations. Some say the special taste is due to the region's water, others guess it is the addition of Multani mitti, and the guesses never stop!

Most famous among all the bhujia varieties is Bikaneri bhujia. Every packet also contains some large chunks of the same ingredients, known as ganthia. In earlier times, many cooks used these chunks as a secret ingredient in many dishes. Apart from relishing these chunks on their own, you can use them to enhance your cooking. Crush and add them to green chutney, kadhi or any curd-based gravy. You can also crush them roughly and sprinkle on khichdi, chaats and dahi vada for a spicy crunch.

4. Papad Khaar

This is a variety of alkaline salt or soda bicarbonate used in preparing papad, dhokla or khaariya. It is available in Rajasthani grocery stores in the form of white cubes or powder. Papad khaar can be stored for up to a year in an airtight container. Many families use another variety known as saaji khaar or sajja khaar.

5. Papad

No meal in Rajasthan is ever complete without roasted papad, smeared with ghee and sprinkled with chilli and cumin powder. This thin, crisp, sun-dried Indian flatbread is commonly served at the end of a meal, adding a crunchy, flavourful element to the dining experience.

The most popular variety is the large-sized Bikaneri papad, available in most Indian grocery stores. Traditionally, papads were made at home and were an excuse for a social gathering where women of the neighbourhood would participate in rolling them out.

There are many varieties of papad which come in different sizes and flavours. They are made with lentils—moong, chana or urad, and range from bland to very spicy. Then, there are tiranga papad, which have three colours and flavours. And not to forget Jodhpuri kaale papad made with the skin of lentils collected while grinding whole lentils in the chakki.

Apart from being eaten on its own, papad forms a base for many sabzis. The dough used for papad is also used in making delicacies such as papad tikli (tiny rounds of papad), papad goli (berry-sized balls of papad) or loye ki roti (roti made from papad dough).

6. Badi (Lentil Nuggets)

Badi, also known as badiya or mangodi, are sundried preserves and a staple in Rajasthani kitchens. These are made by soaking and grinding certain lentils, shaping the batter into nuggets, and drying them in sharp sunlight. Commonly made with either moong dal or moth dal, they are available in many flavours and shapes. These nuggets can be preserved for months and are used in making sabzi, dals, pulav and even pancakes. They are available in online stores as Marwadi badi or mangodi.

7. Rabodi (Wafers from Maize Flour)

A regional speciality of Bikaner, rabodi is available in Rajasthani grocery stores along with badi. Many families make this in batches during the summer months and preserve it round the year. It is prepared by cooking maize flour in buttermilk. Once it thickens but reaches a dropping consistency, the batter is spread out thinly on a plastic sheet or cotton cloth, and sun-dried for a few days. It is then broken into smaller bits and preserved in a dry, clean container for months. Also known as sirabodi, it is used to make a sabzi or a raita.

8. Daana Methi (Fenugreek Seed)

Fenugreek, known as methi, is a very versatile ingredient. Rajasthanis make delightful, unique dishes from its seeds as well as leaves (both fresh and dried). The fenugreek seed, known as daana methi, is a handy ingredient for many sabzis.

Combine fenugreek seeds with raisins to make Daakh Daana Methi (p. 87, variation), with papad to make Papad Methi (p. 90, variation), with dry dates to make Khaarak Methi (p. 87) and with chana dal to make dal daana methi. This plant that can be turned into a vast variety of dishes is also credited with many health benefits such as controlling diabetes and increasing lactation.

9. Red Chilli

In the Rajasthani kitchen, a variety of chillies are used. The types include:

a.   Finely ground red chilli powder.

b.   Coarsely crushed red chilli powder, known as kuti mirchi.

c.   Crushed red chillies with seeds, known as beeja mirchi, similar to Italian chilli flakes but distinct in taste. Beeja mirchi is prepared using an iron mortar and pestle with a few drops of mustard oil for the vibrant colour and perfect texture. The chillies are pressed until the seeds are partly crushed and the chilli skin turns into flakes.

d.   Dry red chilli, the long variety broken into 1-inch bits.

10. Yellow Chilli

Very few people use yellow chillies since the red chilli or Kashmiri chilli is more popular. Yellow chilli is to north Indian food what paprika is to Western culture. When you eat chaats in certain places, especially Aligarh, Banaras, Kanpur, Lucknow, Haridwar and Agra, as well as in Jaipur, there is a distinctive flavour in some dishes imparted by this yellow chilli. We procure it from some old grocery stores in Jaipur. Add it to your special sabzi and dal, and surely in dahi vada.

11. Black Mustard and Yellow Mustard

Mustard is a popular condiment produced from the seeds of the mustard plant. There are many varieties of mustard, but brown or black mustard is mostly used in Indian cooking.

a.   Brown or black mustard: Also known as Indian mustard or rai in Hindi, these are available in different sizes as big mustard seeds (मोटी राई) and tiny mustard seeds (बारीक राई). There seems to be no specific reason to choose among these; mostly, it is a matter of personal preference. These seeds are used across all forms of Indian cuisine, especially in tadka, and to make the famous mustard oil which has a sharp smell and pungent taste.

b.   Yellow mustard: Known as sarson in Hindi, these are used in making pickles, yellow kaanji (fermented probiotic drink like kombucha) and Indian mustard sauce (known as kasundi). It is available in two forms: whole seeds and split seeds or kernels known as rai ki dal. Mustard kernels are used in making many pickles since they impart an ideal flavour and colour to the pickle.

Glossary

In Hindi and English

GRAINS, MILLETS AND PULSES

bajra, bajri—pearl millet
besan—gram flour
chana dal—bengal gram
chawli (lobia)—cow peas
gehun—wheat
jau—barley
jowar—sorghum
kala chana—brown chickpeas
maida—all-purpose flour
makka, makki—maize
masoor—red lentils
moth—dew beans
ragi—finger millet
sabut moong—moong beans
sooji—semolina
soya—soya bean
tuvar dal (arhar dal)—pigeon pea lentils
urad—black gram

DRIED VEGETABLES

aloo ka khelra—dried potato chips
badi (mangodi)—lentil nuggets
fogla—a desert shrub
kachri—wild berry
ker—dried desert capers
rabodi—maize flour wafers
sangri—thin, wild beans from khejari tree

VEGETABLES, GREENS AND FRUITS

adrak—ginger
amrood—guava
chaulai—amaranth greens
gwar phali—cluster beans
gwarpatha—aloe vera
haldi ki jadh—turmeric root
hara pyaaz—onion greens
kachcha aam—raw mango
kari patta—curry leaves
kasuri methi—dried fenugreek leaves
lahsun—garlic
lauki—bottle gourd
methi saag—fenugreek greens
mogra—jasmine flowers
mooli ke patte—radish greens
pakka aam—ripe mango
palak—spinach
sarson ka saag—mustard greens
singhada—water chestnuts
suva bhaji—dill greens
tulsi—basil leaves
turai—ridge gourd

SEEDS AND SPICES

ajwain—carom seeds
amchur—dried mango powder or slices
badi elaichi—black cardamom
chhoti elaichi—green cardamoms
dalchini—cinnamon
dhania—coriander seeds
haldi—turmeric powder
hing—asafoetida powder
imli—tamarind
jaiphal—nutmeg
javitri—mace
jeera—cumin seeds
kala namak—black salt
kali mirch—peppercorns
kalonji—nigella seeds
Kashmiri mirch—Kashmiri chilli powder
kathodi—sour fruit like wood apple
kesar—saffron
kuti mirch—coarse chilli powder
laung—cloves
meetha soda—soda bicarbonate
methi dana—fenugreek seeds
nimbu sat—citric acid
papad khaar (sajji khaar)—an alkaline salt
pippali—long pepper
rai (sarson)—mustard seeds
rai ki dal (rai kuria)—split yellow mustard
sabja—basil seeds, popular as falooda seeds
saunf—fennel seeds
saunth—dried ginger
shahi jeera—black cumin seeds
tej patta—bay leaves
til—sesame

NUTS, DRY FRUITS AND MORE

akhrot—walnuts
badam—almonds
gond—edible gum
kaju—cashew nuts
khaarak (chhuara)—dried dates
khajoor—dates
khopra (sukha nariyal)—dry coconut
kishmish—raisins
makhana—fox nuts
pista—pistachio

DAIRY AND SWEETENERS

batasha—sugar candy
boora—boora sugar
chhaach—buttermilk
gud—jaggery
khoya—reduced milk
malai—milk cream
mishri—rock sugar
paneer—cottage cheese

If you want help with identifying or
procuring any of the ingredients mentioned
in this book, reach out to us:
chefsameer@me.com | (91) 98284 69161
pj@pratibhajain.org | (91) 94440 20011

THANKS FROM THE AUTHORS

Gratitude is not just a word; it is a fragrance that arises when the heart overflows. This book is not merely the labour of a few minds but the confluence of many hearts, hands and energies.

To Prasiddha Rama Rao and Srikant Ranganathan, your editorial insights were not just contributions but a gentle chiselling of thought into clarity. Thank you, Prasiddha, for the poetic translations of the Hindi writings. That you could hear echoes of poetry in them and capture that with such ease it means a lot.

To Chaitanya Sharma and Shireen Vidrohi, your lens did more than capture images; it held the essence of openness, warmth and a quiet willingness to flow.

To Manasvi and Aditi Jain, your unwavering support across various stages of the project—writing, photography, designing and endless brainstorming—has been invaluable.

To Prabodh Jain, Kavitha Shivan and Aruna Vayuvegula, you stood as pillars, reminding us that true support is often felt more than seen. And to Annapurna Mamidipud for helping us grasp the nuances of the dynamic between a chef and an author.

To Rudraksh Lakhwani for your help in sample photography. To Sadhana Chordia and Sharmila Solanki for the immense help with recipe trials in Chennai. And to Nidhi Jha and Pritee Bafna, your attention to the smallest details and tasks is deeply appreciated.

And then, there is family—the space where love takes root. To Sameer's family: Sudha, Natasha and Vipul; and to Pratibha's family: Mahendar and Manasvi—you were not just witnesses but believers, breathing life into this dream, cheering not from the sidelines but from within.

A book is never just written; it is birthed, nurtured and surrendered. To all who played a part, whether named or unnamed, we bow in deep gratitude.

Sameer and Pratibha